# DRINKING FOR ENGLAND

FERGUS LINNANE

# DRINKING FOR ENGLAND

*The Great English Drinkers
and Their Times*

BOOKS

First published in Great Britain in 2008 by
JR Books, 10 Greenland Street, London NW1 0ND
www.jrbooks.com

A catalogue record for this book is available from the British Library.

ISBN 978 1 906217 16 7

1 3 5 7 9 10 8 6 4 2

Printed by MPG Books, Bodmin, Cornwall

# Contents

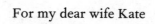

For my dear wife Kate

# *Acknowledgements*

Carolyn Cluskey recalled wine-dark days with Jeffrey Bernard when she worked on the *Sporting Life*, Derwent May foul-mouthed afternoons in the Colony Club. Among the journalists who shared their hazy recollections of Fleet Street before the exodus are Brian Bass, Stephen Boyd, Vic Mayhew, John Patrick, Herbert Pearson, Michael Walker and Pat Welland. Don Walker saved my sanity in many an electronic crisis. My editor at JR Books, Lesley Wilson, has enhanced this one. I admire the publisher, Jeremy Robson, who has started anew at a time when most publishers are thinking of writing *finis*.

# *Introduction*

The pious Normans who spent the night before Hastings in anxious prayer were amazed to see some of their English foes stagger onto the field of battle next day blind drunk. They were not the first to remark the national weakness. The earliest records show the English have always liked getting sloshed. Perhaps this is why the language is so rich in words for drinking and drunkenness: bevvied, blotto, bottled, canned, corked, crapulent, fuddled, hammered, legless, lit up, loaded, maggoty, obfuscated, paralytic, piddled, pie-eyed, pissed, pixillated, plastered, shickered, smashed, soused, sozzled, stoned, stotious, tanked up, tipsy, tight, well-oiled, to name but a few. Drunkards are topers, piss artists, lager louts and pissheads who like to get shit-faced, arseholed, rat-arsed, crocked, off their tits and fluffy.

This applied to all classes, and to the clergy too. Long before the parson-squire with his three bottles a day became a figure of literary fun there were serious complaints that the clergy were setting a bad example. In the middle of the 8th century an archbishop wrote to Cuthbert, Archbishop of Canterbury, saying: 'It is reported that in your diocese the vice of drunkenness is too frequent; so that not only certain bishops do not hinder it, but they themselves indulge in excess of drink, and force others to drink until they are intoxicated. ... This is an evil peculiar to pagans, and to our race. Neither the Franks, nor the Gauls, nor the Lombards, nor the Romans nor the Greeks commit it'. In *Othello* Shakespeare is making the same point when he has Iago say: 'I learned [the song] in England, where indeed they are most potent in potting. Your Dane, your German, and your swag-bellied Hollander ... are nothing to your English ... Why, he drinks you with facility your Dane dead drunk; he sweats not to overthrow your Almaine; he gives your Hollander a vomit, ere the next pottle can be filled.'

Young men and nowadays their Amazonian binge-drinking girlfriends seem to be trying to prove him right as they turn our town centres and urban open spaces into *cloacae* on weekend evenings. There is a kind of desperate triumphalism about the way the young drink. They behave as though they are living in the heroic age of mead halls and warrior kings drinking to the singing of minstrels, an age when life was short and it was worth taking a few risks. Nowadays these risks include confronting foreign football fans, even more ferocious than their English mentors.

The drinking habits of the young have led to a moral panic of a kind seen before. The Gin Mania of the early 18th century led some to predict the imminent doom of the race, or at least the working class. It was an extraordinary outbreak yet the mania burnt itself out, as these things tend to do. Perhaps one day we will speak of binge drinking among the young as something equally unaccountable, but long in the past.

Many people agree that drink, taken in moderation, is one of the great blessings of mankind. This book is a history of drunkenness, and has little or nothing to do with moderation.

# Let No Priest
# Act the Gleeman!

Problem-drinking is an ancient English habit. In the 6th century St David decreed that: 'Those who get drunk through ignorance must do penance fifteen days. If through negligence forty days, if through contempt three quarntains [120 days].' Gildas, a monk who also wrote in the 6th century, lamented that 'not only the laity, but our Lord's own flock and its shepherds, who should have been an example to the people, slumbered away their time in drunkenness, as if they had been dipped in wine'. He advised that if any monk drank so much his speech was too slurred for him to take part in singing the psalms, 'he is to be deprived of his supper'.

The saintly Dunstan, (c.909–988) Archbishop of Canterbury, fought a losing battle against intemperance among his flock and his own clergy. To the former he appealed for an end to drinking in church. Wakes were also a problem, and he urged, 'Let men be very temperate at church-wakes, and pray earnestly, and suffer there no drinking or unseemliness.' His appeal to the clergy is just as direct: 'Let priests beware of drunkeness, and be diligent warning and correcting others in this matter ... Let no priest be an ale-scop, nor in any wise act the gleeman.'

Before the Conquest King Edgar, who died in 975, attempted to regulate the drinks industry. He decreed that there should be only one alehouse per village, and all drinking horns should contain a row of pegs or 'pins' at intervals of about half a pint. No man, he ordered, should drink beyond the next pin in one draught before passing the horn to the next man. Drinkers quickly began to compete to see how many pins they could uncover in one go, and expressions such as 'he is pin-drunk' and 'he is in a merry pin' entered the language. In 1102 the Archbishop of Canterbury forbade priests to get into drinking bouts, 'nor drink to pegs' (Longmate, *The Water Drinkers*).

At a time when the church was the main centre of socialising in a village the villagers found many opportunities to drink there. 'Ales' were celebrations of various kinds, all more or less riotous. At bride-ales the bride provided beer she had brewed herself in exchange for gifts of money. There were also church-ales, tithe-ales, lamb-ales and leet-ales. Scot-ales sound like drinking competitions. The expenses were shared among all the participants, and according to Archbishop Edmund in 1156 'he carries away the credit who hath made the most drunk'.

At the close of the 13th century it was written of a new order of monks at Beverley that they had vowed 'to drink well at their meat, and then afterwards till supper; and afterwards at the collation each must have a piece of candle as long as the arm below the elbow, and as long as there remain a morsel of the candle to burn, the brethren must continue their drinking'. 'A point that they have taken from the Black Monks, that they love drinking forsooth, and are drunk every day, for they know not any other way of living...' Thomas Cromwell acted as Cardinal Wolsey's chief agent in a wide-ranging investigation of corruption in monasteries. 'The scrutiny revealed terrible irregularities in some cases, prominent among which were the vices of gluttony and drunkenness. The result ... was the dissolution of the smaller monasteries [1525]' (French, *Nineteen Centuries of Drink in England*).

Nunneries were little better. Some were hotbeds of drunkenness, feasting, gossiping and worse. The nuns of Coldingham are cited as particularly bad examples by the Rev T.D. Fosbroke in his *British Monachism* of 1817.

'The monasteries were noted for having the best wine and ale, the latter of which they specially brewed for themselves' (French).

Holinshed says the superior wine was called theologicum, because it came 'from the clergy and religious men unto whose houses many of the laity would often send for bottles filled with the same, being sure that they would neither drink nor be served of the worst, or such as was any ways mingled or brewed by the vintner'.

A few historical snapshots:
Walter Mapes, chaplain to Henry II (1133–89), known as 'the jovial archdeacon', confessed his love of good liquor in Bacchanalian verse. This is an English rendering of the original Latin:

> Die I must, but let me die drinking in an inn!
> Hold the wine cup to my lips sparkling from the bin!
> So when angels flutter down to take me from my sin,
> 'Ah, God have mercy on this sot' the cherubs will begin. ...

In the time of King John ( 1167–1216), a monarch who was fond of drink, a writer defined good wine: it should be 'as clear as the tears of a penitent, so that a man may see distinctly to the bottom of his glass. Its colour should represent the greeness of a buffalo's horn. When drunk, it should descend impetuously like thunder, sweet-tasted as an almond, creeping like a squirrel, leaping like a roebuck, strong, like the building of a Cistercian monastery, glittering like a spark of fire, subtle like the logic of the schools of Paris, delicate as fine silk, and colder than crystal'.

On the accession of Richard II (1367) the conduits of the City of London ran with wine for three hours. 'In the upper end of the Cheap was erected a castle with four towers, on two sides of which ran forth wine abundantly. In the towers were placed four beautiful girls dressed in white, who, on the King's approach, blew in his face leaves of gold, and filling cups of gold with wine at the spouts of the castle, presented them to the King and his nobles' (French).

The King was a generous host. At Christmas 1398 at Lichfield when he entertained the Papal Nuncio the guests got through two hundred tuns of wine and two thousand oxen.

When Henry IV came to the throne in 1399 there was a lavish pageant in London. The chronicler Froissart mentions that there were seven fountains in Cheapside and other streets he passed through which perpetually ran with white and red wines.

Prodigious amounts of drink were consumed at public entertainments throughout the 15th century. When George Neville was installed as Archbishop of York in 1464, 300 tuns of ale and 100 tuns of wine were consumed. During the reign of Henry IV 'profusion reigned supreme in high quarters; among the articles which furnished the breakfast table of the nobility were – for a gentleman and his lady, in Lent, a quart of beer and the same quantity of wine at their liveries, a repast taken in their bedrooms immediately before going to roost' (French).

French mentions the Household Book of the Earl of Northumberland, where 'a breakfast bill of fare appears thus: "Breakfast for my lord and my lady: First a loaf of bread in trenchers, two manchets, one quart of beer, a quart of wine, half a chine of mutton else a chine of beef boiled".'

They were dangerous times. To prevent someone slipping poison into the cup of the lord each drink was tested or 'assayed' twice – first by the butler when it was poured in the buttery. This was supervised by the marshall, who covered the cup with its lid, and it was treason for the cup bearer to raise the lid as he bore it to the table. On presenting the cup to his master the cup bearer first removed the lid, poured some of the drink into it and drank it off. Only then was it considered safe for the master to drink.

Another danger was the expense of entertaining the monarch. In one of the *Paston Letters* (cccxliv) Sir John Paston is urged to warn friends to lay in good stocks of wine during a projected royal progress, 'for every man beareth me in hand that the town shall be drank dry, as York was when the King was there'. Among the serious topers helping drink the town dry were the clergy. Pope Innocent VIII sent a Papal Bull to Archbishop Morton in 1490, saying he had heard 'with great grief' from persons worthy of credit that the monks of all the different orders in England had grievously degenerated, that giving themselves up to a reprobate sense they led dissolute lives. 'But the archbishop was fully aware of the evil, for in 1487 he had convened a synod of the prelates and clergy of his province, for the reformation of the manners of his clergy. In this convocation many of the London clergy were accused of spending their whole time in taverns' (French).

## Wallowing in beasty delights

The Tudors certainly knew how to throw a party. When Henry VIII's bride Anne Boleyn was welcomed to the City of London in 1533 a white marble fountain was erected at Gracechurch Corner. Four jets of Rhenish wine rose an ell [about forty five inches] from it and 'met in a cup above the fountain which ran copiously till night'. In the 'great Conduit in Cheap a fountain ran continuously, at one end white wine, at the other claret, all the afternoon' (French). The household books of the kings describe the generous allowance of food and drink for the ladies of the household: a chine of beef, a manchet and a chet loaf was considered enough for breakfast for three. Plus a *gallon* of ale.

Apart from theologicum the ardent drinker had a wide choice: single beer, or small ale; double beer; double double beer; dagger ale; bracket; and most impressive of all, huf cap, which was highly intoxicating. It was also called mad-dog, angels' foot and dragon's milk. In Harrison's *Description of England* (1577) we read: 'These men hale at huf-cap till they be red as cockes, and little wiser than their combs.'

John Taylor, the Water Poet, (1580–1653) wrote:

> There's one thing more I had almost forgot,
> And this is it, of alehouses and innes,
> Wine merchants, vintners, brewers, who much wins
> by others losing, I say more or lesse,
> Who sale of huf-cap liquor do profess.

Gentlemen also brewed the strong March Ale, which took two years to mature. It was usually mixed with spices including nutmeg and ginger. Sometimes a roasted crab was put in it, as in Act 2 of *A Midsummer Night's Dream*:

> Sometimes I lurk in a gossip's bowl,
> In very likeness of a roasted crab;
> And when she drinks, against her lips I bob,
> And on her withered dew-lap pour the ale.

The Puritan writer Philip Stubbes wrote (*The Anatomie of Abuses*, 1583) that the public houses were crowded from morning to night with inveterate drinkers 'whose only care appears to have been where they could obtain the best ale, so totally oblivious to all other things had they become'.

During the reign of James I occurred a famous incident which was grist to the mills of puritanical temperance campaigners. In 1606 James entertained the King of Denmark, and there was a masque or tableau of the arrival of the Queen of Sheba at the court of Solomon. Sir John Harrington described it to Mr Secretary Barlow:

Those whom I never could get to taste good liquor now follow the fashion and wallow in beastly delights. The ladies abandon sobriety and are seen to roll around in intoxication. After dinner the representation of Solomon, his temple and the coming of the Queen of Sheba was made ... or as I may say, was meant to have been made ... the lady who did play the Queen's part did carry most precious gifts to both their majesties, but forgetting the steps arising to the canopy, overset her caskets into his Danish Majesty's lap and fell at his feet ... Much was the hurry and confusion – cloths and napkins were at hand to make all clean. His Majesty then got up and would dance with the Queen of Sheba, but he fell down and humbled himself before her and was carried to the inner chamber and was laid on a bed of state; which was not a little defiled with the presents of the Queen which had been bestowed on his garments; such as wine, cream, cheese, jelly, beverage, cakes, spices, and other good matters. The entertainment and show went forward, and most of the presenters went backward, or fell down, wine did so occupy their upper chambers. Now did appear, in rich dress, Hope, Faith and Charity: Hope did essay to speak, but wine rendered her endeavours so feeble that she withdrew, and hoped the King would excuse her brevity. Faith was then all alone ... and left the Court in staggering condition. ... Charity came to the King's feet, and seemed to cover the multitude of sins her sisters had committed: in some sort she made obeisance and brought gifts, but said she would return home again, as there was no gift which heaven had not already given his majesty; she then returned to Hope and Faith, who were both sick and spewing in the lower hall. Next came Victory, in bright armour, and presented a rich sword to the King, who did not accept it, but put it by with his hand; and by a strange medley of versification, did endeavour to make suit to the King; but ... after much lamentable utterance she was led away like a silly captive, and laid to sleep in the outer steps of the ante-chamber. Now did Peace make entry, and strive to get foremost to the King; but I grieve to tell how great wrath she did discover unto those of her attendants, and much contrary to her own semblance, most rudely made war with her olive branch, and laid on the pates of those who did oppose her coming.

The gunpowder fright [the Gunpowder Plot] is out of all our heads and we are going hereabouts as if the devil were contriving every man should blow himself up by wild riot, excess and devastation of wine and intemperance (Samuelson, *The History of Drink*).

Scenes of wild riot and excess were not confined to high places. In 1617 Thomas Young reported in *England's Bane or the Description of Drunkenness* a drinking competition which would surely have resulted in death from alcohol poisoning if it had been carried to its logical conclusion.

There are in London drinking schools: so that drunkenness is professed with us as a liberal art and science ... I have seen a company amongst the very woods and forests drinking for a muggle [prize]. Six determined to try their strengths who could drink most glasses for the muggle. The first drinks a glass of a pint, the second two, the next three, and so every one multiplieth till the last taketh six. Then the first beginneth again and taketh seven, and in this manner they drink thrice a piece round, every man taking a glass more than his fellow, so that he that drank least, which was the first, drank one and twenty pints, and the sixth man thirty six.

Even in hard-drinking times it was possible to go too far. The Elizabethans paraded persistent topers through the streets in a barrel with the bottom removed and holes cut in the sides for the arms. This was known as 'the drunkard's cloak'. For persistent drunkenness the punishment under a law of 1604 was a fine of five shillings or six hours in the stocks.

# *Pepys is Overheated With Drink*

The diarist Samuel Pepys was as frank about his drinking as his womanising. He struggled with his liking for drink, which fell well short of alcoholism but often left him with a sore head. He would start with his 'morning draught' of ale and then occasionally, unless he was on the wagon, during the day consume a wider variety of drinks than is generally available today. The diary mentions mead, metheglin, various wines, ale, beer and brandy. The wines include Rhenish, muscadine, English, sack, Bristol milk, canary, claret, hippocras, Malaga and Navarre.

On the morning of 8 February 1660, what the comedian Billy Connolly might have called a day of great drink, Pepys practised playing his flageolet, looked at his pigeons and then took Mr Fossan, who had been a fellow student at Cambridge, to the Swan in Palace Yard for a morning draught. They were joined by a Captain Lidcott and had another drink. Afterwards they went to the Rhenish Wine House, and on the way met a Mr Hoole. At the Rhenish 'I paid for my cousin Roger Pepys his wine'. He later went to his father's house, 'and I went down to his kitchen, and there we eat and drank; and about 9 a-clock I went away homewards, and ... to bed with my head not well, by my too much drinking today.'

His descriptions of throwing up and hangovers after drinking too much are perhaps not in the same class as those of Martin Amis (*Money*) and Tom Wolfe (*The Bonfire of the Vanities*) but are good as straightforward reporting: 'I could not sleep ... being overheated with drink ... and quite out of order' (9 March 1660); 'my brains somewhat troubled with so much wine' (1 December 1660); 'About the middle of the night I was very ill, I think, with eating and drinking too much … and vomited in the bason' (27 December 1660).

On 9 October 1663, Pepys went to Guildford and met some friends. Wine was offered and Pepys, who was on the wagon, recorded: 'They drunk, I only drinking some hypocras, which do not break my vow, it being, to the best of my present judgment, only a mixed compound drink, and not any wine. If I am mistaken, God forgive me! But I hope and do think that I am not.'

Pepys greatly enjoyed his drink, but often had misgivings. In September 1665 he was 'much troubled' that he was getting the reputation of being a heavy drinker. His 'late little drinking of wine is taken notice of by envious men to my disadvantage'. At the same time he is proud of his cellar, which he describes lovingly. It reflects his status:

> at this time I have two tierces of claret – two quarter-cask of canary, and a smaller vessel of sack – a vessel of tent [red Spanish wine], another of Malaga, and another of white wine, all in my wine-cellar together – which I believe none of my friends now alive ever had of his own at one time. (July 1665)

Pepys gradually brought his drinking under control. By the end of the diaries he is drinking wine mainly at meals, but then 'liberally'.

Pepys had many a sore head from the seventeenth-century equivalent of business lunches. He was proud of his wine cellar.

# *Last Orders, Please!*

The state began to regulate drinking in 1552, when the first major Licensing Act came into force. Another Act followed two years later, and together they laid down rules for the liquor trade that have survived broadly unchanged until today. Landlords needed a licence from the justices to open a 'tippling house'. The justices could refuse a licence or impose conditions. These varied from place to place: in one parish an alehouse[1] might be open all day every day, and in a neighbouring parish an alehouse might have to close early on weekdays and remain closed on Sundays. 'One almost universal requirement, however, was that licensed premises should be in a spot open to observation, and consist of good-sized rooms where villains could not conspire unseen' (Longmate, *The Water Drinkers*).

However squalid, alehouses, where the poor drank, were only relatively cheap, in comparison with the inns in towns and on the main highways. The historian Peter Clark (*The English Alehouse*) has estimated that in the Middle Ages four pints of the weaker beer would have cost a labourer about a third of his daily wage. The brew was often of poor quality, flat and sour. Clark quotes a 14th-century drinker who complained that it was 'muddy, foggy, fulsome, puddle, stinking'. Better to be employed by the lord of the manor as a servant or day labourer with food and drink as part of the wages. The larger households employed an expert alewife, and the drink served to the workers would be fresh and of better quality than that sold in alehouses.

The quality of the alehouse product improved throughout the Middle Ages, partly owing to the use of hops instead of spices. The number of alehouses grew rapidly, and so did wages. Christopher Hibbert (*The English*) says that while the 13th-century labourer could hardly afford a pint or two, two centuries later a building craftsman in the south of England was earning enough to buy four gallons of good ale with his daily wage. By then, while alehouses were not yet respectable places for a family to go, men and women could relax and sing and gamble, and as Clark points out, the men could pick up a prostitute. With their higher wages the labouring classes were aping their betters. In the 14th-century poem *Piers Plowman* we meet in the ale-seller Breton's house Tim the tinker and two of his apprentices, Hick the hackneyman, Hugh the needleseller, a shoemaker, a warner and his wife, Daw the ditcher, a rat-catcher, the priest, a ropemaker and a dozen whores and 'a whole heap of upholsterers'.

One of those present is Glutton, whom Breton has enticed in when he was on his way to church. He drinks more than a gallon of her wares:

He could neither step nor stand till a staff held him,
And then began to go like a gleeman's bitch,
Sometimes aside and sometimes backwards ...
And he drew to the door all dimmed before him,
He stumbled on the threshold and was thrown backwards.
(*Piers Plowman*, modernised by H.W. Wells, 1935)

The march of the alehouse continued, in spite of competition from brandy and gin shops and various kinds of pub. A government survey in 1577 deduced that there were about 24,000 alehouse keepers in England – one for every 142 inhabitants. Early in the 17th century one observer commented that London's streets were 'replenished' with them, and in Bristol in about 1700 there was one for every 56 people. At a later date the growth was clear to John Howard, the prison reformer, who wrote of the 'great and increasing number of alehouses' he saw in his travels around the country. Because alehouses had red-painted windows they were conspicuous. In 1632 the dramatist Thomas Dekker wrote that 'a whole street was in some places but a continuous alehouse, not a shop to be seen between red lattice and red lattice'.

Not yet under the control of the justices were taverns[2], described by an 18th-century writer as 'a degree above an alehouse'. There you might get drunk with 'more credit and apology'. They too were regulated in the 18th century. Drinking was strictly stratified socially. The poor drank in alehouses, the better off in inns. In between there were taverns. Timothy Nouse left an unflattering picture of alehouses in *Campania Felix* (1706).

> The superfluous number of such petty inns and alehouses seems to proceed from two causes: the first is from the application [for a licence] which is made frequently on behalf of some broken, half-starved merchant or idle fellow who rather than beg or stand and be hanged or at best become chargeable to the parish hopes to get a subsistence by the little cheating and degenerate shifts of ale-selling. The other course is much of the same figure, it being commonly no other than sordid interest of some mean-spirited justice who, to maintain a superfluous or indigent member of his family, or acquaintance, is tempted easily to licence alehouses for the sake of the fees.

## Slumming with Ned Ward

Ned Ward, the author of the *London Spy* (1698–1709), himself a tavern keeper and an acute observer of the London scene, wrote of an unsavoury Billingsgate alehouse:

> In a narrow lane, as dark as a burial vault, which stunk of stale sprats and Sir-reverence, we groped around like a couple of thieves in a coal-hole, to find the entrance to that nocturnal theatre in whose delightful scenes we proposed to terminate the night's felicity. At last we stumbled upon the threshold of a gloomy tavern ...
>
> We no sooner entered but heard such a number of female tongues so promiscuously engaged in a mess of tittle-tattle, that had a waterman knocked down his wife with his stretcher, and been tried for the fact by a parliament of fishwomen they could not have exercised their nimble instruments with more impatience.
>
> We turned ourselves into the smoky boozing den among them: where round the fire sat a tattered assembly of motherly flat-caps [Billingsgate fishwomen] ... with everyone her nipperkin of warm ale and brandy.
>
> The one looking behind her and spying me over her shoulder accosts

me after this manner. 'God save you honest master, will you pledge me?' 'Aye, Dame,' says I, 'with all my heart.' 'Why then,' says she, 'here's a health to mine arse and a fart for those that owe no money.'

His friend urged him to leave.

'Come, come away,' says my friend, 'these saucy tongued old whores will tease us to death.' Which unhappy words one of them overheard, and starting up like a fury, thus gives her lungs a breathing. 'You white-livered son of a Fleet Street bumsitter, begot upon a chair at noonday between Ludgate and Temple Bar. You puppily offspring of a mangy night walker, who was forced to play the whore an hour before she cried out, to pay the bawd her midwife, for bringing you, you bastard, into the world, who is it that you call whores?'

Ned and his friend escaped to a nearby room, packed with 'as many sorts of rakes as you may see whores at a buttock ball'.

Respectable people would go to such an establishment only when slumming, if at all, although in the 19th century upper-class swells would organise outings to the sailors' drinking dens along London's Ratcliffe Highway for an exotic evening out.

After the all-conquering Puritans defeated the Royalists in the Civil War they launched a moral crusade. Drunkenness became a serious offence, adultery and incest were liable to the death penalty, fornication could be punished with three months' imprisonment, and prostitutes could be whipped, branded and jailed for a first offence, and excuted for a second. A proposed law to ban face make-up and the wearing of patches and immodest dress was dropped.

Serious drinking went on, however, particularly among the better-off. There was an Everlasting Club devoted to singing and drinking. It was said to have 'smoked fifty tons of tobacco, drunk 30,000 bottles of ale, 1,000 hogsheads of red port and 200 bottles of brandy'.

The kill-joy Puritans also failed to completely suppress the fleshpots that were beginning to earn the Drury Lane area a bad reputation. Some tavern-brothels, such as 'Oxford Kate's' in Bow Street, continued to trade, probably because their owners had powerful and influential customers.

The politician Sir Ralph Verney ate there despite its reputation because the food was so good. From 1652 the ever-resourceful whores found a new outlet: the new coffee houses became meeting places for them and their clients. A Frenchman reported during the Commonwealth: 'Drinking is the afternoon diversion ... As for taverns, London is composed of them.'

There were as many euphemisms for drunkenness in the 17th century as there are today, but most of the old ones have fallen out of use. In 1635 *The Drunkard Opened* listed some of them: 'He is foxt [as foxed, still used facetiously today], he is flustered, he is subtle, cupshot, he hath seen the French king, he hath swallowed a tavern-token, he hath whipt the cat, he hath been at the scriveners, he is a bit of a barne-weasell.' 'If you were foolish enough to get hicksius-dixious on rough spirit, you might feel womblety-cropt the next day' (Lisa Picard, *Dr Johnson's London*).

When the reign of the godly finally came to an end, many people prepared to get subtle and cupshot.

# Good King Charles's Golden Days

Eleven years of sour puritanism left most of the English with a great thirst and a hatred of the excesses of puritanism that has lasted. The Restoration of Charles II in 1660 brought back the colour and glamour that had been missing in their lives, and a king who was, in the words of the historian Macauley, 'addicted beyond measure to sensual indulgence'. When he entered London in May the streets were literally running with wine and while Charles received the great men of state the common people made up for a lot of lost time. Many of them availed themselves of the hospitality of the Venetian ambassador, who kept wine on tap outside his residence all day.

What kind of regime did Charles's hungover subjects wake up to the next day? Charles's court was dissolute, and the manners of that court have affected society to this day. With him came a group of young aristo-crats who were if anything more profligate, and much harder drinkers. In fact the king, libidinous to a degree, was reputed to be a moderate drinker.

The man who would eventually earn the reputation of being the most dissolute at the court of King Charles was John Wilmot, Earl of Rochester. He wrote to his friend Henry Savile in June 1674:

Of the three businesses of this age, Women, Politics and Drinking, the last is the only exercise at which you and I have not proved ourselves arrant fumblers. If you have the vanity to think otherwise,

17

when we meet next let us appeal to friends of both sexes and as they shall determine, live and die sheer drunkards, or entire lovers; for as we might mingle the matter, it is hard to say which is the more tiresome creature, the loving drunkard or the drunken lover.

Rochester was a rake, and perhaps he sells himself short as a lover. Chancellor (*Rakes*) tells a story of heartless seductions planned by him and his friend the Duke of Buckingham. They rented an inn and passed themselves off as the landlords, getting gentlemen drunk on free wine so they could seduce their wives. They decided to close their campaign with one further seduction. Nearby lived an old miser with a 'very pretty young wife'.

The old man was exceedingly jealous of his charming spouse, and kept her carefully under the surveillance of himself or of an elderly maiden sister who lived with him. He was one of the few whom Rochester and Buckingham never could prevail upon to accept of their hospitality – at least in company with his wife. As, however, he liked good cheer (when it cost him nothing) as well as most, it was arranged by the two reprobates that Buckingham should invite him to the inn while Rochester, disguised as a woman, should go to his house and do his best to deceive the dragon (otherwise the maiden sister) who guarded it, and thus gain admittance to the young wife.

Rochester went to the house, drugged the maiden, seduced the young wife and persuaded her to steal all the miser's money. He took her back to the inn and after enjoying her again handed her over to Buckingham, who also seduced her. When they tired of her they kicked her out, telling her to go to London 'to follow the only trade for which she was now fitted'. The miser returned to his house to find his wife and his money gone, and hanged himself. The courtiers reportedly laughed heartily when Rochester and Buckingham told this tale.

Drink got Rochester and his cronies into trouble on many occasions. Two of them, Sir Charles Sedley and Lord Buckhurst, tested the very limits of official tolerance one day at the appropriately named Cock Tavern (also known as Oxford Kate's) in Bow Street. After bingeing for hours the two stepped onto the balcony and exposed their genitals to angry onlookers. In his diary Pepys described how Sedley acted ...

all the postures of lust and buggery that could be imagined, and abusing of scripture and, as it were, from whence preaching a mountebank sermon from that pulpit, saying that there he had to sell such a powder as would make all the cunts in the town run after him. And that being done he took a glass of wine and washed his prick in it and then drank it off; and then took another and drunk the king's health.

The furious crowd stormed the tavern and the two men narrowly escaped lynching. When they were brought before the courts the Lord Chief Justice told Sedley that it was because of wicked wretches like him 'that God's anger and judgement hangs over us'. Clearly puritanism, though defeated, was still a powerful strand in the fabric of everyday life. Sedley was bound over with a forfeit of £5,000 (about £50,000 today) for bad behaviour. It doesn't seem to have cramped his style.

On another occasion, in October 1668, Sedley and Buckhurst ran about the streets showing their backsides after a drinking binge. They brawled with the parish police, the Watch, and were held in jail overnight. The King intervened and the constable was given a reprimand for arresting them.

Young men usually grow out of this kind of behaviour. Rochester and his friends didn't, and there was a streak of cynical cruelty in them: they were true rakes.

## I spew in her lap

In a poem of 1673 Rochester describes the daily routine of a debauched man-about-town:

> I rise at eleven, I dine about two,
> I get drunk before seven, and the next thing I do,
> I send for my whore, when for fear of a clap,
> I spend in her hand, and I spew in her lap;
> Then we quarrel and scold, till I fall fast asleep,
> When the bitch growing bold, to my pocket does creep.
> Then slyly she leaves me, and to revenge the affront,
> At once she bereaves me of money and cunt.
> If by chance then I wake, hot-headed and drunk,
> What a coil do I make for the loss of my punk!
> I storm and I roar, and I fall in a rage.
> And missing my whore, I bugger my page ...

Rochester wrote searing satires against the King, but the monarch always forgave his young friend in the end, because he was such entertaining company. However, the moral anarchy of Rochester's life sometimes drove the King to helpless fury. In June 1675 the Earl had been drinking in the King's apartments at Westminster with Buckhurst and some other young rakes. As they left they came across the King's sundial in the Privy Garden. This elaborate and valuable artefact was really a device for measuring celestial motions. The King, who was deeply interested in astronomy, treasured it. Rochester and his friends smashed it to pieces. It has been suggested that it looked rather phallic, and Rochester is reported as saying: 'Dost thou stand there to fuck time?'

The Earl of Rochester, perhaps the most licentious of Charles II's dazzling courtiers. His short life was a chaos of drink, sex and brawls, much of his poetry often so obscene that it wasn't printed for many years.

When he sobered up Rochester realised he had gone much too far, and left town. The King too, in his grief and rage, left the court – and vanished. He had gone to Plymouth, where he set out cruising on his yacht *Greyhound*. For ten days nothing was heard of him, and there was consternation. Pepys at the Admiralty feared he had been lost at sea, and the King's mistresses were distraught. The King was after all their meal-ticket.

Charles eventually returned safe to harbour and to court, and he and Rochester were reconciled, but the young rake was dying of syphilis. He died in July 1680, seemingly after a deathbed conversion. His scepticism about everlasting life was evident in a poem he had written just four months before:

Dead we become the lumber of the world,
And to that mass of matter shall be swept
Where things destroyed with things unborn are kept.
Devouring time swallows us whole;
Impartial death confounds body and soul.
For Hell and the foul fiend that rules
God's everlasting fiery jails
(Devised by rogues, dreaded by fools)
With his grim, grisly dog that keeps the door,
Are senseless stories, idle tales,
Dreams, whimsies and no more.

## The gentleman and the rake

Rochester's life is an example of the price genius pays for alcohol. His drinking companion Buckingham lived longer and perhaps drank less but his life can also be seen as a tragic waste. He was an accomplished poet, a statesman and wit. He also had a European reputation as a depraved and extravagant rake, who killed the Earl of Shrewsbury in a duel over the Earl's wife and dissipated a great fortune.

Louis XIV described the Duke of Buckingham as the only true English gentleman that he had ever met, and others were equally dazzled. Bishop Burnet, who disapproved of him, wrote of his noble presence, adding: 'He was a man of ... a most lovely wit, wholly turned to mirth and pleasure.' The Puritan cleric Dean Lockier told Pope that Buckingham 'was

The Duke of Buckingham had
matchless charm and a taste for
squalid debauchery. He and his
friend Rochester took over an
inn to get men drunk and
seduce their wives.

reckoned the most
accomplished man of
the age in riding,
dancing and fencing.
When he came into the
Presence Chamber, it was
impossible for you not to
follow him with your eye, he
moved so gracefully.'

Buckingham's father had been a
favourite of King James I. He was assassinated by a disgruntled soldier,
and the young Duke was taken into the royal household and brought up
with the future Charles II. They were to have a complicated and
sometimes difficult relationship when Charles became King.

After the royalists lost the Battle of Worcester Buckingham went into
hiding in London, and Chancellor (*Rakes*) tells a strange tale of an
encounter with Bridget Cromwell, daughter of the Protector and wife of
his chief lieutenant, Ireton. According to Chancellor, Buckingham
impersonated a kind of busker, giving public performances of ballads so
that he could move around the city gathering intelligence. Bridget
Cromwell, says Chancellor, saw him and was strongly attracted. Not of
course realising who he was she invited him to her home and tried to
seduce him. He escaped her attentions by saying he was a Jew. Once out
of danger he wrote her a letter, telling her who he was.

*Chambers Biographical Dictionary* says that for the next 25 years
Buckingham excelled all the other courtiers in depravity and wit. He took
up with the lovely and vicious Anna Maria, Countess of Shrewsbury,
where many others had been before him. Anthony Hamilton wrote of her:

'Though nobody could brag that he alone had been kindly entertained by her, there was no one who could contend that his suit had been ill received' (*Memoirs of the Comte de Gramont*).

Men fought duels over her, and in January 1668 Buckingham fatally wounded her husband after the Countess engineered a duel between them. Eventually the countess abandoned him and he let himself go, drinking with tosspots and whores. His friend Nell Gwynn, the King's mistress, pleaded with him to smarten himself up. She asked him to 'buy new shoes that he might not dirty her rooms, and a new periwig that she might not smell him stink two storeys high when he knocks at the outward door'. His extravagance cost him his great estates and houses, but this once-great nobleman seemed happy with the life of a country squire, hunting, living in a ruin and spending his nights trying to turn base metal into gold. He died after catching a chill while hunting. He had written his own epitaph in his commonplace book: 'Fortune filled him too full, and he run over.'

It is not altogether surprising that there was heavy drinking in Restoration England. Almost everyone drank some alcohol, partly because water was unsafe to drink. The French visitor Cesar de Saussure like many foreigners was astonished at how much the English drank. He clearly had not heard about the water when he wrote in *A Foreign View of England in the Reigns of George I and George II*:

Would you believe it, though water is to be had in abundance in London and of fairly good quality, absolutely none is drunk? The lower classes, even the paupers, do not know what it is to quench their thirst with water. In this country nothing but beer is drunk, and it is made in several qualities. Small beer is what everyone drinks when thirsty; it is used even in the best houses, and costs only a penny the pot. Another kind of beer is called porter, meaning carrier, because the greater quantity of this beer is consumed by the working classes. It is a thick and strong beverage, and the effect it produces, if drunk in excess, is the same as that of wine; this porter costs threepence the pot. In London there are a number of alehouses, where nothing but this sort of beer is sold. There are again other clear beers, called ale, some of them being as transparent as fine old wine, foreigners often mistaking them at first for the latter ... it is said that more corn is consumed in England for the making of beer than for making bread.

The poor sick in St Bartholomew's Hospital were entitled to three pints of beer a day, and boys at Eton were admonished if they did not get through their daily allowance.

Until the arrival of the Dutch King William III in 1688 the English drank fermented liquors – wine, beer, mead and cider. The Dutch and the English soldiers who had served in the Low Countries brought back with them a taste for gin, a spirit distilled from grain. The English had a surplus of low-grade corn unsuitable for brewing but capable of being made into gin. The government imposed heavy duties on imported spirits to encourage a new English distilling industry, and created a free-for-all by leaving it uncontrolled. They had, in a sense, opened the gates of Hell.

# The Gin Mania

Daniel Defoe wrote in 1728: 'Our common people get so drunk on a Sunday that they cannot work of a day or two following. Nay, since the use of Geneva [gin] has become so common many get so drunk they cannot work at all, but run from one irregularity to another, till at last they become arrant rogues.'

He was writing about the craze for drinking cheap spirits, which afflicted London's poor from the 1720s to the 1750s.

Parliament was dominated by gentlemen farmers, the country was producing a glut of grain and distilling it into gin was vastly profitable. Taxes on gin were reduced. The duty was only 2d a gallon, sellers didn't need a retail licence and soon the drink was being sold in thousands of premises of varying degrees of respectability – in 1725 there were 6,187 in the capital excluding the City and Southwark. By contrast, the vastly bigger London of 1945 had only 4,000 pubs.

A committee of justices reported in 1726 that gin was being sold 'even in the streets and highways, on bulks [stalls] set up for that purpose, in wheelbarrows and privately in garrets, cellars, backrooms and other places … Such who sell fruit or herbs in stalls sell Geneva, and many inferior tradesmen begin now to keep it in their shops for their customers, whereby it is scarce possible for soldiers, seamen, servants or others of their rank, to go anywhere without being drawn in … In the hamlet of Bethnal Green above forty weavers sell it. And if we may judge what will happen in other workhouses now erecting, by what has already happened in that of St Giles in the Fields, we have reason to fear the violent fondness and desire of this liquor, which unaccountably possesses all our poor, may prevent in great measure the good effects proposed by them.'

Gin was cheap — 'Drunk for a Penny, Dead Drunk for two pence, Clean Straw for Nothing' was the boast of the gin shops. Most of the distilling of gin took place in London, and most of the drinking. Among the poor, almost everyone drank it — men, women and children, even infants. It was used as an anaesthetic to silence starving children. It was a food substitute for their starving parents. The drink's vile taste and lethal potency — it was sold at the strength it came from the still, much stronger than the gin sold today — were disguised by heavy sweetening with sugar and flavouring with cordials. A cheap skinful brought a few hours escape from misery.

The results were appalling. Judith Defour, a wretched dipsomaniac, 'never in her right mind but always roving', fetched her two-year-old child from a workhouse where it had been given new clothes. She strangled it, sold the clothes for 1s 4d, left the naked body in a ditch at Bethnal Green, split the money with the woman who had suggested the crime and spent the rest on gin. The *Gentlemen's Magazine* reported: 'There were executed at Tyburn, July 6, Elizabeth Banks for stripping a child; Catherine Conway, for forging a seaman's ticket; and Margaret Harvey for robbing her master. They were all drunk.'

People reeled about the streets or collapsed in gutters at all hours of the day and night. In the middle of the day men, women and children lay stupefied by the roadside in slum areas such as St Giles and Whetstone Park. Inside the gin shops unconscious customers were propped up against the walls until they came round and could start again. In 1743 more than eight million gallons of the fiery spirit were consumed, according to official estimates, but some thought the figure was as high as 19 million gallons. And by far the greatest part of it went down the throats of the poor of London. As well as the thousands of outlets described above it was sold in prisons. In Newgate and London's other prisons it was known as Strip Me Naked, Kill-Grief, Cock-My-Cap, Comfort, Poverty, Meat-and-Drink, Diddle, Heart's Ease, A Kick In The Guts, Tape, White Wool and Washing and Lodging.

## A new kind of drunkenness

The novelist and magistrate Henry Fielding wrote in *An Inquiry in the Causes of the late Increase of Robbers etc*:

A new kind of drunkenness, unknown to our ancestors, is lately sprung up amongst us, and which, if not put a stop to, will infallibly destroy a great part of the inferior people. The drunkenness I here intend is that acquired by the strongest intoxicating liquors, and particularly by that poison called Gin; which I have great reason to think is the principal sustenance (if it may be so called) of more than a hundred thousand people in this metropolis. Many of these wretches there are who swallow pints of this poison within the twenty four hours; the dreadful effects of which I have the misfortune every day to see, and to smell too. But I have no need to insist on my own credit, or on that of my informers; the great revenue arising from the tax on this liquor (the consumption of which is almost wholly confined to the lowest order of people), will prove the quantity consumed better than any other evidence.

Particularly disturbing was the extent to which women were 'habituated' to gin. 'We find the contagion has spread among [women] to a degree hardly possible to be conceived,' reported a committee of the Middlesex magistrates in 1736. 'Unhappy mothers habituate themselves to these distilled liquors, whose children are born weak and sickly, and often look old and shrivelled as though they had numbered many years; others, again, give [gin] daily to their children, whilst young, and learn them, even before they can go [walk] to taste and approve of this great and certain destroyer.'

London had long sucked in healthy young people from the countryside, used them up and spat them out into graveyards. At the height of the Gin Mania in the 1740s, there were twice as many burials as baptisms in the city. Corbyn Morris commented: 'Enquire from the several hospitals in the City, whether any increase of patients and what sort, are daily brought under their care. They will all declare, increasing multitudes of dropsical and consumptive people arising from the effects of spirituous liquors.'

The government made clumsy efforts to curb the mania it had created. In 1729 following a campaign led by the Middlesex magistrates a licence fee of £20 for retailing spirits was imposed, and the spirit duty was raised from 2d to 5s a gallon. These measures were found to be unworkable and repealed in 1733, a move which was followed by another wave of drunkenness and disorder. This in turn led to the more draconian 'Gin Act' of 1736 requiring a £50 licence for retailing.

There was rioting, an explosion in Westminster Hall and threats to the life of the Master of the Rolls, Joseph Jekyll, seen as the chief initiator of the Act. Five informers under the Gin Act were stoned to death, one of them in New Palace Yard. A particular hate figure was the magistrate Sir Thomas de Veil, loathed among other things for his attempts to implement the Gin Act. In William Hogarth's print *Night* a figure which would have been clearly recognisable to contemporaries as Sir Thomas has the contents of a chamber pot poured over his head. This refers to a story that Sir Thomas was one day sampling gin, only to find that an ill-wisher had replaced it with piss. In January 1738 a mob besieged his house in Frith Street, threatening to burn it and kill his informers.

Popular violence effectively killed the law, and in seven years only three of the expensive licences were paid for. The law spawned a horde of informers: in a period of less than two years there were 12,000 cases, and nearly 5,000 convictions.

The rage for gin gradually subsided. In 1751 some gin-shops were suppressed, and the increase in taxes was eventually so effective that in 1757 an observer commented: 'We do not see the hundredth part of poor wretches drunk in the street since the said qualifications.' An American visitor to London noted that the common people were still drinking heavily, but beer and porter rather than spirits, 'because its excessive dearness placed it almost beyond their reach'. Consumption of British spirits fell to one million gallons a year by 1784.

The Restoration had also unleashed a tidal wave of beer drinking across the country. Licences for new alehouses were granted 'almost on demand' (Longmate, *The Water Drinkers*). Throughout the 18th century one of the few things rich and poor had in common was a joy in getting drunk.

The Gin Mania was almost wholly a London phenomenon. Up and down the land, the poor drank in alehouses, as they had for generations. Alehouses were still often sordid, with earthen floors and just a table or two and a few chairs for furniture. Here the common man drank his solace for a life of unending toil and hardship. He was only copying, as far as he could afford, the behaviour of his betters. The Sussex shopkeeper Thomas Turner described rural revels in his diary (*Diary of Thomas Turner, 1754-1765*). 'We continued drinking like horses, as the vulgar phrase is, and singing till many of us were very drunk, and then we went to dancing, and pulling wigs, caps and hats; and thus we continued in this frantic manner, behaving more like mad people than they that profess the name of Christians.'

## Walpole's wine bill

Members of Parliament would loll or snore drunkenly on their benches, as would magistrates. Hibbert (*The English*) says that when the Mutiny Act was framed it included a clause saying court martials should take place at times of the day when its members were likely to be sober. In 1774 guests at the Lord Mayor's dinner at London's Mansion House drank 626 dozen bottles of wine. Prime Minister Robert Walpole spent a small fortune on wine, even though he was also smuggling large quantities into the country for his own use. In 1733 he spent the enormous sum of £1118 with the wine merchant James Bennett, and £48 with another vintner, Schaart and Co. That year his household consumed 1200 bottles of white wine alone. Two years later Lord Hervey wrote to Frederick, Prince of Wales: 'Our company at Houghton [Walpole's magnificent new stately home] swelled at last into so numerous a body that we used to sit down to dinner with a snug little party of thirty odd, up to the chin in beef, geese, turkeys etc; and generally over the chin in claret, strong beer and punch.'

In fact drunkenness was so common that it could sometimes excuse even homicide. The *Gentlemen's Magazine* reported in 1748:

At a christening at Beddington in Surrey the nurse was so intoxicated that after she had undressed the child, instead of laying it in the cradle she put it behind a large fire, which burnt it to death in a few minutes. She was examined before a magistrate and said she was quite stupid and senseless, so that she took the child for a log of wood; on which she was discharged.

Alehouses gradually became less disreputable. By the middle of the 18th century some became almost indistinguishable from taverns: both began to be referred to as public houses. They served food, tobacco and snuff, and newspapers were provided for customers. They were respectable enough for women to be seen there. In Smollett's *The Life and Adventures of Sir Launcelot Greaves*, 1760, there is a description of the kitchen of a country alehouse[1], 'paved with red bricks, remarkably clean, furnished with three or four windsor chairs, adorned with shining plates of pewter and copper sauce-pans nicely scoured, while a cheerful fire of sea-coal blazed in the chimney.'

   The seductive image of the tavern as a haven of warmth, good drink and food and male good fellowship, untouched by fashion, long predates the *Pickwick Papers*. (The modern rage to re-create it has led to the destruction of thousands of interesting but later interiors.) It is the invention of course of writers, and it is hardly surprising that writers were particularly the prisoners of this fantasy. An evening spent tippling in the company of one's friends in a jolly tavern or by a comfortable domestic fireside could not be harmful, surely? Jonathan Swift was startled to be told by a friend that he drank too much. He said he never drank more than his physician prescribed, but his physician was a two-bottle man himself. A satire of 1715 says Swift 'was heard to make some self-denying promises in prayer, that, for the time to come, he would stint himself to two or three bottles in the evening'. An invitation from the Archbishop of Cashel suggests he had a reputation among his friends as a drinker. Giving him minute directions about the route, the archbishop mentions that he would pass the home of a parson who kept a good cellar, in which he always had a hogshead of the very best wine. Swift's 'Country Quarter Sessions' begins:

   Three or four parsons full of October,
   Three or four squires between drunk and sober.

William Somerville, author of the once-popular poem 'The Chace', had this memorial in a letter by his friend William Shenstone: 'For a man of high spirit, conscious of having, (at least in one production) generally pleased the world, to be plagued and threatened by wretches that are low in every sense; to be forced to drink himself into pains of the body, in order to be rid of the pains of the mind, is a misery.'

   The actor James Quin, who once had to flee the country after a brawl, and was described by French (*Nineteen Centuries of Drink*) as a *bon vivant*, is recalled more vividly in Garrick's amusing epitaph than in any review of his great tragic roles:

   A plague on Egypt's arts! I say;
   Embalm the dead, on senseless clay

Rich wines and spices waste!
Like sturgeon, or like brawn, shall I,
Bound in a precious pickle, lie,
Which I shall never taste.

Let me embalm this flesh of mine
With turtle fat and Bordeaux wine,
And spoil th' Egyptian trade.
Than Humphry's Duke more happy I;
Embalm'd alive, old Quin shall die,
A mummy ready made.

The convivial poet James Thomson, author of once-famous *Seasons*, was a friend of Quin. French tells an anecdote about him: 'Mr H. of Bangor said he was once asked to dinner by Thomson, but could not attend. One of his friends who was there said that there was a general stipulation agreed on by the whole company that there should be no hard drinking. Thomson acquiesced, only requiring that each man should drink his bottle. The terms were accepted unconditionally, and when the cloth was removed a three-quart bottle was set before each of his guests. Thomson had much of this agreeable kind of humour.'

## Boswell dead drunk

James Boswell was frank about his weakness for wine and women. He practised law briefly and unsuccessfully. Lord Eldon, the Lord Chancellor, recalled in his *Anecdote Book* how Boswell was found lying dead drunk on the pavement at Lancaster assizes about the year 1782. Eldon and his colleagues next morning sent him a guinea and a brief, supposedly from a client, instructing him to appear in court 'to move for the writ of "*Quare adhesit pavimento*". In vain did the perplexed and bibulous barrister apply to all the attorneys of his acquaintance for information as to the nature of the writ for which he was instructed to move, and great was the astonishment of the Judge when the application was made to him. At last one of the Bar, amidst the laughter of the Court, exclaimed: "My Lord, Mr Boswell *adhesit pavimento* last night. There was no moving him for some time. At length he was carried to bed, and has been dreaming of what happened to himself."'

Boswell's friend Dr Johnson, who came from Lichfield in Staffordshire, recalled that in his youth 'all the decent people in Lichfield got drunk every night, and were not the worse thought of'. Johnson explained his own abstinence by admitting that he could not drink in moderation. He said the point of getting drunk was 'to lose self, to throw self away'. He also, when asked if a man could be happy 'in the moment that was present', replied: 'Never but when he is drunk'.

In conversation with an old college friend named Edwards in April 1778 Johnson became humorously preachy:

Edwards: How do you live, sir? For my part, I must have my regular meals and a glass of good wine. I find I require it.

Johnson: I now drink no wine, sir. Early in life I drank wine; for many years I drank none. I then for some years drank a good deal …

Edwards: I am grown old: I am sixty-five.

Johnson: I shall be sixty-eight next birthday. Come sir, DRINK WATER AND PUT IN FOR A HUNDRED.

## Savage drinker

Johnson's poet friend Richard Savage was a ferocious drinker. He narrowly escaped the gallows after killing a gentleman in a drunken brawl. He dissipated the £50 pension Queen Anne awarded him in 1732 in a week's drinking. Johnson wrote his *Life*, and let him off lightly:

An irregular and dissipated manner of life had made him the slave of every passion that happened to be excited by the presence of its object, and the slavery to his passions reciprocally produced a life irregular and dissipated. He was not master of his own motions, nor could promise anything for the next day.

He also said that Savage 'in no part of his life was it any part of his character to be the first of the company that desired to separate'. Lord Tyrconnel left a less diffident portrait:

It was the constant practice of Mr Savage to enter a tavern with any company that proposed it, drink the most expensive wines with great profusion, and when the reckoning was demanded, be without money: if, as it often happened, his company were willing to defray his part, the affair ended without any ill-consequences; but if they were refractory, and expected that the wine should be paid for by him that drank it, his method of composition was to take them with him to his own apartment, assume the government of the house, and order the butler in an imperious manner to set the best wine in the cellar before his company, who often drank till they forgot the respect due to the house in which they were entertained, indulged themselves in the utmost extravagance of merriment, practised the most licentious frolics and committed all the outrages of drunkenness.

Savage eventually lost the friendship of even these companions, 'and wandered about the town, slighted and neglected, in quest of a dinner, which he did not always obtain'. He went to Bristol, and suffered there. 'He received a remittance of five pounds from London, with which he provided himself a decent coat.' He decided to spend some of the remainder on the journey back to London, but instead spent it in his 'favourite tavern'. The tale goes on: 'Thus was he again confined to Bristol, where he was every day hunted by bailiffs. In this exigence he once more found a friend, who sheltered him in his house, though with the usual inconveniences with which the company was attended; for he could neither be persuaded to go to bed in the night nor to rise in the day.' Savage died at Bristol after being imprisoned for debt.

While Dr Johnson was never in Savage's league he said that when he was at University College he could drink three bottles of port without ill effects.

# *Vice and Drink*

The link between drink and vice is obvious. London had luxury inns which were also brothels from at least the 16th century on. Elizabeth Holland ran the large and successful Holland's Leaguer on Bankside in the 1630s. Holland, known as Mother like other bawds of the time, made much of her fortune by selling food and drink at exorbitant prices.

In the 18th century the main hot-spot of vice was Covent Garden. The Commonwealth had been a setback for the sex industry there. A contemporary observer wrote:

> If you step aside into Covent Garden, Long Acre and Drury Lane, where these Doves of Venus, those Birds of Youth and Beauty – the Wanton Ladies – do build their nests, you shall find them in such a dump of amazement to see the hopes of their trading frustrate ... [before the success of the Puritans] ten or twenty pound suppers were but trifles to them ... they are now forced to make do on a diet of cheese and onions ... the ruination of whoring was why the London Bawds hated 1641 like an old Cavalier.

### List of wanton ladies

With the change in the moral climate after 1660 the sex industry quickly recovered, and the Covent Garden area became like a Wild West town, with drinking, gambling and every vice catered for. Sir John Fielding, brother of the novelist and a fellow magistrate, said the perambulating harlotry was so dense it was as if all the whores in the country had gathered there.

For the man-about-town looking for a pick-up there was a guide, *The List of Covent Garden Ladies or The New Atlantis*, written by Jack Harris.

He is believed to have been head-waiter at the Shakespeare's Head tavern. He subtitled his guide *Containing an exact Description of the Persons, Tempers and Accomplishments of the several Ladies of Pleasure who frequent Covent Garden and other Parts of the Metropolis*. He began selling handwritten lists in the 1740s and by the time of his death in 1765 was getting a useful income from the 8000 printed copies he sold each year. He was also paid a fee by the women, who in effect were advertising their wares. Among them was the most famous of all 18th century courtesans, Fanny Murray.

Harris's descriptions are entertaining. He writes in a seafaring vein of a Miss Devonshire of Queen Anne Street: 'Many a man of war has been her willing prisoner, and paid a proper ransom; her port is said to be well-guarded by a light brown *chevaux-de-frieze* ... the entry is rather straight; but when once in there is very good riding ... she is ever ready for an engagement, cares not how soon she comes to close quarters and loves to fight yard arm and yard arm, and be briskly boarded.'

He is even more explicit about a Miss Wilson of 10 Bull and Mouth Street:

A pair of sweet lips that demand the burning kiss and never receive it without paying interest ... descend a little lower and behold the semi-snowballs ... that want not the support of stays; whose truly elastic state never suffers the pressure, however severe, to remain but boldly recovers its tempting smoothness. Next take a view of nature *centrally*; no *folding lapel*, no *gaping orifice*, no *horrid gulph* is here, but the *loving lips* tenderly kiss each other, and shelter from the cold a small but easily stretched passage, whose *depth* none but the *blind boy* can fathom ...

Harris was really a gangster, a criminal exploiter of women on a large scale, like the 20th-century vice czars of Soho. One of his innovations was the Whores' Club, the necessary counterpart of the men's clubs which were becoming a notable feature of fashionable London. It met each Sunday night at the Shakespeare's Head tavern. It was a mutual-aid organisation, and had about a hundred members. The main benefactor was Harris himself.

The aim of the Shakespeare's Head club was to help whores who were down on their luck or in prison. The apparently contradictory rules suggest what a gulf there is between us and the 18th century.

1. Every girl must have been 'debauched' before she was 15.
2. All members must be on Harris's *List*.
3. No *modest* woman to be admitted.
4. Members must not have been in Bridewell more than once.
5. Any girl tried at the Old Bailey for any crime except picking pockets could remain a member as long as she had not pleaded her belly [told the court she was pregnant].
6. Any member who became pregnant would be struck off.
7. Each member to contribute half a crown, one shilling of which to go to support members who cannot earn a living because they are being treated for venereal disease, or who cannot get into the Lock Hospital. Another sixpence to go to Harris for 'his great care and assiduity in the proper conducting of this worthy society'. The remaining shilling was to be spent on drink, 'gin not excluded'.
8. Any member who finds a wealthy protector to make a suitable donation to the club before quitting.
9. No men to be allowed in except Harris, who can choose any girl he fancies for his bedfellow that night.
10. No religion or politics to be discussed.
11. Any member who gets too drunk to walk to be sent home in a coach or sedan chair at the expense of the society, the fare to be paid back at the next meeting.
12. Any member who breaks glasses, bottles, etc. or behaves in a 'riotous manner' to be expelled until she pays for the damage.
13. Any member 'overcharged' with liquor who in 'clearing her stomach' soils another's clothes must replace them.

We can get some idea of the atmosphere in the club when these spirited young women, many in their teens, let their hair down from Hogarth's print of a riotous gathering of whores at the Rose Tavern, No. 3 from the *Rake's Progress*. There girls are behaving in a 'riotous manner' and some will soon be 'clearing their stomachs'.

The sexual underworld Harris presided over was lawless. Drunken men with drawn swords fought in the Piazza, screeching whores tore at each other in the competition for clients. Jaded aristocrats seeking a doxy for the night in a low drinking den could not be sure what was in their glass. Ned Ward describes a visit to a 'coffee house' with a doctor friend who has treated some of the girls there for venereal diseases. His friend called for a bottle of cock-ale, a drink in which a cock and other ingredients had been boiled. Ned tasted it and protested to the ancient bawd that it was no more than a mixture of weak beer and treacle:

'If this be cock-ale, said I, let coxcombs drink it. Prithee, give me a glass of brandy, or something that will dart like lightning into my spirits, and not fill my guts with thunder.'

With that the reverend doctress of debauchery (after she had approved my choice with a cheerful smile) signified her sympathizing appetite in these words:

'Sir, you are of my mind: I think there's nothing like a dram of true Nantes [Nantes brandy, which was scarce because of war with France] or some such comfortable cordial. Of the former, indeed, I have none, by reason of its scarcity, but I have an excellent distillation of my own preparing, which some call Aqua Veneris. It will restore an old man of threescore to the juvenility of thirty, or make a girl of fourteen, with drinking but one glass, as ripe as an old maid of twenty four. Twill make a parson dance … a Puritan lust after the flesh, and a married man oblige his wife oftener in one night than without it he should be able to do in seven. I sell it to most citizens wives in Town, who are seldom without it in their closets to oblige their husbands or gallants.'

Ned and his friend ordered some of this elixir, but disappointingly he does not comment on its taste or effect.

Besides elite brothels Covent Garden had some notable taverns. The Rose in nearby Russell Street had a mixture of respectable and disreputable clients, including whores and their customers. Pepys, needing refreshment while attending a performance of a play by Rochester's friend Sedley at Drury Lane Theatre, got a boy to keep his place and slipped out to the Rose. There he ate 'half a breast of mutton off the spit'. On other occasions he ate there with his mistresses. The Rose was also popular with actors and managers from the nearby theatres, including David Garrick, Richard Brinsley Sheridan, Jack Kemble, Sarah Siddons, Peg Woffington, George Ann Bellamy – an actress in spite of the name – and Sophia Baddeley. Not surprising then that through its doors over the years passed the great whores and courtesans, Sally Salisbury, Betsy Carless, Lucy Cooper and Fanny Murray, 'as well as princes and paupers, poets and playwrights, merchants and broken servants, conmen, mountebanks, rakes, lawyers and distinguished foreigners.'

The rake and a friend are giving a party for a roomful of whores in Hogarth's *Rake's Progress*. He is drunk and will soon be oblivious to the chaos around him, but the revels will go on. The woman undressing in the foreground is a posture moll, preparing for her obscene striptease act. A servant brings a brass platter and a candle.

## The 'posture molls' strip off

While fairly orderly and respectable during the day at night the Rose was one of the most dangerous places in London, a scene of riot and even murder, a 'very sink of iniquity' where 'the real Rake gambles, fucks, drinks and turns night into day'. Hogarth catches this in the print mentioned above, from the *Rake's Progress* series. It shows whores and their customers in an upstairs room, the girls robbing their drunken clients, one girl spitting gin at a rival, another attempting to set fire to a map with a candle.

'Posture molls' were a speciality of the Rose. These were women who simulated sex as warm-ups for the whores and their customers. The woman would strip naked, dance on an enormous brass plate, then lie on her back and draw her knees under her chin. At some point, as the customers crowded round, sweating in the overheated room, the candlelight flickering on their faces, the woman would snuff out a lighted candle 'in an obscene mockery of sex'. Hogarth's print depicts the woman as she is stripping off. A servant is seen in the doorway, bringing in the platter and the candle.

The Rose was described as 'the Resort of the worst Characters in Town, male and female, who make it the Headquarters of Midnight Orgies and Drunken Broils where Murders and Assaults frequently occur'. In 1700 Sir Andrew Slanning, who had the immense income of £20,000 a year, picked up a young whore in Drury Lane Theatre. As he left the theatre he was followed by a gentleman named John Cowland and some of his friends. Cowland put his arm around the girl's neck and Slanning objected, claiming that the girl was his wife. Cowland, who knew that he was married to a 'woman of honour', accused him of lying. Before they could draw their swords their friends parted them, and they all agreed to go to the Rose to settle the quarrel over a glass of wine. As they climbed the stairs Cowland drew his sword and stabbed Slanning fatally in the stomach. The *Newgate Calendar* reports: 'Mr Cowland being found guilty on the clearest evidence received sentence of death and, though great efforts were made to obtain a pardon for him, he was executed at Tyburn on the 20th of December 1700.'

Another notorious drinking haunt was the Ben Jonson's Head tavern in Russell Street, known as Weatherby's after its proprietor, Elizabeth Weatherby. The *Nocturnal Revels* of 1779 called it 'a receptacle' for rakes, highwaymen, pickpockets, swindlers and prostitutes, 'from the charioted kept mistress to the twopenny bunter [prostitute] who plies under the Piazza'.

## The first nightclubs

Respectable men went armed to such hostelries, knowing their reputation for sudden deadly violence. Respectable women did not go there at all, with the exception of a few famous actresses. They went instead to Carlisle House in Soho Square or the Pantheon in Oxford Street. Carlisle House was run by Madame Theresa Cornelys, once the mistress of Casanova. It was a kind of nightclub, renowned for the opulent extravagance of its balls and masquerades. There were real pines and fountains, 'an elegant erection of Gothick arches', and 'a moving spiral pillar of lights'. A fast set of society beauties, led by the wholly scandalous Elizabeth Chudleigh, Duchess of Kingston[1], patronised it.

The Pantheon in Oxford Street, which opened in January 1772, competed for the same aristocratic and wealthy clientele as Carlisle House. It was even more magnificent – the main room was an enormous rotunda based on the church of Santa Sophia in Constantinople. Horace Walpole called it 'the most beautiful edifice in England' and confessed: 'It amazed me myself. Imagine Balbec in all its glory!' (A Marks and Spencers store stands on the site today.) Yet however hard the management of both the Pantheon and Carlisle House tried to keep the *demi-monde* at bay courtesans found their way in. The Pantheon announced that such women would be barred, but on the opening night the actress-courtesan Sophia Baddeley turned up with a posse of noblemen who drew their swords and made it clear they were prepared to use them. She was allowed in, and joined other women of her profession who had somehow already been escorted inside.

During the later 18th century the centre of gravity of pleasure shifted westwards, to Pall Mall and the St James's area. The obsessions of the man of pleasure, drinking, sex and gambling, were all catered for in a small area. The Rev Sydney Smith said a 'parallelogram between Oxford Street, Piccadilly, Regent Street and Hyde Park encloses more intelligence and human ability, to say nothing of wealth and beauty, than the world has ever collected in such a space before'. He was talking about the world of fashion and culture but if he had added Pall Mall as the base of his

Two wealthy young gentlemen prepare to sample the goods on offer in a genteel London bagnio in an engraving of 1787. The room is well-furnished and the presence of a Black servant suggests the night's entertainment will be expensive.

parallelogram he would have defined that small self-contained world which contained all that the man of pleasure desired – gentlemen's clubs, where he could drink and gamble, and elite brothels where he could take the expensive whores to a private room. If he dabbled in politics Parliament was but a short walk away through St James's Park.

A man could stagger from his club, where he might have won or lost a fortune, to one of the exclusive brothels in King's Place, an insignificant alley off Pall Mall where almost all the houses were elite bordellos. There, if he had enough money left, he could enjoy the loveliest young women of the town, or sit and drink and eat in rooms furnished in the latest taste by Chippendale[2]. In *A Picture of England* the German traveller Baron J.W. von Archenholz described what the men-about-town would find in these establishments. He uses the current terms nuns and abbesses for prostitutes and bawds:

> The noted houses situated in a little street in St James's, called King's Place, in which great numbers of nuns are kept for people of fashion, living under the direction of several rich Abbesses .... You may see them superbly clothed at public places, even those of the most

expensive kind. Each of these convents has a carriage and liveried servants, since these ladies never deign to walk anywhere except in St James's Park.

The Baron adds that prices in the King's Place nunneries were so exorbitant 'as to exclude the Mob entirely'. The same was true of the clubs of St James's, although class played its part in keeping them exclusive.

# The Hell-Fire Clubs

Nights for the customers of the establishments described by von Archenholz would usually begin in what became known as gentlemen's clubs. The peace of these well-furnished, mostly masculine establishements might occasionally be broken by an oath or a challenge to a duel, but mostly men went there to drink or gossip or gamble with members of the same class and tastes. However, the wildness of 17th-century manners took some time to subside, and by no means all the drunken roisterers in the early 18th century were, or behaved like, gentlemen. In March 1712 five peers and 'persons of quality' were involved in a brawl in a tavern in the Strand, in London. Swords were drawn and in the scuffle the landlady was killed. 'The gentlemen laughed and ordered that she should be added to their bill.' This was an example of an outbreak of upper-class thuggery that terrorised the capital for several months. Bullies attacked innocent men and women in the streets, raping, slitting noses, cutting off ears and rolling people downhill in barrels. According to Christopher Hibbert (*The Roots of Evil*) one gang, The Bold Bucks, who specialised in rape, got so drunk before erupting into the streets that 'they were quite beyond the possibility of attending to any notions of reason or humanity'. Swift called the gangs 'a race of rakes' and L.O. Pike, in a *History of Crime in England*, described the antics of 'the roisterers who made the night hideous in the eighteenth century. The "Mohocks", the "Nickers", the "Tumblers", the "Dancing Masters" and the various bully-captains ... If they met an unprotected woman they showed they had no sense of decency; if they met a man who was unarmed or weaker than themselves they assaulted and perhaps killed him.' Other groups called themselves the Sweaters, the Scowerers, the Hectors and the

Muns. The Mohocks had the worst reputation. Led by a man with a Turkish crescent tattooed on his forehead, they would get drunk in a tavern before surging into the streets to slash faces and gouge out eyes. They defeated the Watch in pitched battles. Jonathan Swift wrote in a letter in March 1712: 'Our Mohocks go on still, and cut people's faces every night, but they shan't cut mine.' John Gay wrote in his poem *Trivia*:

> Now is the time that rakes their revels keep;
> Kindlers of riot, enemies of sleep …
> Who has not heard the Scowerer's midnight fame?
> Who has not trembled at the Mohock's name?
> Was there a watchman took his hourly rounds
> Safe from their blows, or new-invented wounds?
> I pass their desperate deeds, and mischiefs done
> When from Snow Hill black steepy torrents run;
> How matrons hooped within the hogshead's womb
> Were tumbled furious then, the rolling tomb
> O'er the stones thunders, bounds from side to side …

In April 1712 the *Spectator* published a manifesto said to have been written by the Mohock emperor himself. He said their aim was to cleanse the streets of 'loose and dissolute lives'. But his reign was rapidly coming to an end. In June that year 20 Mohocks attacked a member of the Watch, John Bouch, in Essex Street. They threatened to nail him into his guard box and take it away. Bouch counter-attacked, arresting three of the Mohock leaders and driving the rest off with his sword. The men he arrested were fined three shillings and fourpence each at their trial at the Old Bailey. The ease with which they were routed and the paltry fines must have made them seem ridiculous.

After that the trouble subsided as suddenly as it arose. The emperor was thought to have married a wealthy woman and settled down. His followers ceased to riot. They may have been among the 'persons of quality' who founded the first hell-fire clubs.

These emerged in London in the 1720s as sinister alternatives to the Whigs' Kit Cat Club, the Tories' Board of Brothers and the Cocoa Tree. The Rump Steak was confined to those who had been publicly snubbed by George II. The hell-fire clubs gave their members stronger meat. An anonymous pamphlet of 1721 called *The Hell-Fire Club, kept by a Society of Blasphemers* hints at dark secrets:

> Among the worst, the very worst of men,
> Those men who of the Hell-Fire Club will be
> Infernal Members, where in jollity
> Each man strives who in sin shall most abound
> And fill his mouth with oaths of dreadful sound.

## Twenty very pretty fellows

In 1720 it became common knowledge that Philip, Duke of Wharton, had been elected president of one of these clubs. There seem to have been three, with a total of 40 upper-class members. Wharton was certainly such: his father Thomas, the first Marquess of Wharton, was one of the heroes of the Glorious Revolution. He wrote its hit song *Lilibulero*, and boasted that he had 'sung King James out of three kingdoms'. His brilliant son Philip was brought up to be a pillar of the Whig establishment, intensively educated in science, mathematics, metaphysics, languages and classical literature. But the boy was a born troublemaker, and at the age of 16 broke his father's heart by making a runaway marriage with the daughter of a mere major general. The Marquess tried to get the marriage annulled and when he failed, parted the couple by sending his son away on the Grand Tour.

His father's timely death gave young Wharton the title and he set out without his wife but with seven footmen. On the Continent he dabbled in Jacobite politics, accepting a knighthood of the Garter from the Old Pretender. When he returned he sat in the Irish House of Lords, supporting the government. In 1718 a grateful George I made him a duke, an astonishing honour for a non-royal minor, but he did not know his man. Back in England, Wharton became a gadfly, denouncing ministerial guilt over the South Sea Bubble scandal in which the court was involved. Lord Stanhope collapsed on the floor of the House as he attempted to counter Wharton's accusations. Wharton also founded a newspaper, the *True Briton*, to castigate Sir Robert Walpole's government. It had little effect.

In 1721 the King had issued an order in council suppressing the hell-fire clubs. Wharton, clutching a Bible, made a speech in the Lords denying he was a patron of blasphemy. He took himself off to live in Twickenham where he ran another permissive club, the Schemers. The intrepid Lady Mary Wortley Montague wrote in a letter to her sister: 'Twenty very pretty fellows (the Duke of Wharton being president and chief director) have formed themselves into a committee of gallantry, who call themselves Schemers and meet regularly three times a week to consult on gallant schemes for the advancement of that branch of happiness.' She adds that the renown of the club 'ought to be spread wherever men can sigh or women can wish … 'Tis true that they have the envy and the curses of the old and ugly of both sexes, and a general persecution from all old women; but this is no more than all reformations can expect in their beginning.'

Wharton went to Spain, where he became a Catholic and married an Irish maid of honour at the Spanish court, his first wife having died. The King of Spain gave him command of a regiment of Irish exiles. His picaresque progress continued. One night in France he met a young English peer who had a coach. Wharton persuaded him to drive from St Germain to Paris on what he called 'important business'. There the Duke hired a second coach, drove to the Opéra, hired six musicians, drove back to St Germain and although it was past midnight got the musicians to serenade some ladies in the palace. He then drove to Poissy with his peer and the musicians and serenaded an Englishman who lived there. The Englishman invited them to breakfast, but the musicians said they would be fined if they did not get back to the Opéra. Wharton explained to the peer that he had no money, and asked him to pay the musicians for the night's entertainment, promising to return the favour if an opportunity arose. The peer, pointing out ruefully that such an opportunity was unlikely to arise, paid up.

Wharton died in 1731. He was an insubstantial and marginal figure, but his intemperance and mad spending were examples to later rakes and his clubs were a template for Sir Francis Dashwood's more infamous Hell-Fire Club.

## Revels at the abbey

Dashwood founded the Society of Dilettanti in 1732. The members were connoisseurs and a qualification was having been to Italy, but Horace Walpole said the real one was being drunk. Fox, Garrick, Sir Joshua

Reynolds and many Whig grandees were among the members. Dashwood's inclinations were however better served by the Hell-Fire Club he founded in a ruined abbey at Medmenham by the Thames in Buckinghamshire. About all we know for certain from documentary evidence is that a great deal of drinking took place there, but it was an open secret that the other real business of the members was sexual indulgence with the 'nuns' they took there for that purpose. Members included some of the highest servants of state: Dashwood was Chancellor

Sir Francis Dashwood was an important politician and also founder of the Hell-Fire Club. It was said of his sex-drive that he had 'the staying power of a stallion and the impetuousity of a bull'.

of the Exchequer and later Postmaster General, Lord Sandwich was First Lord of the Admiralty and Thomas Potter, Paymaster General. Perhaps the most important political figure involved was John Wilkes. Horace Walpole was one of the many notable visitors, including, it was suggested, Benjamin Franklin, who was a friend of Dashwood's.

We get some glimpses of the rituals of the monks of Medmenham, as they were called, in a curious book of 1779, *Nocturnal Revels, or, The History of King's Place and Other Modern Nunneries*, written by 'A Monk of the Order of St Francis', that is, Sir Francis Dashwood. The book surveys the London sex industry and its customers. It tells of men and women members of the Hell-Fire Club parading in masks as they made their choices and of women secluded there while they had the offspring of these brief sexual unions. The *Revels* says the women considered themselves 'as the lawful wives of the brethren during their stay within the monastic walls; every monk being religiously scrupulous not to infringe upon the nuptial alliance of any other brother'.

Medmenham Abbey, where Dashwood and his disciples drank deep. Their blasphemous rites were said to include sex orgies with celebrated London courtesans.

Grave statesmen would not have indulged in this outrageous behaviour without copious 'libations'. Horace Walpole wrote that 'Bacchus and Venus were the deities to whom they almost publicly sacrified', and the cellar accounts of the club, some of which have survived, suggest deep toping.

The women involved were usually the wives, sisters and girlfriends of the monks. When the men wanted variety they sent to London for professionals. Fanny Murray once mentioned that she had 'waited on the Monks at Medmenham'. She had been a mistress of the Earl of Sandwich, and the obscene *Essay on Woman*, written by Wilkes[1] and Potter, was dedicated to her.

Another celebrity whore believed to have entertained the monks was the one-eyed Betty Wemys. She would get drunk in the Rose Tavern in Covent Garden, lose her glass eye and start fights as she scrambled about looking for it. Lucy Cooper, who may have been one of Dashwood's mistresses, was another.

Some girls were sent by the brothel-keeper Charlotte Hayes, the best-known of 18th-century London bawds. She achieved wealth and acceptance rare in her profession, entertaining the Prince Regent and one of his brothers at her mansion at Epsom. She and her girls would have been well-known to some of the monks, who were customers at her elite brothel in King's Place, St James's. Lord Sandwich said of her: 'She keeps the Stock Exchange supplied with real, immaculate maidenheads.' This was naive of the great lord – Hayes was an expert re-virginiser of shop-worn girls.

What the locals made of the arrival of coachloads of colourfully dressed London harlots in their sleepy rural retreat is not known, but there was gossip, and the abbey continued to be a focus for rumour long after the monks had ceased to meet there. Dashwood built a church nearby, St Lawrence's, whose decor owed more to pagan examples than Christian piety. It had an 80-foot tower topped by a 20-foot golden ball which could be seen for miles around. Inside the globe was a chamber with benches round the sides. Dashwood would sit there with Wilkes and other survivors of the abbey, tippling and singing songs. Wilkes wrote:

> Some churches have been built for devotion, others from parade of vanity. I believe this is the first church which has ever been built for a prospect ... built on the top of a hill for the convenient devotion of the town at the bottom of it ... I admire the silence and secrecy which reigns in that great globe, undisturbed by [Dashwood's] jolly songs very unfit for the profane ears of the world below.

He also referred to the church as 'the best Globe Tavern I was ever in'.

By the time Dashwood died in 1781 most of the other monks were already dead. Although they cannot bear comparison with the rakes of Charles II's court they were men of wit and charm and taste. Some were poets, others successful politicians. Above all they were rebels and perhaps harbingers of that example of picturesque egotism, the romantic rebellion.

## The hell-fires die down

As the fires of the Hell-Fire Club at Medmenham died down, embers of the fantasy flickered into life elsewhere. A follower of the Medmenhamites, John Hall Stevenson, set up his own fraternity at Skelton Castle near Saltburn in Yorkshire. He renamed it Crazy Castle and his followers called themselves the Demoniacals.

Like Dashwood, Stevenson was bitterly anti-Catholic. Admonished by Wilkes for not believing his account of proceedings at Medmenham, he had replied:

> *Le Diable d'Ennuie* possessed me all at once and drove me as he did my Brethren ye swine down a precipice where I am now suffering among the damned that are bathing in sulphur at Harrogate for not believing that there was anything miraculous in the shrine of St Francis. Say a mass for me ... Do give me a line with yr. absolution for my transgressions to St Francis, and a hint of the world to come.

Dashwood acted as adviser to the Demoniacals, but they seem to have had none of the talent for dissipation of their southern exemplars. The only other person of note associated with them was the novelist Laurence Sterne, who was vicar of Sutton-on-the Forest in Yorkshire, and he seems to have been mainly interested in the castle library. The Demoniacals began by holding satanic rituals, but they lacked the gusto of the Medmenhamites and Crazy Castle became a drinking club where the members gambled and told dirty stories.

There were hell-fire clubs at Oxford and Cambridge early in the 19th century. Byron, who had just left Trinity College, Cambridge, held a meeting at his home, Newstead Abbey, in 1809 to commemorate Medmenham. During it he drank wine from a human skull. With this melodramatic gesture the hell-fire movement could be held to have guttered and died. The wild spirit of the 18th century was giving way to the formality and preening of the dandy. The era of the gentlemen's clubs as we know them had begun.

# High Stakes

The rakes of Dashwood's abbey were rumoured to have seduced virgins by the light of flickering tapers on altars dedicated to Venus. The clubmen of St James's behaved much more self-destructively. They gambled 'deep' and drank deeper and many an ancient fortune changed hands on the turn of a card or the roll of dice.

Of the great gambling clubs, White's, established in St James's Street in 1693, set the pattern. Later came Boodle's and Crockford's, also in St James's Street, and Almack's and Brooks's in Pall Mall (it later moved to St James's Street). Sheridan wrote of Brooks's:

> Liberal Brooks, whose speculative skill
> Is hasty credit and a distant bill,
> Who, nursed in clubs, disdains a vulgar trade,
> Exults to trust and blushes to be paid.

This tactic paid off. The generous Brooks presided over the greatest gambling den of the age. Lord Lauderdale spoke of £70,000 being lost there in a single night. Horace Walpole, who was a member, said 'a thousand meadows and cornfields are staked at every throw [of the dice], and as many villages lost as in the earthquakes that overwhelmed Herculaneum and Pompeii.'

Originally Brooks's had 27 members, all Macaronis or dandies. In an age of dandy dressing they were the most outrageous. Enormous wigs were part of their uniform. They were all young, and all rich; Fox joined when he was just 16. The club acquired a reputation for 'wild behaviour and sensational gambling' (Murray, *High Society*). One of the founders, a

Mr Thynne, retired in disgust because he had won only £12,000 in two months. An old betting book at the club contains a note: 'That he may never return is the ardent wish of members.'

Heavy gambling and the drinking which accompanied it was characteristic of the three main clubs, White's, Brooks's and Boodle's. A passion for gambling gripped society high and low from the reign of Anne to that of Victoria. Clubs grew out of coffee houses, but as gambling became more socially exclusive it became necessary to keep out professional card-sharps and cheats. One observer pointed out that in a coffee house the man holding a hand of cards next to you might turn out to be a notorious highwayman. 'Judges there were liable to meet the man whom they might afterwards have to sentence in the dock. It was no uncommon thing ... to recognise a body swinging in chains on a heath outside London as a man with whom you had called a main at hazard a few weeks before at White's or the Cocoa Club' (Boulton, *The Amusements of Old London*).

So the rich formed members-only clubs and lost their fortunes to each other. Lord Lyttelton dreaded that the rattling of a dice-box at

Pall Mall's clubland in the 1840s, when it had cast off its reputation for reckless gambling. It was the solid Victorian respectability of such establishments that eventually led to the forming of various Bohemian boltholes for rebels of both sexes.

White's may one day or other (if my son should be a member of that noble academy) shake down all our fine oaks. It is dreadful to see not only there, but almost in every [gaming] house in town, what devastations are made by that destructive fury, the spirit of play.

And since Walpole believed that when an heir was born in a rich and aristocratic family, the butler was sent to White's to put his name down for membership, it was likely that Lyttelton's son would one day be a member of that 'noble academy'. Whole estates, the accumulation of generations, could change hands in an evening. As a young man Admiral Harvey lost £100,000 gambling at White's. He offered to sell his estate to pay the debt, but in a rare act of clemency in those flinty hearted circles his gambling companion, an Irishman with a conscience, would accept payment of only £10,000, and suggested they play again for the other £90,000. This time Harvey won and regained his fortune. He went on to serve under Nelson at Trafalgar.

Gambling was also heavy, or deep, as the current term had it, at Almack's, Brooks's and elsewhere. Walpole wrote in a letter in February 1770:

The gaming at Almack's … is worthy of the decline of our empire … the young men of the age lose ten, fifteen, twenty thousand pounds in an evening there. Lord Stavordale, not one and twenty, lost £11,000 there last Tuesday, but recovered it in one great hand at hazard. He swore a great oath – 'Now if I had been playing deep I might have won millions.'

For the foolish drink was an invariable accompaniment to gambling, and the more astute found easy pickings by staying sober. General Scott, Canning's father-in-law, won £200,000 playing whist at White's, 'thanks to his notorious sobriety'. This is over £10 million today. Perhaps the most successful gambler of the age, William Douglas, Duke of Queensberry, was also abstemious. Drink did not mix well with either of his main interests, gambling and sex.

## Charles James is foxed

Charles James Fox, the leading Whig politician, was passionately interested in drink, sex and gambling, and reckless in all three. The son of an enormously rich man who amassed much of his fortune while Paymaster-General of the Forces, an expected if not seemly form of corruption, he was by character and inclination the inspiration of a glittering circle of fledgling aristocrats and significant politicians. They included George, Prince of Wales and the playwright and politician Richard Brinsley Sheridan.

Not surprisingly, a man who stayed up all night drinking and gambling was not always at his best in the House of Commons. Walpole reported that on one occasion his formidable oratory failed him ...

Nor could it be wondered at. He had sat up playing at hazard at Almack's, from Tuesday evening the 4th, till five in the afternoon of Wednesday, 5th. An hour before he had recovered £12,000 that he had lost, and by dinner, which was at five o'clock, he had ended losing £11,000. On the Thursday he spoke in the above debate: went to dinner at past eleven that night; from thence to White's, where he drank till seven the next morning; thence to Almack's, where he won £6,000; and between three and four in the afternoon he set out for [the races at] Newmarket. His brother Stephen lost £11,000 two nights after, and Charles £10,000 more on the 13th; so that in three nights, the two brothers, the eldest not 25, lost £32,000.

All this time at the tables he was drinking heavily. Fox[1] had inherited £154,000 from his father to pay his debts. Soon it was all gone, and he had to rely on friends to keep him afloat. When the bailiffs moved into his house in St James's his friends organised a whip-round which raised £65,000 to pay off his creditors.

The historian George Otto Trevelyan gives a sense of the heavy drinking among statesmen in his *Early History of Charles James Fox*:

These were the days when the Duke of Grafton, the Premier, lived openly with Miss Nancy Parson [a notorious courtesan]. Rigby, the Paymaster of the Forces, had only one merit, that he drank fair. He used brandy as the rest of the world used small beer. Lord Weymouth, grandson of Lord Cartaret, had more than his grandfather's capacity for liquor, and a fair portion of his abilities. He constantly boozed till daylight, even when a Secretary of State. His occasional speeches were extolled by his admirers as preternaturally sagacious, and his severest critics admitted them to be pithy. Walpole made the following smart hit at him: 'If I paid nobody, and went drunk to bed every morning at six, I might expect to be called out of bed by two in the afternoon to save the nation, and govern the House of Lords by two or three sentences as profound and short as the proverbs of Solomon.' 'They tell me, Sir John,' said George the Third to one of his favourites, 'that you love a glass of wine.' 'Those who have so informed your majesty', was the reply, 'have done me great injustice; they should have said a bottle.' Two of the friends of Philip Francis, without any sense of having performed an exceptional feat, finished between them a gallon and a half of champagne and Burgundy, a debauch which in this unheroic age it almost makes one ill to read of.

A London clubman might lose in a night the equivalent of the lifetime income of whole villages, and hardly spare it a thought. In London's clubland, and in great houses throughout the land, men were in too much of a hurry getting, spending and losing great fortunes to care about the less fortunate. The upper classes were going through a phase of conspicuous consumption, including drink, perhaps unequalled until the great age of City bonuses at the beginning of the 21st century. For the more dissolute members of the aristocracy the leader of these revels was George, Prince of Wales.

# The Prince of Whales

Some men give a certain tone to their times and leave a legacy of manners. George IV was the last true profligate to sit on the English throne, although his grand-nephew Edward VII might have emulated him if he had been allowed to. George left his stamp on the upper reaches of society, and his behaviour affects us today in that the Victorian values foolish politicians invoke were largely a reaction to it.

The poet and essayist Leigh Hunt was jailed with his brother John for describing George thus when he was Prince of Wales:

> This Adonis in loveliness is a corpulent man of fifty … a libertine over head and ears in debt and disgrace, a despiser of domestic ties, the companion of gamblers and demireps, a man who has just closed half a century without one single claim on the gratitude of his country or the respect of authority.

He might also have mentioned George's addiction to food, drink and drugs. By the time of his death in June 1830 he was a bloated recluse, skulking at Windsor Castle and forbidding the servants to look at him.

George when Prince of Wales was a natural leader for the rakes who clustered around his dissolute court, which was a marked contrast to the cheese-paring, stuffy establishment of his parents, King George III and Queen Charlotte. He was handsome, a successful womaniser, a dandy, and apart from a strong strain of sentimentality, utterly heartless.

His gross appetites took a toll on his looks, his figure and his health. In 1818 the Duke of Wellington said of the overweight Prince to Creevey the diarist: 'By God, you never saw such a figure in your life as he is.' By 1821, no longer by any means an Adonis, George weighed at least 20 stone, and would encase himself in 'a Bastille' of whalebone corsets before appearing in public. Three years later his waistline had increased to 50 inches and his great stomach hung around his knees. The essayist Charles Lamb painted a devastating word picture of the corpulent old gent:

> Not a fatter fish than he
> Flounders round the polar sea.
> See his blubbers – at his gills
> What a world of drink he swills …
> Every fish of generous kind
> Scuds aside or shrinks behind;
> But about his presence keep
> All the monsters of the deep …
> Name or title what has he?
> Is he Regent of the sea?
> By his bulk and by his size
> By his oily qualities
> This (or else my eyesight fails)
> This should be the Prince of Whales.

Prodigious drinking was partly responsible for his physical deterioration. The cartoonist James Gillray published a caricature of him as 'A Voluptuary Undergoing the Horrors of Digestion', surrounded by

decanters of port and brandy, empty bottles, an overflowing chamber pot and unpaid bills. In March 1830, just months

Gillray's devastating caricature of the Prince of Wales as A Voluptuary Under the Horrors of Digestion. Every detail builds up the picture of depravity – the overflowing chamber pot, the dice, the bills, the bottles and not least, the use of a fork to pick his teeth. The latter detail shocked the Prince's contemporaries.

before the Prince's death, Wellington, then Prime Minister, reported that one night after going to bed George had consumed 'two glasses of hot ale and toast, three glasses of claret, some strawberries!! and a glass of brandy'. As George's health waned his gluttony did not. The following month Wellington wrote to a friend:

> What do you think of his breakfast yesterday for an invalid? A pigeon and beef steak pie of which he eat two pigeons and three beefsteaks, three parts of a bottle of Moselle, a glass of dry champagne, two glasses of port and a glass of brandy.

This strange 'breakfast' was followed by a large dose of laudanum, opium dissolved in brandy. By the end of 1829 he was taking a hundred drops or more of this addictive opiate before important state occasions. In the weeks before his death he was taking more than 250 drops in a period of 36 hours and although he could still hold a conversation the effects were disastrous. They included 'bouts of over-excitement, depression, severe lethargy and confusion of mind' (Parissien, *George IV*). Heavy drinking must have added to his confusion. The artist Joseph Farington had recorded in his diary in April 1799 that George drank barely diluted gin in half-pint measures. In addition to bottles of wine and his measures of gin he later as king began to drink copious quantities of whisky, then something of a novelty in England. Finally he acquired a taste for the sweet cherry liqueur Maraschino, for which he seemed to have a limitless capacity. Port gave him gout at an early age, and by 1826 his bed had 'eleven gouty pillows'.

## Partying with the Prince

George's addictions began early. While dancing at a party when he was in his early twenties he fell over and was then sick in front of the guests. At a ball at Lady Hopetoun's he was so stupified by drink that he could only sit and gaze vacantly about him, 'pale as ashes, with glazed eyes set in his head'. Supper and a bottle and a half of champagne roused him. He 'posted himself in the doorway, to the terror of everybody that went by, flung his arms around the Duchess of Ancaster's neck and kissed her with a great smack, threatened to pull Lord Galloway's wig off and knock out his false teeth, and played all the pranks of a drunken man upon the stage, till some

of his companions called for his carriage and almost forced him away'
(Huish, *Memoirs of George the Fourth*).

Huish, his first and most critical biographer, tells of another drunken
party when the Prince was a youth. At the Earl of Chesterfield's house at
Blackheath when the company all 'drank to excess' one of them released a
large ferocious dog. After savaging a servant it seized the Prince's coat
tails. He was saved by a tipsy companion, who felled it with a blow to the
head. In the meantime the Earl had fallen down the steps and badly injured
his head. The Prince stumbled to his phaeton and fell into a stupor. He was
driven back to town by his wicked uncle, the Duke of Cumberland, who
could hold his drink better.

At his daughter Princess Charlotte's 16th birthday party he got so
drunk and abusive the girl wept and was led away by her father's friend
Richard Brinsley Sheridan. On another occasion the Prince and some of
his more disreputable companions, including George Hanger, Sheridan
and Fox, invited 'some dashing Cyprians', in other words harlots, to a
tavern called the Staffordshire Arms. Sheridan got so intoxicated he was
put to bed. The others found they could not pay the bill, and slipped away.
When Sheridan woke the next morning 'he found himself in the character
of a hostage for the expenses of the previous night's debauch' (Huish).

The Prince played childish pranks, often when drunk. He called on a
Miss Vaneck with two equerries. On entering her room he was heard to
exclaim, 'I *must* do it, I *must* do it.' When Miss Vaneck asked him what it
was he was obliged to do, he winked at the equerries and they seized her
and laid her on the floor, while the Prince whipped her. This was the result
of a bet. At Newmarket with the Duc d'Orleans and his brother the Abbé
de la Fai, the Abbé declared that he could charm a fish out of the water. He
bent over a stream to tickle a fish with a twig, then noticing something in
the Prince's manner, said he hoped the Prince was not going to push him
in. The Prince declared upon his honour that he would not. The Abbé, who
was standing on a little bridge, leaned over the water again. The Prince
caught him by the heels and threw him in (Philipps, *Bad Behaviour*).

In his journals, Augustus Hare quotes the reminiscences of the Hon.
Augusta Barrington:

George IV as Prince Regent was very charming when he was not
drunk, but he generally *was*. Do you remember how he asked Curran

to dinner to amuse him – only for that? Curran was up to it, and sat silent all through dinner. This irritated the Prince, and at last, after dinner, when he had had a good deal too much, he filled a glass with wine and threw it in Curran's face, with 'Say something funny, can't you?' Curran, without moving a muscle, threw his own glass of wine in his neighbour's face, saying, 'Pass his Royal Highness's joke.'

This is almost identical to an incident recorded by the artist Joseph Farington in his diary in 1803. Perhaps it was the Prince's favourite party trick.

At one of the entertainments given by the Prince, His Royal Highness filled a glass with wine and wantonly threw it in [Colonel George] Hanger's face. [Hanger] without being disconcerted immediately filled his glass and throwing it in the face of the person who sat next to him bid him pass it round – an admirable instance of presence of mind and judgement upon an occasion of coarse rudeness.

## Tears at the altar

Occasionally his drunken frolics turned more serious. One night in 1812, drinking with the super-rich Earl of Yarmouth and the Earl's principal mistress at the time, Fanny Wilson, the Prince went too far. He 'capped his unmannerly conduct by embarrassing advances' to Fanny[1]. Yarmouth gave the Prince a violent push. The Prince, although usually prickly about his dignity, chose to overlook this insult, probably realising that publicity would be disastrous. However, someone in his household talked, and the satirist John Wolcot, under his pseudonym Peter Pindar, set the episode to verse. His account, with the title 'Royal Stripes, or a Kick from Yarmouth to Wales', was embellished with an offensive illustration by George Cruikshank.

The Prince was at his very worst in 1794 when he first met Caroline, his German bride-to-be. He had agreed to marry if Parliament would pay off his debts of £650,000. His friend Lord Malmesbury was sent to Brunswick to collect Caroline, and the couple first met in St James's Palace. She was confronted by a handsome man of 32, already going to seed, renowned for good manners which failed on this occasion. He saw a strapping, hoydenish young woman who would prove to be foul-mouthed and far from clean. He whispered to a companion, 'Harris, I am not well; pray get me a glass of brandy.' At the wedding ceremony in April 1795 George was clearly drunk, and almost passed out twice. When he made his vows he hiccupped, and gazed meaningfully at his mistress, Lady Jersey. When the Archbishop of Canterbury asked whether anyone knew any reason why the marriage should not take place George burst into tears. According to Caroline the Prince then drank himself into unconsciousness and 'passed the greatest part of his bridal-night under the grate, where he fell'.

The Prince was a conspicuous consumer of luxury goods, including sex. And in most cases he paid late, if at all. A caricature shows him being dunned by the bawd Mrs Windsor and other brothel-keepers, who are presenting him with their bills. One demands £1000 for 'first slice of a young tit only 12 years' and £1000 for 'uncommon diversions'. A coloured whore named Black Moll is holding out a bill itemising her services to His Royal Highness, including 'Tipping the Velvet' for £100. A young waif holds a paper asking for payment for her lost maidenhead. Rowlandson was one of several caricaturists who showed the Prince with prostitutes. In 1786 another artist pictured him demanding 'a brisk wench in clean straw'.

He was usually accompanied on these escapades by some of the most notorious rakes in England. The artist Benjamin Robert Haydon observed: 'The people [George] liked had all a spice of vice in their nature.' As a group they were more disreputable even than the rakes who attended Charles II's court, and significantly lacked their literary talents. Some must have been chosen simply because his father despised or feared them for their influence over his son. However, most found the Prince a treacherous friend.

George's mentor Charles James Fox, leader of the Whigs, was detested by the King, and men like Richard Brinsley Sheridan, George Beau Brummell, Richard Cosway, Jack Payne, Anthony St Leger, George Hanger and the Barrymores would not have been welcome at the staid and stuffy court. Worse, the King's sinister brother, the debauched Duke of Cumberland, was an intimate drinking companion of the Prince. The Duke had seduced Lady Henrietta Grosvenor and was sued by her husband. According to Horace Walpole, she had 'rendered herself too accessible' to the Duke. Cumberland's puerile love-letters were a feature of the case. Lord Grosvenor was awarded a colossal £10,000. Cumberland's other transgressions included marrying a commoner and seducing a woman whose daughter afterwards insisted on being called

Princess Olive of Cumberland. When the great actress-courtesan Sophia Baddeley found she could no longer maintain her price he sent her a peremptory summons to a Covent Garden brothel. Sophia, who once had the wealthiest aristocrats among her lovers and could command hundreds of pounds a night, indignantly refused. She retorted: 'Go and tell the Duke to send for Lady Grosvenor.' Horace Walpole declared that 'unbounded freedom reigns at Cumberland House'.

Even more worrying for the King was his son's friendship with Fox. It was Cumberland who introduced the young Prince to gambling, but it was the wenching, drinking, talking, non-sleeping and gambling-mad Fox who showed him the extremes of libertine behaviour. The Prince was captivated by Fox's extraordinary charm and good nature, and impressed by the way he threw away his own fortune and the considerable sums he borrowed from his friends. Fox was a brilliant orator and a formidable statesman, but he was the worst possible role-model for the weak Prince of Wales. Trying to emulate the drinking feats of Fox and Sheridan was an early mistake.

When he was 21 the satirical poem *The Devil Divorced* was published. (I have inserted the words 'Prince' and 'Wales', which are indicated by dashes in the original):

> First on my list a man of rank appears,
> Far versed in wickedness above his years.
> The Prince of Wales, if I can ought foretell,
> Will most assuredly come down to hell.
> Whenever vice or lewdness lead the way,
> With what officious zeal doth he obey!
> Him no ambition moves to seek renown;
> To be esteemed the greatest buck in town
> Appears to be his wish and sole delight.
> Full many times at twelve o'clock at night
> I've known him drunk, with half a dozen more,
> Kick up a row, break lamps, perhaps a door,
> And to conclude the night, to bilk his whore.

Before he developed a taste for portly aristocratic matrons, some of them grandmothers, George's appetite for whoring was great. A contemporary caricature, 'King's Place, or a View of Mr Fox's Best Friends' (1784), shows the Prince talking to two of his mistresses, the actress Perdita Robinson and the courtesan Elizabeth Armistead. The bawd Mrs Windsor is saying of Fox: 'He introduced his R— H— to my house.' (When Fox eventually married and settled down it was with Armistead.)

All this was the stuff of gossip columns and news reports, which the King read with growing dismay. The Prince and his cronies had the misfortune to live through the great age of caricature, from the late 18th century to about 1830, and although the King was unlikely to have seen many of them his better-off subjects did, and they laughed. The artists who made a living by caricatures were talented, and two, James Gillray and George Cruikshank[2], were at times touched by genius.

## Lady Lade's lovers

As a young man the Prince was surrounded by a group of raffish serving officers whom he admired, mostly for their worst tendencies, and they often appeared with him in caricatures. Sir John Lade was remarkable for drinking, driving a coach-and-four with great skill and for marrying the high-class courtesan Letitia Smith. She had been involved with George's younger and favourite brother Frederick, and more famously with the highwayman Sixteen-String Jack Rann, who was executed in 1774. He was so called because of the silk tassels he attached to the knees of his breeches, and ever the dandy he went to his execution in a new pea-green suit, a ruffled shirt and a hat surrounded with silver rings. In his buttonhole he wore a huge nosegay. The night before his execution he was allowed to entertain seven girls in his cell. Letitia was present when he was hanged at Tyburn.

Lady Lade was also noted for driving her phaeton furiously and for swearing in public. 'He swears like Letty Lade', the Prince once remarked of a man whose language was particularly expressive. George gave the Lades an annual pension of £300, which may have been partly for services rendered. Letitia was rumoured to have been among his lovers before her marriage in 1787, and after it she acted as his procurer, introducing him to the beautiful Elizabeth Harrington, leading to her briefly becoming, in Huish's words, a 'victim' of the Prince's 'libidinous desires'. The Prince, who admired Letitia's expert and daring horsemanship, commissioned an equestrian portrait of her by George Stubbs. Huish didn't share this enthusiasm – he thought she represented 'all that was vile and despicable

Sir John Lade cutting a dash with his coach-and-four at Tattersall's Yard in Grosvenor Place in 1796. Lade was one of the Prince of Wales's disreputable companions. His foul-mouthed wife, Letitia, a former whore, was the lover of the highwayman Sixteen-String Jack Rann. She was present at his execution.

in woman'. She once danced with the Prince at a public assembly in Brighton, whereat the more conservative aristocratic women present, including the Duchess of Rutland, walked out and left the town. The incident brought a fusillade from *The Times*, which deplored the fact that the Prince should dance with 'a woman who lived in the style of a mistress to one-half of his acquaintance ... among those acquaintances, his own brother made one of that very woman's keepers'.

George shared the Lades' passion for carriage-driving. During the 1780s and 1790s he was often seen driving his carriage along Brighton seafront accompanied by Sir John. Thackeray recalled that the Prince once drove a carriage from Carlton House to Brighton in four and a half hours, and the Prince himself boasted of driving a phaeton-and-four 'twenty-two miles in two hours at a trot'.

In October 1795 a newspaper report caught something of the attraction of Sir John Lade for the Prince:

A curious circumstance occurred at Brighton on Monday. Sir John Lade, for a trifling wager, undertook to carry Lord Cholmondeley on his back, from opposite the Pavilion twice round the Steyne. Several ladies attended to be spectators of this extraordinary feat of the dwarf carrying the giant. When his Lordship declared himself ready, Sir John desired him to strip. 'Strip!' exclaimed the other; 'why surely you promised to carry me in my clothes.' 'By no means,' replied the Baronet; 'I engaged to carry you, but not an inch of clothes. So therefore, my Lord, make ready, and let us not disappoint the ladies.' After much laughable altercation, it was decided that Sir John had won his wager, the Peer declining to exhibit himself *in puris naturalibus*.

Such harmless high spirits kept the Prince amused for a while, and for once he showed his gratitude, granting Lade the pension[3] mentioned above in 1814 when he emerged penniless from a debtors' prison.

Not everyone shared George's amused tolerance for Lade. Lord Thurlow, the gruff Lord Chancellor, said on finding that he had been invited to dinner at the same time as Sir John: 'I have, Sir, no objection to Sir John Lade in his proper place, which I take to be your Royal Highness's coach-box, and not your table.'

Another exception to the rule of sundered friendships was George's First Equerry, Colonel Gerard Lake, who remained close to him until his death. The King considered Lake a bad influence, and had him posted to a series of appointments abroad. Lake was reprimanded for the savagery of his suppression of the United Irishmen in 1797–8, yet was later appointed Commander-in-Chief in India, and when he returned to Britain was created a viscount. On hearing of Lake's death in 1808 George fainted, something he could do at will.

## Hanging out with Hanger

Colonel George Hanger, a hero of the American War of Independence, was another of the Prince's boon drinking and gambling companions. He was basically a decent but weak man born into an age of temptation, as he tells us in his autobiography:

I was early introduced into life, and often kept both good and bad company; associated with men both good and bad, and with lewd women and women not lewd, wicked and not wicked; – in short with men and women of every description and every rank, from the highest to the lowest, from St James's to St Giles's [a notorious slum around the present New Oxford Street]; in palaces and night cellars; from the drawing room to the dust cart. The difficulties and misfortunes I have experienced, I am inclined to think, have proceeded from none of the above-mentioned causes, but from happening to come into life at a period of the greatest extravagance and profusion ... I could not stand the temptations of that age of extravagance, elegance and pleasure: indeed, I am not the only sufferer, for most of my contemporaries, and many of them of ten times my opulence, have been ruined.

Nathaniel Wraxall left this vignette of Hanger when the Prince had dropped him:

The Hon. George Hanger, now become an Irish baron in his old age by the successive decease of his two brothers, the Lords Coleraine, might rather be considered as a humble retainer at Carlton House than justly numbered among the friends of the heir apparent. Poor even to a degree of destitution, without profession or regular employment, subsisting from day to day by expedients, some of them not the most reputable, he was regarded as a sort of outcast from decent society.

Hanger's lifelong interest in women began as a schoolboy at Eton. He tells us:

A carpenter's wife was the first object of my early affections; nor can I well express the nature of my obligations to her. Frequently have I risked breaking my neck in getting over the roof of my boarding house at night, to pass a few hours with some favourite grisette at Windsor.

He was clearly an engaging companion, and he also helped the Prince kill time, sometimes by devising what Beresford Chancellor calls curious wagers. Hanger may have been innocent or naive, but among the Prince's circle were several professional gamblers, who successfully used such contests to fleece the royal dupe. Chancellor tells of one contest devised by Hanger, which cost the Prince thousands of pounds. During a convivial party at Carlton House Hanger suggested that turkeys could walk further in a given time than geese. Since the Prince respected his judgement, he wagered a large sum on the outcome. Twenty geese were matched against twenty turkeys, and at first the latter seemed the likely winners, gaining at least two miles on the geese. But as evening drew on the turkeys flew into nearby trees to roost, and the geese won. Anyone who had done a little research would have predicted this result, and successful gamblers of the time, such as Lord Queensberry, were noted for their meticulous pre-contest research.

Hanger had a touching modesty, particularly given the circles he moved in. In 1814 he succeeded his brother as Lord Coleraine, a title which gave him no pleasure. One day in Bond Street an acquaintance said to him: 'I hope I have the honour to see your Lordship in perfect health.' Hanger replied: 'What do you mean, you scoundrel, by calling a man names he is ashamed of? Whether Lord Coleraine be up there' (pointing to the sky) 'or down there' (pointing to the ground) 'I know not, or care not; but I am, as I always was, plain George Hanger.' When he was pitifully poor he once entertained the Prince, one of the royal dukes and some of their friends in his Soho lodging house. They ate baked shoulder of mutton and baked potatoes, and

Col. George Hanger, raffish friend of the Prince of Wales. He showed a touching modesty when the Prince dropped him. When he fell on hard times he married his housekeeper, refused to use his title and spent his days reminiscing in a north London pub.

drank porter. The Prince, noted for serving some of the most elaborate and expensive meals ever seen in England, said he had never enjoyed a meal so much.

Hanger's modesty served him in old age, when the Prince had long abandoned him for a younger, more fashionable and amusing set. He married his housekeeper, spent much of his time at a pub near his lodgings in unfashionable Somers Town telling tales of his war service in America and died in 1824, aged 72.

Another of the Prince's louche companions was Captain Jack Payne of the Royal Navy. Although he rose to be a rear-admiral and was MP for Huntingdon, he was *persona non grata* with the court because of his drinking and gambling. He was notoriously unreliable where money was concerned, and when the Prince proposed him for membership of Brooks's Club he was blackballed. Yet the Prince appointed him Comptroller of his household, and let him use a private apartment at the Brighton Pavilion. He was given the valuable sinecure of Treasurer of Greenwich Hospital.

Payne was dismissed in 1796 for his support of Princess Caroline and opposition to George's mistress, Lady Jersey. The Jerseys were given Payne's house next door to George's residence, Carlton House. (He later got his job back and was remembered in the Prince's secret will 'with truest affection'.)

George's principal guide in aesthetic matters in his early twenties was the 'extrovert and eccentric' miniaturist Richard Cosway. He was a frequent visitor to musical soirées Cosway and his wife Maria held at their home in Berkeley Street. It was widely rumoured that he was having an affair with the vivacious Maria, but it has to be admitted his name was linked to many women. In 1785 Richard Cosway was appointed Principal Painter to His Royal Highness the Prince of Wales.

## That scoundrel Weltje

George's choice of companions reached its nadir, as far as the King and just about everyone else were concerned, with Louis Weltje. He was a cook and co-owner with his brother of a cake shop in St James's Street when George met him. George had always shown an alarming tendency to treat servants as friends, and in 1828 it was reported that 'he talks to his pages with far more openness and familiarity than to anybody'. Weltje, whom the King described as a 'scoundrel', wormed his way into the Prince's confidence, performing secret services which were too sordid for the equerries. He acted as pander and bought off outraged husbands and mothers, and fobbed off creditors.

Weltje began his career as a cook in the court of the Duke of Brunswick. After he arrived in London he tried his luck as a street musician, then opened a gingerbread stall. Eventually he became the Prince's Comptroller at Carlton House, at the same time running an exclusive gambling club at 64 Pall Mall.

By the early 1780s Weltje had made himself indispensable to the Prince, and in 1784 was sent to find suitable accomodation for his master in Brighton. He was heavily involved in the Prince's development of a villa that eventually became Brighton Pavilion, and for years they sought to maintain the fiction that the vastly expensive project was Weltje's.

His arrogance was breathtaking. In 1778 there was an installation supper for Knights of the Bath at the Pantheon, with the Prince and the Duke of York attending. Weltje refused to do the catering, saying 'for the one thousand guineas offered he could supply only sandwiches'. When he procured the *Morning Post* as the Prince's mouthpiece *The Times* commented: 'go back to keeping your gingerbread stall ... an itinerant German music-grinder, raised from earning halfpennies ... to a great German Toad-eater who amassed a great fortune by dubious practices.' Weltje had indeed amassed a fortune, but he lost it all gambling. He died penniless in 1810, and the prince granted his widow a pension of £90 a year.

Perhaps the most outrageous of all the Prince's friends were the Barrymores. Richard Barry, seventh Earl of Barrymore, had estates and a handsome income of £20,000 a year. Eventually it seemed hardly enough for his extravagance. He was known as 'Hellgate' because of his profligacy, particularly in gambling. (Wags dubbed his foul-mouthed and savage-tempered sister 'Billingsgate', his clerical brother, a compulsive gambler who was seldom out of trouble for debt, 'Newgate', and his club-footed brother 'Cripplegate', all of course well-known London landmarks.) In 1791 during Ascot races Barrymore spent £1785 laying on two banquets for the Prince, who attended neither. In the course of his brief racing career he is believed to have run through £300,000. He annoyed another great gambler and horseracing man, the Duke of Queensberry, by buying a mansion in Piccadilly larger and grander than the Duke's home nearby. Barrymore married – at Gretna Green – Letitia Lade's niece, the daughter of a sedan-chairman. He was fond of acting, and spent a fortune on this harmless pursuit, building a full-sized theatre at his country home at Wargrave in Berkshire.

Barrymore and his brothers and sisters were notorious for playing hair-raising practical jokes, which sometimes amused the Prince. They shared his love of Brighton, which was the scene of many of their frolics. They would race down in their coach, 'sometimes stopping to uproot or displace signposts, at other times screaming "Murder! Rape! Unhand me, villain!"'(Hibbert, *George IV*).

When they reached Brighton they raised hell, going about at night with a coffin to terrify the citizens. They called themselves the 'Merry Mourners' and knocked at doors, telling servants they had come to collect their dead masters. One night they placed the open coffin, with a servant inside, outside a house, rang the bell and ran away. The terrified house-owner opened fire with a pistol, narrowly missing the servant's head.

'Cripplegate' charged his horse into the house of Maria Fitzherbert, secret wife of the Prince of Wales, up the stairs and into an attic. It was later brought down by two blacksmiths. 'Hellgate' dressed up in his cook's clothes and sang a serenade under Mrs Fitzherbert's bedroom window at three o'clock in the morning.

By the spring of 1792 Barrymore was in financial trouble. He had to sell his Piccadilly mansion and its contents – it was bought by his great rival on the turf, the Duke of Queensberry. Creditors snapped at his heels, getting court orders against him. The Wargrave theatre, where the Prince of Wales had often been a guest, was pulled down and the materials sold. The props and costumes were sent to auction at Christie's. His stables, on which he lavished a fortune, were closed and the horses sold.

In 1793 Barrymore's short and 'feverish existence' ended suddenly and mysteriously at the age of 24. While he was driving in a carriage a hunting gun propped against the side went off, shooting him in the eye. When his affairs were finally tidied up it was found that he was still solvent, a mystery as great as his death.

A lurid and scurrilous publication, *The Jockey Club, or a Sketch of the Manners of The Age*[4], depicts the Prince's friends as the 'very lees of society'. 'If a man of the most depraved, the vilest cast were, from a vicious sympathy, to choose his company, it were impossible for his choice to fix anywhere else.' *The Jockey Club* attacked the Prince over Mrs Fitzherbert, his debts – 'a national disgrace' – his dissipation, extravagance and dishonesty in promising to reform. The attack on his friends was even more venomous. The rowdy Barrymores, George Hanger and Sir John Lade were described as 'creatures with whom a man of morality or even common decency' would not be seen. Lady Lade was a 'common prostitute'. The Prince's brother the Duke of York spent his time 'amongst the nymphs of Berkeley Row'. Weltje was a 'brute'.

## Brummells' fashion statement

His callous indifference to the fate of two of his closest friends, the dandy George Brummell, known as Beau, and the playwright Richard Brinsley Sheridan, shows the Prince at his worst. At the least he should have been grateful to Brummell for teaching him restraint in dress. When he first met Brummell, the Prince, now regarded as a man of exquisite taste, wore multi-coloured clothes and considered himself the leader of the dandies. After coming under the Beau's sway he was less gaudy.

Brummell did more than anyone to restrain the exuberance of dandy taste. He insisted on simplicity in cut and style. He went to ridiculous lengths over minor details of dress and dressing. Apart from the cut and congruity of colours his greatest contribution to style was the tying of the neckcloth, or stock. These had been made of limp cloth, and usually looked messy. Brummell favoured starched muslin, which was tricky to work with. 'Brummell's dressing room was always thronged with fashionable spectators trying to see how he did it: they included the Prince Regent and the Dukes of Bedford, Beaufort and Rutland, all of whom were his personal friends' (Murray, *High Society*). The slightest mistake and the whole thing had to be undone and a new start made. This is how one of Brummell's friends described the operation:

> The collar, which was always fixed to the shirt, was so large that, before being folded down, it completely hid his head and face, and the white neckcloth was at least a foot in height. The first *coup d'archet* was made with the shirt collar, which he folded down to its proper size, and then, standing before the looking glass, with his chin poked up towards the ceiling, by the gentle and gradual declension of his lower jaw he creased the cravat to reasonable dimensions.

The Brummell stock created a sensation. The young men who followed him so slavishly were mostly wealthy, they had little to do all day except indulge themselves. After Brummell's fashion revolution the more dedicated dandies among them could no longer be seen in public with a crumpled stock without losing face.

Brummell cannot have been wholly serious. One night at dinner, sitting next but one to a nobleman who was so encased in a colourful oriental tie he could not see those to either side, Brummell asked a waiter: 'Is Lord Worcester here?'

'Yes, sir.'

'Tell Lord Worcester I would be happy to drink a glass of wine with him.'

'Yes, sir.'

'Is his lordship ready?'

'Yes, sir.'

'Then tell him I drink his health,' said Brummell, without turning his head to look at Worcester. It was a rebuke, but an amusing one. He would never have been guilty of Worcester's sartorial solecism. Brummell said: 'If John Bull turns round to look after you, you are not well dressed; but either too stiff, too tight, or too fashionable.'

The man who held sway over this constellation of rich young aristocrats was himself a commoner. Brummell's grandfather was a valet who later ran a lodging house. One of his lodgers was the father of a future Prime Minister, and through him Brummell's father got a job as a Treasury clerk. He became private secretary to Lord North, acquired a number of government sinecures, married a beautiful and wealthy woman and mixed in the highest Whig circles. He sent George to Eton. When the boy left, at the age of 15, he met the Prince, who promised him a commission in his own regiment, the highly fashionable 10th Hussars.

Brummell duly joined the army, and when he was 20 sold his commission. According to legend the regiment had been posted to Manchester, social death for a dandy like Brummell, and so he resigned. He had inherited £30,000, was a good-looking young man with a dry wit and great charm, and soon established himself as the arbiter of taste. The Prince, who was dazzled, was said to have burst into tears when Brummell criticised the cut of his new coat. He could only have agreed with Brummell's dictum, 'A life of leisure is a most difficult art ... boredom is as depressing as an insistent creditor.'

Brummell's sayings, often repeated among the *ton*, are examples of Regency wit at its best. Asked for the address of his hairdresser Brummell replied: 'I have three: the first is responsible for my temples, the second for the front and the third for the occiput.' When he was asked at a dinner whether he liked vegetables, he said he had never eaten any, adding, after a pause: 'No, that is not quite true – I once ate a pea.' He was said to have jilted a woman because she ate cabbage. When a wealthy merchant invited him to dinner he replied: 'With pleasure, if you will promise faithfully not to tell anyone.' At a house where the champagne was not of the quality he was used to he asked for 'some more of that cider', but was entreated to come again.

There was another story which he denied, although it has the ring of his insolent humour. A *nouveau riche* invited him to dinner, and asked him to name the guests. Brummell did so. The host said: 'Good, that will make an even number. Your ten friends, yourself and myself – twelve in all.'

'Good God, sir,' the Beau is said to have replied, 'you surely don't mean you are to be one of the party!'

This parvenu held sway for a time at the top of society by his cool narcissism and wit, but was undone by a weakness for gambling and for pricking the egos of men with a more secure social standing. Making the Prince cry about the style of his coat was bad enough, but from time to time Brummell treated him with a cutting lack of respect which the touchy Prince eventually could not bear. At a ball in 1812 the Prince arrived with Lord Alvanley. He stood talking to Alvanley, pointedly ignoring Brummell. At last Brummell could stand it no longer, and called out, 'Alvanley, who's your fat friend?'

## The Beau's last bet

Given the Prince's tendency to drop his friends, even the most sycophantic, they would have fallen out sooner or later. Brummell's arrogance and lacerating wit hastened the break, and those four fatal words 'who's your fat friend?' sundered what had been a long and close friendship. There is no doubt that Brummell annoyed the Prince with unkind remarks about the well-upholstered Mrs Fitzherbert. He had coined the nickname Benina for her, after the gigantic Carlton House porter known as Big Ben.

Brummell once said 'I made [the Prince] what he is and I can unmake him', words he had long years to regret. It was debt, however, rather than the withdrawal of royal favour that ruined him. It was said that two emperors, Napoleon and Brummell, fell at the same time, but Brummell really abdicated. He was as popular as ever. He was even successful in minor wagers. The famous Betting Book at White's records some of them:

Mr Charles Bouverie bets Mr Brummell one hundred guineas that the Empress Maria Louisa is not in Paris within six months of the present date – April 9, 1815. [Bouverie paid]

Mr Brummell bets Mr [Paul] Methuen twenty-five guineas that the Allies make peace with Buonaparte. [Methuen paid in 1814]

Mr Brodrick bets Mr Brummell twenty five guineas to two hundred that Buonaparte is not alive this day six weeks – January 10, 1814. [Brodrick paid]

Mr Brummell bets Mr Blackford thirty guineas to twenty-five guineas that Sir William Guise beats Mr Dalton for the county of Gloucester, now contesting between them – February 1811. [Blackford paid]

Brummell could easily afford to lose these comparatively small sums. And his luck seemed to be in at the hazard table. One night he won £26,000, almost as much as his whole inheritance of thirty thousand. Then one night after a long losing streak he announced he had lost every penny he had in the world. He wished someone would make him promise never to play again. His friend Pemberton Mills gave him a ten-pound note, saying he expected a thousand if Brummell ever gambled. For a while the Beau tried to stay away from the tables but about two weeks later Mills saw him gambling again. Sadly he touched his friend on the shoulder and asked, not for the thousand but for the return of his ten. Brummell began to borrow heavily at ruinous interest rates. One evening in 1816 he made a last appeal to a friend, Scrope Davies.

My Dear Scrope, Lend me two hundred pounds; the banks are shut, and all my money is in the three per cents. It shall be paid tomorrow morning. Yours, George Brummell.

My Dear George, Tis very unfortunate; but all my money is in the three per cents. Yours, S Davies.

That night he fled to Calais to escape his creditors, and never returned. His property was sold at auction to help pay his creditors, and raised £1100. One of the items was a handsome snuff-box, in which there was a note in his handwriting: 'This was intended for the Prince Regent, if he had conducted himself with more propriety towards me.' George helped him financially from time to time, but with such small amounts that it was little help. On his way to Hanover in 1821 George passed through Calais but refused to visit Brummell, who had left his name in the visitors' book at the Prince's hotel as an indication that he hoped to be reconciled. Thackeray said of George's way of casting off his friends and lovers:

> On Monday he kissed and fondled poor Perdita[5], and on Tuesday he met her and did not know her. On Wednesday he was very affectionate with the wretched Brummell, and on Thursday forgot him.

The *Dictionary of National Biography* says that in 1837 Brummell 'began to show signs of imbecility; he held phantom receptions of the beauties and magnates of the old days. Soon all care of his person went, and from carelessness and disease his habits became so loathsome that an attendant could hardly be found for him.' This once most fastidious dandy died in a lunatic asylum in Caen in 1840.

## A glass with Sherry

Brummell was a minor if amusing character. Richard Brinsley Sheridan, the Irish playwright, wit, theatre impresario and politician, was a major figure in several fields whose biggest mistake was devoting himself to the service of an ungrateful prince. For years he was George's closest political adviser. He was also a hard-drinking womaniser, a political schemer and unreliable about money, a strange mixture of charlatanry and integrity.

His friend Tom Moore, the poet, told amusing anecdotes about Sheridan's bad behaviour in his biography of the playwright.

Lord John [Russell] told a good trick of Sheridan's upon Richardson – Sheridan had been driving three or four hours in a hackney coach, when seeing Richardson pass, he hailed him and made him get into it – he instantly contrived to introduce a topic upon which Richardson (who was the very soul of disputatiousness) always differed with him – and at last, affecting to be mortified by R's arguments, said 'You really are too bad – I cannot bear to listen to such things – I will not stay in the same coach with you' and accordingly got out and left him – Richardson hallooing out triumphantly after him 'Ah, you're beaten, you're beaten' – nor was it till the heat of his victory had a little cooled that he found he was left in the lurch to pay for Sheridan's three hours' coaching.

The diarist Joseph Farington tells a story which redresses the balance. In August 1815 Sheridan was imprisoned for debt in the Fetter Lane sponging house. He received between £400 and £500 to obtain his release and then one of his old tenants whose own goods had been seized because of debts called on him. Farington says: 'Sheridan asked him what sum would relieve him. The man replied that £300 would restore him to his former state. Sheridan gave him the money.'

He was as witty as Oscar Wilde, and more economical. One day two royal dukes approached him in Piccadilly. 'I say, Sherry,' said one, 'We're just discussing whether you are more rogue or fool.' Sherry took them both by the arm and replied: 'Why faith, I believe I am between both.' With a courage which is still touching he watched his Drury Lane Theatre burning down one night in 1809 and replied to a man who wondered that he could stand there so calmly drinking: 'Surely a man may be allowed to drink a glass of wine by his own fireside?'

At a time when eloquence was measured in days rather than hours Sheridan had exceptional stamina. He made his mark with the impeachment for corruption of Warren Hastings, the East India Company administrator, which lasted more than seven years. On 7 February 1787, Sheridan rose to speak. He sat down five hours and forty minutes later. The speech was a triumph and he was offered £1000 for the copyright. Unfortunately for him there was no text to sell – he had departed freely from whatever notes he had used. Twenty years later Fox said it was the greatest speech he had ever heard. Windham thought it the finest ever made. One of Hastings' defenders, Logan, sat through the first hour and thought: 'All this is declamatory assertion without proof.' After the second, 'This is a most wonderful oration.' After the third, he thought: 'Mr Hastings has acted very unjustifiably.' After the fourth, 'Mr Hastings is a most atrocious criminal,' and after the fifth, 'Of all the monsters of iniquity, the most enormous is Warren Hastings.' Later in the trial after speaking for four days Sheridan 'contrived with a knowledge of stage effect ... to sink back, as if exhausted, in the arms of Burke, who hugged him with the energy of generous admiration'. Burke, no mean gasbag himself, called it 'the most astonishing effort of eloquence, argument and wit united, of which there is any record or tradition'.[6]

Sheridan was born in Dublin in 1751, of a native Irish family which had converted to Protestantism. His grandfather Thomas Sheridan was a close friend of Swift, and his father, also Thomas, was a writer, a noted teacher of elocution, actor and author of a *Life of Swift*. The family moved to Bath, Richard was educated at Harrow, and after leaving school tried writing for the theatre. In 1773 he married the beautiful opera singer Elizabeth Linley, after fighting two duels with a Welsh beau who was pursuing her, and they settled in London, living way beyond their means. In his early twenties he wrote 'the two best comedies of the age' (J.B. Priestley): *The Rivals* and *The School for Scandal*. With the exception of *The Critic* (1779) 'teeming with sparkling wit' (*DNB*) he wrote nothing else of note. In 1778 he became the proprietor of Drury Lane and in 1780 he was elected for Stafford, and afterwards held some minor government posts. His political importance, however, was much greater, as confidential adviser to the Prince. He was a Whig follower and then rival of Fox, and the three of them gambled and drank deep together.

Sheridan met the Prince when the latter was just 21, at Brooks's Club or at Devonshire House, home of Georgiana, Duchess of Devonshire. It had become the powerhouse of Whig politics, and Fox was a frequent guest. The Prince found the relaxed attitudes to sex, drinking and gambling there congenial. Since Fox and his Whig friends were detested by the King the Prince had an added reason to go there. He and Sheridan were soon close and genuine friends, sharing an 'interest in drinking, music, literature and practical jokes' (O'Toole, *A Traitor's Kiss*). But from Sheridan's point of view it was a hopelessly unequal friendship. The Prince used him and then, when he abandoned his Foxite political views, discarded him.

Sheridan led the campaign for a Regency Bill when the King seemed incurably ill in 1788. His 'ready wit and adept political management proved invaluable to the Prince' (Parissien) and it was Fox whose clumsy demand in the Commons that the Prince be given unfettered powers strengthened the Pitt government's case for delaying. In the event the King recovered before the Bill could become law, but Sheridan continued to be indispensable to the Prince of Wales. 'When George heard a rumour that, in view of his recent conduct ... his parents planned to shift the succession to the Duke of York, he asked Sheridan to negotiate with his brother' (Parissien).

## Sheridan's fall

Sheridan's moment seemed to have come in 1801. Pitt resigned because of the King's obdurate opposition to his plan to give Irish Catholics full citizenship, including the right to stand for Parliament. Bizarrely, Sheridan was now in favour at court, having conducted the Queen and her daughters to safety when there was an attempt on the King's life at the theatre in May 1800. The King praised Sheridan, 'who he verily thought had a respect and regard for him'. 'Sheridan's name was once more talked of in connection with government office – the Chancellorship' (Parissien). The King became seriously ill again in 1804, and although Sheridan did not get high office he was still close to the Prince, acting as his intermediary with the government. Perhaps more important, in view of his pressing debts, the Prince made him Receiver of the Revenue of the Duchy of Cornwall, a sinecure bringing him at least £1200 a year. Thanking him, Sheridan pledged that 'to the end of my Life I will strenuously employ every Faculty of my Mind in your service'.

By now Sheridan was drinking heavily. He lost his compelling good looks and his face became red and bloated. The orator who had often held the Commons spellbound was now usually too drunk to be an effective speaker, although he occasionally reached his old heights. He had quarrelled with Fox and had stopped writing plays. His Drury Lane theatre burned down in 1791 and was rebuilt at great expense (it was destroyed by fire again in 1809). When George became Prince

Sheridan's Drury Lane Theatre. When it burned to the ground in 1809 the great playwright, wit and politician watched from a nearby tavern and remarked: 'Surely a man may be allowed to enjoy a glass of wine before his own fireside.'

Regent in 1811 Sheridan very reasonably hoped for high office. But Fox had died in 1806 and after a show of uncontrollable grief George began quietly to change his politics. His old Foxite beliefs and circle became an embarrassment, and Sheridan was mortified to be directed by his royal patron to write to Spencer Percival, the Prime Minister, to say his Tory administration would stay in power for the time being. When Percival was assassinated the Prince offered Sheridan a minor post in the new government, 'an insulting offer which [he] proudly refused' (Parissien).

Sheridan was a stauch supporter of Catholic emancipation, which the Regent opposed, and deciding to end his parliamentary dependence on the court he fought Stafford in 1812, coming last in the poll. Without a seat he lost his parliamentary immunity to arrest, and in May 1814 he was held in the sponging house over a debt of £600. He was eventually released, living with his wife 'in a state of filth and stench that was quite intolerable'.

Sheridan died in June 1816. It was said he called down 'shame on the Regent for abandoning me'. The Prince had his last glimpse of his old friend in August 1815. George was passing through Leatherhead in his coach: he saw Sheridan about thirty yards ahead, and turned to his companion, saying, 'There is Sheridan.' At that point Sheridan turned aside into a lane, and the Prince made no attempt to follow or attract his attention. So parted for ever the Prince, mighty ruler of his country, and his broken friend, 'the man on whom he had depended so much for nearly forty years' (O'Toole).

Why did Sheridan, so gifted, fail? He backed a series of wrong horses. He attached himself to the Whig party when the Tories were just becoming dominant. When Fox was dismissed by the King Sheridan followed him into the wilderness. His worst error of judgement was to attach himself to the Prince of Wales. And eventually his drinking, particularly after the death of his beloved wife Betsy in 1792, robbed him of his old wit and sparkle.

As he lay dying the bailiffs were about to carry him to prison in a blanket when a doctor came to his rescue with the threat of a murder charge. Two royal dukes and half the peerage followed his coffin to the Abbey, and his pall-bearers included five peers and a bishop.

## Disreputable dukes

The unsuitable companions the Prince of Wales chose included two of the most notorious dukes in England, Queensberry and Norfork. They were of another generation, Norfolk being 16 years older than the Prince and Queensberry 38 years older. Queensberry was a great gambler and the lecher of the age. Norfolk was a celebrated drunkard, ignorant and with an aversion to washing. The only time his servants could wash him was when he was drunk.

Charles Howard, eleventh Duke of Norfolk, known as 'Jockey', was uneducated. Yet he had qualities that were admirable, at least in an Englishman. Wraxall says that when he was in the Commons he displayed 'a sort of rude eloquence, analogous to his formation of mind and body', and that in later years in the Upper House he 'maintained the manly independence of his character, and frequently spoke with ability as well as information'. He was a staunch supporter of Fox, and briefly held a Lordship of the Treasury in 1783. He refused the Prince Regent's offer of the Garter as a bribe to support Lord Liverpool's Tory administration in 1812.

However, he is remembered for devoting most of his energy 'to the gratification of his sensual appetites' (Melville, *Beaux*). He fathered innumerable bastards, and paid maintenance to their mothers 'as the wages of their shame'.

> It was said that the money was paid quarterly, at a certain banker's, the cheques to be cashed on the same day, to all the parties. Such frail pensioners were not likely to postpone their receipts; and aware of this, the Duke used to sit in a back parlour, to have a peep at his old acquaintances, the names of whom, as each applied, he knew, as the clerk was appointed to bring the cheque as presented, for the Duke's inspection. There he would make his comments to a confidential person at his elbow. Of one he would say, 'She looks as young as twenty years ago!' of another, 'What a dowdy!' and of another 'What an old hag!' Occasionally, however, a feeling of compunction, or perhaps of caprice, would seize him when he would desire the party to step in, and there, after inquiring of their welfare, strange to say, he would sometimes entertain them with a gratuitous lecture on morality! (Angelo, *Reminiscences*).

Once when he was driving through the village of Greystoke in Cumberland he saw hordes of children waving to him from both sides of the road. 'Whose are all those children?' he asked. His steward answered, 'Some are mine, Your Grace, and some are yours.'

Even more remarkable than his sexual prowess was his capacity to 'swill wine like a Silenus, and gorge beefsteaks like a Buckhorse' (Richardson, *Recollections*). When still a lad he often dined with his father at the Thatched House tavern and drank him and his friends under the table before 'sallying forth to begin the night' (Melville, *Beaux*). He ate at the Beefsteak Club, whose members though formidable in their own potations could not match him bottle for bottle. Once when he was casting about for a new and unusual character to use at a masquerade there were many suggestions, all of which were rejected. Then Sam Foote, the wit and playwright, suggested: 'Go sober!' There is no record that he took this up.

Wraxhall attributed his drunkenness to a hereditary weakness, 'transmitted down, probably, by his ancestors from Plantagenet times, and inherent in his blood'. His appetite amazed those who watched him eat. Charles Marsh never forgot the sight:

> His appetite literally grew by what it fed on. Two or three succeeding steaks, fragrant from the gridiron, rapidly vanished. In my simplicity, I thought his labours were over. I was deceived, for I observed him rubbing a clean plate with a shallot, to prepare it for the reception of another. A pause of ten minutes ensued, and his Grace rested upon his knife and fork; but it was only a pause, and I found that there was a good reason for it. Like the epic, a rump of beef has a beginning, a middle and an end. The palate of an experienced beefeater can discern all its progressive varieties, from the first cut to the last; and he is a mere tyro in the business who does not know that towards the middle there lurks a fifth essence, the perfect ideal of tenderness and flavour ... for this cut the Duke had wisely tarried, and for this he re-collected his forces. At last he desisted, but more, I thought, from fatigue than satiety (*The Clubs of London*).

Before one of these orgies the Duke would usually stop at Covent Garden for a dish of fish.

### Toasting a toper

He was a drinking companion of the Prince of Wales, and Thackeray recalled a trick played on him by that habitually mean-spirited individual. The Prince had invited Jockey to dine and sleep at the Pavilion in Brighton. He and his brothers had a plan to get the old man drunk. It was the custom at the time for men to drink toasts to each other. They decided that each guest in turn would call on the Duke to drink a toast, and it was a challenge that the old toper could not refuse.

> He soon began to see there was a conspiracy against him; he drank glass for glass; he overthrew many of the brave. At last the First Gentleman of Europe [as the Prince liked to think himself] proposed large glasses of brandy. One of the royal brothers filled a

great glass for the Duke. He stood up and tossed off the drink. 'Now,' says he, 'I will have my carriage and go home.' The Prince urged upon him his previous promise to sleep under the roof where he had been so generously entertained. 'No,' said he, he had had enough of such hospitality. A trap had been set for him; he would leave the place at once and never enter its doors more. The carriage was called, and came; but in the half-hour's interval, the liquor had proved too potent for the old man; his host's generous purpose was answered, and the Duke's old grey head lay stupified upon the table. Nevertheless, when his post-chaise was announced, he staggered to it as well as he could, and stumbling in, bade the postillion drive to Arundel. They drove him for half and hour round and round the pavilion lawn; the poor old man fancied he was going home. When he awoke that morning he was in bed at the Prince's hideous house at Brighton ... I can fancy the flushed faces of the royal princes as they support themselves at the portico pillars and look on at old Norfolk's disgrace; but I can't fancy how the man who perpetrated it continued to be called a gentleman. (Thackeray, *The Four Georges*).

In 1792 the caricaturist James Gillray depicted Norfolk sitting on the knees of two mountainous courtesans, whom E.J. Burford (*Wits, Wenchers and Wantons*) identifies as the 40-stone Royal Sovereign and her companion Nelly Hutton, who weighed just under 30 stone. In spite of these and other excesses the Duke lived until 1815, when he was 69.

Others who did not have his constitution died young. The popular Jack Talbot, son of Lord Malahide, fought bravely in the Peninsula but didn't find a role in peacetime.

The Duke of Beaufort, who knew of his fondness for liquor, found him in his lodgings in Mount Street drinking sherry for breakfast, and pointed out to him his folly. 'It will be the death of you,' his Grace remonstrated. 'I get drunk every night,' retorted Talbot, 'and find myself the better for it next morning.' The morning soon came when he did not feel better, and the regimental doctor was called in. Lord Alvanley, who was fond of the lad, asked the medical man how his patient fared. 'My lord,' was the reply, 'he is in a bad way, for I was obliged to make use of the lancet this morning.' 'You should have tapped him, doctor,' said the witty peer, 'for

I am sure he has more claret than blood in his veins.'

How very Regency to make a grisly joke over a dying man. Talbot was found dead in his chair shortly afterwards, a half-empty sherry bottle by his side. He was 27.

When George died at Windsor Castle in June 1830 he was friendless and surrounded by sycophants and men and women who were blatantly on the make. His chief physician, Sir Henry Halford, was a cynical careerist. Three days earlier his coachman had been fined £60 (about £3700 today) after being caught making off with furniture from the castle in his master's carriage at five o'clock in the morning. The King's last mistress, Lady Conyngham, had hurried away from the dying man's bed with a coachful of loot. The King died friendless, as he had lived.

# Six-Bottle Men

The hard drinking of the Prince of Wales and his set was not exceptional, or even unusual. The 18th century was rich in prodigious drinkers, among them the highest servants of state. A later commentator wrote: 'Anyone who will take the trouble to go carefully through the columns of the ill-printed newspapers of the last century will find that drunkenness, dissoluteness, and the sword hanging on every fool's thigh ready to do his bidding were the characteristics of the period. People got drunk at dinners and then slew one another, or in some other way broke the law.'

Sir Gilbert Elliot wrote to his wife in 1787: 'Men of all ages drink abominably. Fox drinks what I should call a great deal, though he is not reckoned to do so by his companions; Sheridan excessively; and Grey [later an Earl and reforming Prime Minister] more than any of them. But it is in a more gentlemanly way than our Scotch drunkards, and it is always accompanied with lively clever conversation on subjects of importance. Pitt [the Younger, Prime Minister] I am told drinks as much as anybody.' Pitt sometimes drank more than three bottles of port a day. He once arrived at the House of Commons completely drunk and was sick behind the Speaker's chair. In his *Life of George IV* Percy Fitzgerald said that in 1788 Pitt 'broke down in the House [of Commons] owing to a debauch the night before at Lord Buckingham's, when, in company with Dundas and the Duke of Gordon, he took too much wine.'

Fitzgerald tells a story of 'three young men of fashion' who turned up drunk as dinner guests. They were Orlando Bridgman, Charles Greville and a Mr Gifford, and were so intoxicated 'as to puzzle the whole assembly'. Gifford he described as 'a young gentleman lately come out, of a good estate of about five thousand a year the whole of which he is in the act of spending in one or two years at least, and this without a grain of sense, without any fun to himself or entertainment to others. He never uttered a word, though as drunk as the other two, who were both riotous, and began to talk at last so plain that Lady Francis and Lady Valentine fled from the side table to ours, and Mrs Sheridan would have followed them, but did not escape till her arms were black and blue and her apron torn off.'

The Regency memoirist Captain Rees Howell Gronow wrote of the dinners of his youth ...

> The dinner-party, commencing at seven or eight, frequently did not break up before one in the morning. There were then four, and even five-bottle men; and the only thing that saved them was drinking very slowly, and out of very small glasses. The learned head of the law, Lord Eldon, and his brother Lord Stowell used to say that they had drunk more bad port than any other two men in England; indeed, the former was rather apt ... to speak occasionally somewhat thicker than natural, after long and heavy potations. The late Lords Panmure, Dufferin and Blayney, wonderful to relate, were six-bottle men at this time, and I really think that if the good society of 1815 could appear before their more moderate descendants in the state they were generally reduced to after dinner, the moderns would pronounce their ancestors fit for nothing but bed ... a perpetual thirst seemed to come over people, both men and women, as soon as they had tasted their soup; as from that moment everybody was taking wine with everybody else, till the close of the dinner; and such wines as produced that class of cordiality which frequently wanders into stupefaction. How all this sort of eating and drinking ended was obvious, from the prevalence of gout, and the necessity of every one making the pill-box their constant bedroom companion.

## Wild John Mytton

There was, around the turn of the 18th century, a general acceptance that someone who drank six bottles or more of port a day was a serious drinker[1].

John Mytton, squire of Halston, near Shrewsbury, who was born in 1796 and died 38 years later 'amid the horrors of delirium tremens'

(Sitwell, *English Eccentrics*) was an eight-bottle-a-day man. Port that is, before he changed to brandy. He was wild beyond all reason. Perhaps it was the port which made this great sportsman impervious to the bitterest winter weather. In pursuit of game he would wade through icy water or stride out in snowstorms wearing only the scantiest clothing, or none at all. On one occasion the keepers on his uncle's estate at Woodhouse were astonished to see Squire Mytton, stark naked, chasing ducks across a stretch of ice.

Sitwell wonders that he reached even the age of 38. Charles James Apperley, the sporting author who used the pseudonym Nimrod, wrote an account of his progress.

How often has he been run away with by gigs, how often struggling in deep water without being able to swim? How was it that he did not get torn to pieces in the countless street brawls in which he was engaged? On one occasion he nearly was torn into two pieces, at a race-course meeting in Lancashire, for one gang of thieves took it into their heads to pull Squire Mytton into a house at the very moment when a rival gang of thieves took it into *their* heads to pull him out of it. In this encounter neither side won, because the squire's enormous physical strength kept him stationary and, in the end, one of the gentlemen engaged in the struggle was transported to the Colonies as a reward for his violence and the attempted robbery.

The squire was constantly riding at dangerous fences, falling off his horse when drunk, driving his tandem at a frantic speed and paying no more attention to crossroads and corners than he did to creditors. 'There goes Squire Mytton', the country people would say, when they saw a crazily driven tandem, rushing along like the north wind; and they would raise a cheer, for the squire was warm-hearted and beloved. Once he galloped at full speed over a rabbit-warren, to find out if his horse would fall. He found out. Rolling over and over, after a time both horse and squire rose to their feet unhurt.

He liked causing accidents. When a passenger in his gig suggested that they might moderate their speed, the squire asked: 'Were you ever much hurt then, by being upset in a gig?' The passenger shocked Mytton by admitting he had never been in such an accident. 'What, never upset in a gig? What a damned slow fellow you must have been all your life.' With that he ran the inner wheel up a bank, overturning the vehicle. Neither of them was very badly hurt.

He loved animals, when he was not shooting or eating them. He once rode into the dining room on a large brown bear. When he applied his spurs the bear objected, and bit him badly through his calf. On another occasion he was sharing a bottle of mulled port with his horse Sportsman when the animal dropped dead. His most painful adventure followed a bout of hiccups. The inimitable Apperley describes it:

> You have read that somebody set fire to Troy, Alexander to Persopolis, Nero to Rome, a baker to London ... but did you ever hear of a man setting fire to his own nightshirt to frighten away the hiccup? Such, however, is the climax I have alluded to, and this is the manner in which it was performed. 'Damn this hiccup,' said Mytton, as he stood undressed on the floor, apparently in the act of getting into his bed; 'but I'll frighten it away'; so seizing a lighted candle he applied it to the tab of his shirt, and, it being a cotton one, he was instantly enveloped in flames.

Two men rescued him by tearing off the fragments of nightshirt and rolling him on the ground. The squire, appallingly burnt, reeled into bed with the words: 'The hiccup is gone, by God.' The following morning he greeted his friends with a loud 'view-haloo' to show his contempt for the pain he was in.

He had run through a great fortune, literally throwing money away. He would crunch handfuls of banknotes into a ball and throw them to his servant. Returning from Doncaster races he left a pile of banknotes, amounting to several thousand pounds, on the seat of his open carriage. He fell asleep, and the money was blown away.

He died penniless in a debtors' prison, his wife, whom he loved, having left him. Sitwell says he was worn out by 'too much foolishness, too much wretchedness and too much brandy'.

## Athletes of liquor

One of Dashwood's companions at Medmenham was the uncouth satirical poet Charles Churchill. He consumed his short life [1731–64] in a frenzy of toil, poverty, fame and dissipation. He married a girl named Martha Scott in the Fleet Prison and she made him miserable. Burdened with two unwanted children, he followed his father's wishes and became a clergyman although he had no vocation: he 'prayed and starved on forty pounds a year' at Rainham in Essex. He was not a success – it was said he eked out his stipend by selling cider to the villagers, and despite his literary talents his sermons were dull:

> Whilst, sacred dullness ever in my view,
> Sleep at my bidding crept from pew to pew.

In 1761 his *Rosciad* and *The Apology*, poems satirising actors and critics, made him briefly affluent. He used the money to introduce his lifelong friend, the poet Robert Lloyd, to the stews of London, and they became very scandalous. Wilkes said in a letter to the Duke of Grafton that they were 'generally employed in celebrating the mysteries of the god of love'. He might have added the god of wine, but that went without saying in those circles at that time. Churchill wrote to Wilkes: 'Though I will not get drunk with every Fool, I am above being thoroughly sober with an honest fellow like you.' Wilkes introduced him to the Medmenham rites in the summer of 1762, and the renegade priest shared his friend's healthy contempt for them. However, he enjoyed himself among the nuns, and from time to time had to retire from the fray to recover from a dose of the pox. In July 1762, only a month after his introduction to the club, he writes of his penitential regime for what must have been a monumental hangover if not worse: 'Breakfast at nine – two dishes of tea and one thin slice of bread and butter – dine at three – eat moderately – drink a sober pint – tumble the bed till four – tea at six – walk till nine – eat some cooling fruit and to bed.'

When Wilkes launched his anti-Bute newspaper the *North Briton* in June 1762 he recruited Churchill and Lloyd to help him harry the Ministry. With his eye as ever on the main chance Wilkes offered to desist if he were given the governership of Canada – he would take the two friends with him, Churchill as chaplain, Lloyd as secretary. It is fascinating to speculate how the duo would have fared in the bracing atmosphere of the frontier. The deal was rejected, perhaps by minds with a keener sense of the ridiculous.

*

To return to the politicians at the top of the chapter. They were all known as six-bottle men, although they may not all have drunk that much, or not all the time. It is only fair to note that port was not as strong as it is today, and the bottles were smaller.

Many parsons, squires, army officers and university dons were what one historian has called 'athletes of liquor'. Sheridan could presumably have matched them, if he had bothered to count. His biographer Tom Moore said that he drank for inspiration. 'If the thought (he would say) is slow to come, a glass of good wine encourages it, and when it does come, a glass of good wine rewards it.' The poet and journalist Leigh Hunt remarked that when Sheridan was drinking, 'he was thoroughly in earnest'. Byron, though in a deplorable condition himself, would help Sheridan to bed, lamenting: 'Poor fellow! he got drunk very thoroughly and very soon. It occasionally fell to my lot to convey him home – no sinecure – for he was so tipsy that I was obliged to put on his cocked hat for him – to be sure it tumbled off again, and I was not myself so sober as to be able to pick it up again.' Sheridan told him that on the night of the 'grand success' of his play *The School for Scandal* 'he was knocked down and put into the watch house [jail] for making a row in the street & being found intoxicated by the Watchmen'. Even when sozzled his wit and presence of mind did not desert him. One night the Watch found him drunk in the gutter and demanded his name, and the playwright answered: 'Wilberforce'. The famous anti-slavery campaigner was a noted teetotaller.

Lady Holland, at whose great mansion in west London, the political powerhouse of the Whig ascendancy, Sheridan was a constant guest, told Moore that he would take a bottle of wine and a book to bed with him; 'the *former* alone intended for use'. He drank spirits with breakfast, and on his way into town invariably stopped at an old roadside inn, the Adam and Eve, where he ran up a long bill. This 'Lord Holland was left the privilege of paying' (French, *Nineteen Centuries of Drink*).

While Byron found Sheridan a delightful companion he had reservations: he contrasts the playwright's staying power with that of the playwright George Colman.

I have got very drunk with both – but if I had to *choose* – and could not have both at a time – I would say – 'let me begin the evening with

Sheridan and finish it with Colman'. – Sheridan for dinner – Colman for Supper – Sheridan for claret or port – but Colman for everything – from the Madeira and champagne – at dinner – the claret with a *layer* of port between the glasses – up to the punch of the night – and down to the grog – or gin and water of day-break ... Sheridan was a Grenadier Company of Life-Guards – but Colman a whole regiment, of light infantry to be sure – but still a regiment.

In a letter to the poet Thomas Moore in October 1815 Byron tells how he and another man helped Sheridan down a corkscrew staircase 'which had been constructed before the discovery of fermented liquors, and to which no legs, however crooked, could possibly accommodate themselves ... I carried away much wine, and the wine had previously carried away my memory; so that all was hiccup and happiness for the last hour or so, and I am not impregnated with any of the conversation.'

Byron confessed that after the *Edinburgh Review* rejected an early piece of his, 'Hours of Idleness', he tried to drown his mortification with three bottles of claret after dinner. He was the author of the lines 'On A Carrier who died of Drunkenness':

John Adams lies here, of the parish of Southwell:
A carrier who carried his can to his mouth well;
He carried so much, and he carried so fast,
He could carry no more, and was carried at last;
For the liquor he drank was too much for one,
He could not carry off, so now he's carrion.

The *Reminiscences* suggest that to end the evening drunk was almost a point of principle with some of the great personages of state:

Many of the follies and extravagances that marked the life of this gifted but reckless personage [Sheridan] must be attributed to the times in which he existed. Drinking was the fashion of the day. The Prince, Mr Pitt, Dundas, the Lord Chancellor Eldon and many others who gave the tone to society would, if they now appeared at an evening party 'as was their custom of an afternoon', be pronounced fit for nothing but bed. A three-bottle man was not an unusual guest at a fashionable table; and the night was invariably spent in drinking bad port wine to an enormous extent.

## Carousing with Lamb

Many 18th-century writers were immoderate drinkers. Wordsworth, a noted water-bibber, described his friend Samuel Taylor Coleridge as a 'rotten drunkard' 'rotting out his entrails with intemperance'. When Charles Lamb recalled wistfully bibulous nights round the table –

> I have been laughing, I have been carousing,
> Drinking late, sitting late, with my bosom cronies
> All, all are gone, the old familiar faces.

– he was thinking in particular of Coleridge. Lamb wrote of the poet in a letter:

> Coleridge has powdered his head, and looks like Bacchus, Bacchus ever sleek and young. He is going to turn sober, but his clock has not struck yet, meantime he pours down goblet after goblet, the 2nd to see where the 1st has gone, the third to see no harm comes to the second, a fourth to say there's another coming, and a 5th to say he's not sure he's the last.

The artist and diarist Benjamin Haydon recalled an 'immortal dinner party' he held on 28 December 1817: present were Wordsworth, Keats, Lamb, Thomas Monkhouse, 'a merchant of Budge Row', and an explorer named Joseph Ritchie. A man named John Kingston, a deputy comptroller of the Stamp Office, gatecrashed the party by saying he knew Wordsworth, and became the butt of Lamb's peculiar humour. 'Lamb got exceedingly merry and exquisitely witty; and his fun in the midst of Wordsworth's solemn intonations of oratory was like the sarcasm and wit of the fool in the intervals of Lear's passion ...'

The stamp man asked Wordsworth whether he thought Milton was a great genius. The others looked embarrassed and Lamb, who was dozing by the fire, woke and told Kingston he was 'a silly fellow' before dozing off again. The stamp man then asked: 'Don't you think Newton a great genius?' Again great embarrassment, and again Lamb woke.

He took up a candle and asked: 'Sir, will you allow me to look at your phrenological development?' He then turned his back on the poor man, and at every question of the comptroller he chanted:

Diddle diddle dumpling, my son John,
Went to bed with his breeches on.

At this point the stamp man revealed to Wordsworth, who had a connection to the Stamp Office, who he was. The poet, who knew nothing about him, was nonplussed, but before he could reply Lamb called out:

Hey diddle diddle
The cat and the fiddle.

Embarrassed, Wordsworth said to him: 'My dear Charles!' Lamb chanted, 'Diddle diddle dumpling, my son John.' Then 'Do let me have another look at that gentleman's organs.' Haydon and Keats hurried Lamb into another room, shut the door 'and gave way to inextinguishable laughter'. From time to time Lamb called out: 'Who is that fellow? Allow me to see his organs once more.'

We went back, but the comptroller was irreconcilable. We soothed and smiled, and asked him to supper. He stayed, though his dignity was sorely affected. However, being a good-natured man, we all parted in good humour, and no ill effects followed ... It was indeed an immortal evening.

Many of Lamb's letters record drunken episodes and apologise for drunken behaviour. To Thomas Manning (February or March 1801) he writes: 'Last Sunday ... as I was coming to town from the Professor's inspired with new rum, I tumbled down and broke my nose. I drink nothing stronger than malt liquors.' He once wrote: 'The drinking man is never less himself than during his sober intervals.'

On another occasion he writes to Manning apologising for his irreverence and folly at a party. 'You knew me well enough before, that a very little liquor will cause a considerable alteration in me.'

*

## Damn temperance

Lamb's beloved sister Mary had stabbed their mother to death in a fit of madness. She was released into Lamb's care, and he devoted his life to looking after her, grinding out 30 years in a clerical job he hated at India House. Although he fell in love he appears to have abandoned all hope of marrying, because of his devotion to Mary. He wrote to Dorothy Wordsworth of the tension that would build up between them when a new bout of her madness was coming on: 'irritable and wretched with fear ... I constantly hasten the disorder ... She lives but for me; and I have been wasting and teasing her life for five years incessantly with my cursed drinking and ways of going on.' He wrote to Dorothy in autumn 1810 after Mary had tried to persuade him to drink water: 'Must I then leave you, gin, rum, brandy, aqua-vitae, pleasant jolly fellows? Damn Temperance, and he that first invented it!'

Not everyone found his tipsy jocularity attractive. Carlyle called the 57-year-old Lamb 'a confirmed, shameless drunkard [who] asks vehemently for gin and water in strangers' houses, tipples till he is utterly mad, and is only not thrown out of doors because he is too much despised for taking such trouble with him. Poor Lamb! Poor England, that such a despicable abortion is named genius!'

Behind the façade there was a serious artist, and Lamb resented being patronised by the great men who were his friends. When Coleridge addressed his as 'my gentle-hearted Charles' three times in one poem he responded by writing to him: 'For God's sake (I never was more serious) don't make me ridiculous any more by terming me gentle-hearted in print, or do it in better verses. ... In the next edition of the Anthology ... please to blot out gentle-hearted and substitute drunken dog, ragged-head, seld-shaven, odd-eyed, stuttering, or any other epithet which truly and properly belongs to the gentleman in question.' On the other hand he was deadly accurate in his affectionate description of Coleridge as 'an archangel, a little damaged'.

Lamb told a story about Coleridge which captures his essence. One day on his way to his job in South Sea House he met the poet, 'brimful of some new idea, and in spite of my assuring him that time was precious, he drew me within the door of an unoccupied garden by the roadside, and there, sheltered from observation by a hedge of evergreens, he took me by the button of my coat, and closing his eyes commenced an eloquent discourse, waving his right hand gently, as the musical words flowed in an unbroken stream from his lips. I listened entranced; but the striking of a church-clock recalled me to a sense of duty. I saw it was of no use to attempt to break away, so taking advantage of his absorption in his subject, I, with my penknife, quietly severed the button from my coat, and decamped. Five hours afterwards, in passing the same garden on my way home, I heard Coleridge's voice, and on looking in, there he was, with closed eyes – the button in his fingers – and his right hand gracefully waving, just as when I left him. He had never missed me!' This caricature tells us more about the two men than the strictest truth.

Lamb died in 1834 after stumbling in Edmonton High Street and grazing his face. An acute skin infection set it, and he was dead a week later. There were suggestions that he was drunk. He had been deeply upset by the death of his friend Coleridge earlier in the same year, and he had been carried home drunk several times since.

Coleridge could probably have matched Lamb drink for drink. William Jerdan tells us in his *Autobiography* (4 vols, 1852–3) of a dinner party at which Coleridge and the versatile writer and wit Theodore Hook were among the guests. The wine glasses on the table were generally felt to be too small. The guests smashed them, all but one, which was reserved for 'a poetical fate'.

Tumblers were substituted, and might possibly contribute their share to the early hilarity and consecutive frolic of the night; for ere long Coleridge's sonorous voice was heard declaiming on the extraordinary ebullitions of Hook – 'I have before in the course of my time met with men of admirable promptitude of intellectual power and play of wit, which, as Stillingfleet tells,
*The rays of wit gild whereso'er they shine*
but I never before conceived such amazing readiness of mind, and resources of genius to be poured out on the mere subject and impulse of the moment.' Having got the poet into this exalted mood the last of the limited wine-glasses was mounted up on the bottom of a reversed tumbler, and, to the infinite risk of the latter, he was induced to shy at the former with a silver fork, till after two or three throws he succeeded in smashing it to fragments, to be tossed into the basket with its perished brethren

... The exhibition was remembered for years afterwards by all who partook of it; and I have a letter of Lockhart[2]'s alluding to the date of our witnessing the roseate face of Coleridge, lit up with animation, his large grey eye beaming, his white hair floating, and his whole frame, as it were, radiating with interest, as he poised the fork in his hand, and launched it at the fragile object (the last glass of dinner) distant some three or four feet from him on the table!

## Port at High Table

French (*Nineteen Centuries of Drink*) describes the drinking that went on at universities in the 18th century as *terrible*. He quotes Henry Gunning, a college official at Cambridge for more than 60 years, until his death in 1854. In his *Reminiscences of the University, Town and Country of Cambridge from the Year 1780* Gunning recalled: 'Drunkenness was the besetting sin of the period when I came to college. I need scarcely add that many other vices followed in its train.' Speaking of a college friend, he wrote: 'I do not remember ever to have seen him guilty of drunkenness, at that time almost universal.' He is sometimes more specific:

For many years during the Rev Charles Simeon's ministry (I speak from my own personal knowledge) Trinity Church and the streets leading to it were the scenes of the most disgraceful tumults. On one occasion an undergraduate who had been apprehended by Simeon was compelled to read a public apology in the church. Mr Simeon made a prefatory address: 'We have long borne during public worship with the most indecent conduct from those whose situation in life should have made them sensible of the heinousness of such offences; we have seen persons coming into this place in a state of intoxication; we have seen them walking about the aisles, notwithstanding there are persons appointed to show them into seats; we have seen them coming in and going out without the slightest reverence or decorum; we have seen them insulting modest persons, both in and after divine service; in short, the devotions of the congregation have been disturbed by almost every species of ill conduct.

\*

George Pryme, the first Professor of Political Economy at Cambridge, who was born in 1781, confirms this picture in his posthumous *Autobiographic Recollections* of 1870:

> When I first went to Cambridge [in 1799] the habit of hard drinking was almost as prevalent there as it was in country society ... 'Buzzing', unknown in the present day, was then universal. When the decanter came round to any one, if it was nearly emptied, the next in succession could require him to finish it; but if the quantity left exceeded the bumper [large glass], the challenger was required to drink the remainder, and also a bumper out of the next fresh bottle. There was throughout these parties an endeavour to make each other drunk, and a pride in being able to resist the effects of the wine.

Richard Porson, who was elected regius professor of Greek at Cambridge in 1792, was a remarkable man, not least in his appearance. A writer in *The Montly Magazine* was much struck by this, describing 'a large patch of coarse brown paper on his nose, the rusty black coat hung with cobwebs'. In 1807 a friend noted 'his fiery and volcanic face, and ... his nose, on which he had a perpetual efflorescence, and which was covered with black patches; his clothes were shabby, his linen dirty'.

His smoking, drinking, and rumoured propensity for settling arguments with a poker made him an alarming guest. He was said to have carried a young lady round the room in his teeth. John Timbs, author of *Club Life of London*, said that at Cambridge 'his passion for smoking, which was then going out

Richard Porson's formidable intellect and habit of settling arguments with a poker made him an alarming companion. His capacity for drink and non-stop talking were also daunting, but many found this Cambridge professor's wit irresistible.

among the younger generation, his large and indiscriminate potations, and his occasional use of the poker with a very refractory controversialist had caused his company to be shunned by all except the few to whom his wit and scholarship were irresistible'.

Porson had been a child prodigy with an extraordinary memory. Admirers paid for his education, sending him to Eton. In early manhood he was something of a ladies' man. He was also a noted scholar, of whom the *Dictionary of National Biography* says he advanced Greek scholarship. It adds that he 'gave way to intemperance' and indeed he would drink anything when the mood was on him, including embrocation. One night he dined with the artist John Hoppner, one of the friends who tried to keep Porson sober. There was no wine for dinner, because Mrs Hoppner had gone out taking with her the keys of the wine cellar. Porson insisted that Mrs Hoppner probably kept a bottle for her own use in her bedroom. Hoppner, knowing his wife's abstemiousness, humoured his guest by searching the bedroom, and to his amazement found a bottle. Porson emptied it and pronounced it to have been the best gin. When Mrs Hoppner returned her husband told how the guest had polished off her hidden cache. 'Drunk every drop of it!' she replied: 'Good God! It was spirits of wine for the lamp!'

Porson would sit talking all night, and eventually his hosts had to stipulate that he would stay no later than eleven in the evening. He did not always keep his promise. Horne Tooke once invited him to dinner, knowing that on the three preceding nights the professor had refused all requests by his hosts to go home to bed. Tooke reasoned that Professor Porson must be exhausted, and would be no trouble. He was wrong.

As the night wore on, the learned professor ranged over many topics. Dawn came, and still he talked. Tooke, worn out, told him he had arranged to meet a friend for breakfast in a coffee house in Leicester Square. Porson said he would come too. After they were seated in the coffee house something distracted the professor and Tooke seized the opportunity to flee back to his home, where he commanded the servants to barricade the door and not to let Porson in, for a man who could 'sit up four nights successively could sit up forty'.

Tooke got a sort of revenge. When Porson threatened to 'kick and cuff' him, and even mentioned the poker, Tooke insisted that if they must have a duel it should be in brandy-drinking. When they had had two quarts each the professor sank under the table. Tooke drank his health in another glass and joined the ladies.

## The devil, or Porson

Porson was a wit. Once he was walking with a friend discussing the Trinity when a buggy passed with three men in it. 'There is an illustration of the Trinity,' said his friend. 'No,' said Porson, 'you must show me one man in *three* buggies, if you can.' When someone who had been bested in argument said to him, 'Dr Porson, my opinion of you is most contemptible' the great scholar replied: 'Sir, I never knew an opinion of yours that was not contemptible.' He refused to argue with a scholar named Dodd, saying 'Jemmy Dodd, I have always despised you when sober, and I'll be damned if I argue with you now that I'm drunk.' He was merciless towards pretentiousness. While on a coach journey he heard a young passenger quote some Greek in an effort to impress the ladies. Leaning forward, he said: 'I think, young gentleman, you favoured us just now with a quotation from Sophocles; I do not happen to recollect it there.' The young man, who had no idea who he was dealing with, replied: 'The quotation is word for word as I have repeated it, and in Sophocles too; but I suspect, Sir, that it is some time since you were at college.' The professor produced a pocket edition of Sophocles and invited the young man to find the quotation. After turning the pages for some time he remembered that in fact it was from Euripides. Porson rummaged in his pockets and produced a pocket Euripides. The young man then recalled that the quotation was in Aeschylus. As the professor produced the works of the great playright from his pocket the young man cried out: 'Stop the coach. Let me out – there's a fellow here has got the Bodleian Library in his pocket. He must be the devil, or Porson himself.'

French says that Porson was 'a prominent figure in the Cider Cellars in Covent Garden. It was his nightly haunt.' He is presumably referring to Bob Derry's Cider Cellars, a dangerous haunt of criminals, prostitutes and broken-down actors, a sort of last-chance saloon. A contemporary visitor recorded 'a scene of confusion, drunkenness and stupidity … the many prostitutes … were like so many dressed-up carcasses in the shambles, drinking away to keep up their spirits'. How a noted professor of Greek became accepted there is a mystery. The Cellars feature in the gossip columns and crime reports of newspapers, and in about 1760 Commodore

Edward Thompson, a naval hero and scholar, mentioned them in his *Meretriciad*. This is a verse survey of the sex industry. He enlarged it over the years, and the edition of 1765 mentions the lovely harlot Lucy Cooper[3], who rose higher and sank faster than her sisters:

Lewder than all the whores in Charles's reign ...
At famed Bob Derry's where the harlots throng
My muse has listened to thy luscious song
And heard thee swear like worser Drury's punk,
The man who should have thee, who could make thee drunk,
Cit, soldier, sailor or some bearded Jew
In triumph reeling, bore thee to some stew.

Porson neglected his duties as Librarian to the London Institution. His successor, William Maltby, told the poet and banker Samuel Rogers: 'He was very irregular in his attendance there; he never troubled himself about the purchase of books which ought to have been added to the library; and he would frequently come home dead-drunk long after midnight. I have good reason to believe that, had he lived, he would have been requested to give up the office ... I once read a letter from the Directors of the Institution ... which contained, among other severe things, this cutting remark: "We only know that you are our Librarian by seeing your name attached to the receipts for your salary ..."'

George Fordyce (1736–1802) physician and chemistry lecturer, had something of the same capacity for food and drink as Porson, with an important difference. He was a great admirer of lions, and particularly their habit of eating once a day, and then as much as possible, which he tried to emulate. His favourite restaurant was Dolly's Chop House off Paternoster Row, where he went every day at four. While his pound and a half of rump steak was cooking he would whet his appetite with a large plate of fish or half a chicken. To drink he had a tankard of strong ale, a bottle of port and a quarter of a pint of brandy. On his way back to his house in Essex Street, where he gave his lectures, he would stop at the Chapter Coffee-House in Paternoster Row, the London Coffee-House and the Oxford, at each of which he had a glass of brandy and water.

One day, attending a woman patient with a mysterious illness, Fordyce found that he could not take her pulse. The beats seemed to swim in his head. 'Drunk, by the Lord,' he muttered, attributing the effect to his lunch. To his surprise the woman burst into tears. Next day she sent for him, and confessed that he was right – he had diagnosed her illness correctly.

## The funniest man in England

If the Georgian period was not so rich in bibulous characters Theodore Hook (1788–1841) would deserve a chapter to himself. His life was a fantastic mixture of fame and obscurity, success and failure, which included friendship with the Prince Regent and the high nobility, bankruptcy and prison. His novels rivalled Scott's in popularity, he had his first stage success with a comic opera when he was 16, he was the greatest talker of his times and one of the worst practical jokers of all time. He founded the Tory paper *John Bull* and made it a financial success. He was also a great drinker and the funniest man in England.

If this brief narrative is breathless it simply reflects the pace of his life. This defiant verse from his drama *The Fortress* of 1807 sums him up:

> Then now I'm resolved at all sorrows to blink –
> Since winking's the tippy I'll tip 'em the wink,
> I'll never get drunk when I cannot get drink,
> Never let misery bore me.
> I sneer at the Fates, and I laugh at their spite,
> I sit down contented to sit up all night,
> And when my time comes, from the world take my flight,
> For – my father did so before me.

At the height of his social *eclat* notices like the following appeared in the columns of *The Times* and other papers of record:

> Last night Lord Harrington entertained a small company to meet the Duke of Wellington. Those present included the Duke and Duchess of Bedford, Lord and Lady Southampton, Lord Londonderry, Lord Canterbury, Lord Lyndhurst, Lord Redesdale, Lord Charleville, Lord Strangford, Lord Chesterfield, Count d'Orsay, and Mr Theodore Hook.

*Mr* Theodore Hook – the lone commoner, the Man Without a Title, was there simply for his entertainment value. Parties would not go with a swing without him. Lofty aristocrats would be lured from their country retreats simply by the opportunity to hear him talk, and talk, and talk, and sing. After he died there was a slump at one of his clubs, the Athenaeum, where the number of dinners served fell by 300 in a year.

A.J.A. Symons wrote in *English Wits*: 'When the Earl of Jersey and the Marquess of Hertford received in their vast London houses ... at the special Sunday dinners of that Duke of Cumberland who became King of Hanover: there, prominent in gaeity, irrepressible in spirits, obese, improvident, amusing and amused, sat Mr Theodore Hook.'

He would entertain his fellow guests with a fountain of words, his 'bewilderingly ready tongue', with tales of his past hoaxes – his greatest were yet to come – and with 'fantastic musical improvisations'. He gave his all and it killed him.

Hook was a contemporary at Harrow of Byron and Sir Robert Peel. He was good-looking, could sing, draw and play the piano well. When he went up to Oxford he was already a successful dramatist.

Shortly after arriving he left Oxford and for a time devoted himself to practical jokes. One day, rowing on the Thames with the comedian Matthews, he was angered by a notice in a riverside garden at Barnes forbidding boats to dock. He and Matthews landed and, using their fishing line as a tape, paced up and down the lawn, apparently taking measurements. Confronted by the landowner, an alderman, Hook said he was carrying out a survey for a company which was planning to dig a new canal through the man's garden. It would, he calculated, pass beneath the alderman's window and through his greenhouse.

This hoax is recalled in his own *Gilbert Gurney*, and even now 'there is something fascinating' in the skill with which he recalls the growing consternation of the alderman and his attempts to placate the two stern officials.

Finally he invites them to dinner. Hook charms him, and over the last bottle, confesses all in impromptu verse:

For we greatly approve of your fare,
Your cellar's as prime as your cook;

My clerk here is Matthews the player,
And my name, sir, is — Theodore Hook!

His greatest jape, the Berners Street Hoax of 1809, entitles him to be called the greatest practical joker or the biggest pest in English history, according to taste. He sent out hundreds of letters (thousands in one version of the story) to tradesmen, ordering them to deliver their wares to a Berners Street address at a particular time and date. What ensued must have been one of the biggest traffic jams ever seen. Hook is said to have watched from a private house nearby as the street and the area became clogged with the carts of angry tradesmen. Among the throng were said to have been the Governor of the Bank of England, the chairman of the East India Company and the Duke of Gloucester, all enticed by letters telling them that they would learn something to their advantage if they arrived at the appointed time. Among the last to arrive was the Lord Mayor, who reversed his carriage and went straight to the police. But Hook remained undiscovered and free.

'Something must be done for Hook,' murmured the Prince Regent, and in 1812 at the age of 24 he was appointed Accountant-General and Treasurer of Mauritius, with an income of £2000 a year. He left his considerable debts behind and in 1813 took with gusto to life in a kind of paradise 'not without angels', a life of operas, racing, balls, and claret at ten pence a bottle. The governor was distantly related to him by marriage, and for five years 'the cares of office lay light as thisledown on summer air' on Hook. Then the governor was replaced by a General Hall, a clerk in Hook's office claimed he was guilty of fraud and a large deficit was discovered in the accounts. Hook was arrested, his property was seized and sold and he was despatched under guard to England. On arrival he was released, the Attorney-General having found no grounds for a criminal charge (his accuser, who may have been the embezzler, had cut his throat). There was a cloud on the horizon: the Board of Colonial Affairs began an investigation which lasted for years.

## Hook on the rack

In 1820 Hook, now penniless, helped found *John Bull*, which was soon a success. It took the side of George IV in his quarrel with his wife, Queen Caroline. The flagrant follies of the King made the task of his detractors easy. Hook countered this with an anonymous and unremitting investigation into the private lives of the Queen's supporters. Caroline, who was accused of adultery, was represented by her supporters as a wronged woman. Nevertheless the great Whig ladies were reluctant to visit her court, particularly when those who did so found their frailties exposed in *John Bull*. All efforts to unmask him, even the offer of a reward of £500, failed. Lady Jersey, once the King's mistress, said no one connected with the detested paper would be received by her: the following issue of the paper made it clear her most secret conversations were somehow known to *John Bull*. The printer and publisher were jailed, but they refused to name Hook. All this time he continued to be the darling of society. The circulation soared.

Eventually the secret got out, and political retribution was swift. The angry Whigs remembered Mauritius, the Audit Board at last concluded its investigation against Hook and he was fined the impossible sum of £13,000, his goods were seized for the second time and he was held in a debtors' prison. He was there for two years before being released, at the age of 36, broke but unbowed. He began to write novels, and was soon earning £2000 a year again. He took a fine house in Cleveland Row, living an extravagant bachelor lifestyle. In fact he had a mistress, four daughters and a son about whom he was reticent. When the consequences of his high spending became obvious he left his fine house in central London and went to live at Fulham. In his diary he wondered 'when I look back, that I should have been so foolish as to waste the prime of life in foolish idleness'. He had one last chance: when his old schoolfellow Peel formed his first government in 1834 he offered Hook the post of Inspector of Plays if the incumbent, George Colman, could be persuaded to relinquish it. But Colman was a friend, and Hook did not even ask him.

As he grew older and fatter and his hair fell out, Hook drank more and more. He spent the whole of one afternoon drinking gin and Maraschino cocktails by the pint, before dining, apparently sober, at Lord Canterbury's. He explained that his appetite was poor because of 'a biscuit and a glass of sherry rashly taken at luncheon'. At his club he queried a bill for ten brandies, saying he had drunk only nine. The waiter reminded him of the one he had swallowed before he even sat down.

He kept up this pace for ten years before his liver gave out. A friend called and caught him undressed. Hook observed: 'Well, you see me as I am at last – all the bucklings and paddings and washings and brushings dropped for ever – a poor old grey-haired man, with my belly about my knees.' Catching sight of himself in a mirror at another friend's house he remarked: 'Ay, I see I look as I am; done up in purse, in mind, and in body too at last.' A week later he was dead, in August 1841. He was not quite 53.

The Treasury, whose spite in the Mauritius affair was not spent, seized and sold his goods. His children would have been left penniless, as he feared but for a fund raised by old friends. It was said that the only one of his grand acquaintances to contribute was the King of Hanover.

# The Haunts of Pleasure

Many contemporaries of Sheridan and Porson woke daily with sore heads. One reason was the ubiquity of temptation. Apart from pubs, clubs, taverns and brothels London abounded in tea-gardens and pleasure gardens, of which Vauxhall and Ranelagh, and later Cremorne, were the most famous. Some were noted for the licentiousness of their clients. The Dog and Duck, a tavern in St George's Fields south of the river, was a sort of safe house for crooks. It continued in business from 1642 to 1812. Here aspiring young criminals would go to watch the highwaymen mount up and say goodbye to their 'flashy women' before setting off to earn their living on the highways. Henriques (*Prostitution and Society*) says that it was a favourite resort of whores and their ponces. Another author wrote that 'some of the most beautiful middle-class women of the town, their bullies and suchlike young men, who came there, with no thoughts for the consequences, refresh the thirsty throats of their girls with fiery drinks' (J.P. Malcolm, *Anecdotes*). David Garrick in his *Prologue to the Maid of the Oaks* described the riotous goings-on:

> St George's Fields, with taste and fashion struck,
> Display Arcadia at the Dog and Duck;
> And Drury Misses here in tawdry pride,
> Are there 'Pastoras' by the fountain side;
> To frowsy bowers they reel through midnight damps,
> With fauns half drunk and Dryads breaking lamps.

Vauxhall, one of the most popular of all the pleasure gardens, had its origins in the 17th century. Pepys, who is frank about his own

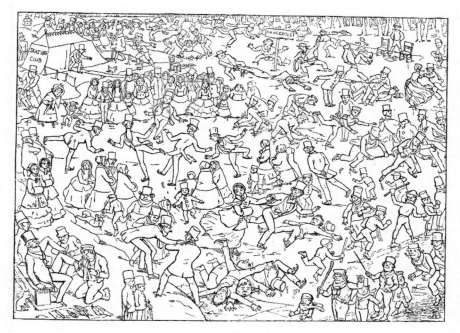

Vauxhall Gardens, where Pepys heard the screams of women 'almost forced' by young gallants. He was a frequent and admiring visitor, and Boswell wrote of the 'good eating and drinking for those who wish to purchase that regale'.

weaknesses, was shocked by the behaviour of the visitors. His diary entry for 27 July 1688 reads: 'Over the water with my wife and Deb and Mercer … and eat there and walked; and observed how coarse some young gallants from the town were. They go into the arbours where is no man and ravish the woman there, and the audacity of vice in our time much enraged me.'

Pepys spent another lively evening there with a group of dissipated young aristocrats known as the Ballers in May 1668. He met Harry Killegrew, 'a rogue, newly come back out of France but still in disgrace with our Court', and other members of the group. He stayed with them to supper in one of the arbours. Pepys called the group 'as very rogues as any in the town, who were ready to take hold of every woman that came by them'. He said their bawdy talk made his head ache. They described a typical night at the brothel of 'my Lady Bennet' and how they had danced naked with her girls, and 'all the roguish things in the world'. However, he justified his presence, just as he justified reading pornography, as something a man should do once. 'But Lord, what loose cursed company was I in tonight; though full of wit and worth a man's being in for once, to know the nature of it and their manner of talk and lives.' Things had certainly not improved in the next century.

Vauxhall's many shady and secluded arbours were ideal for prostitution. 'Those who purposely lost their way in the bushes did not bother to be discreet and made a tremendous uproar, no doubt added to by the screams of respectable women being raped' (Henriques, *Prostitution*). An even greater scandal was the food, the meagreness of the portions being legendary. Dickens wrote in *Sketches by Boz*: 'It was rumoured ... that Vauxhall Gardens by day was the scene of secret and hidden experiments, that there carvers were exercised in the mystic art of cutting a moderate-sized ham into slices thin enough to pave the whole of the grounds ...' Vauxhall, where the entrance charge was 1s, was seen as more democratic than Ranelagh, which cost 2s 6d and was more exclusive and also more raffish. Vauxhall was similar to Cremorne Gardens, which opened on a riverside site in Chelsea in 1830. They were typical pleasure gardens used by families for picnics, fireworks, concerts and so on. At night the atmosphere changed. The *Saturday Review* commented that 'none but an idiot' could fail to notice that at dusk the women there were augmented by 'a large accession of fallen [women] characters'.

Cremorne fell victim to Victorian values: it lost its licence in 1871, and closed six years later. In fairness to whores it should be said that they were many and places of entertainment into which they would be allowed, apart from pubs and taverns, were few. It was inevitable that they would be drawn to places where men went for amusement. Few men at the time knew more about such places than the 18th-century man-about-town William Hickey.

# Hickey Among the Ladies

William Hickey gave his name to a famous 20th-century newspaper gossip column. This was a tribute to his memoirs, which give a vivid and gossipy picture of, among other things, a young man exploring London's seamier side in the second half of the 18th century. Hickey was frankly carnal and fun-loving, quite unable to resist the company of pretty girls or the sound of a pulled cork. His memoirs catch the racy side of London in the age of George III, when vice was probably more self-confident and flagrant than before or since. He knew the gambling hells and bordellos, and among his many affairs was one with a well-known harlot. He was among the men who raised £50 to save the celebrity harlot Lucy Cooper from starving in prison.

The city teemed with whores. One good authority reckoned there were 50,000 in 1800: recently a survey estimated the number in today's vastly bigger London at about 5000 (Prof Matthews). Hickey knew several of the girls. At the Rose Tavern he would have seen the Posture Molls and the Great Impures of the day such as Fanny Murray, and the actors from the nearby theatre, including Mrs Siddons and David Garrick.

Hickey first saw Emily Warren at Charlotte Hayes's brothel in 1776, when the bawd was grooming the young girl for her future career as a harlot by teaching her deportment and manners. At the time she was 'an unripe and awkward girl, but with features of exquisite beauty'. Hayes had spotted her as an 11-year-old, leading her blind father through the streets, begging. She bought the girl from her father. In spite of Hayes's efforts

William Hickey with his black servant. Hickey's frank memoirs of life in late eighteenth century London highlight its seamier side. He visited the brothels and knew many of the bawds and their girls.

Emily never learned to read. Hickey guessed the truth when he noticed that she left the room whenever a letter was delivered to her. Otherwise the transformation was total and the beggar child became one of the ornaments of Hayes's bordello.

Emily was the mistress of Hickey's friend Bob Pott, who left her in Hickey's care while he set out for India. As soon as she heard Pott had sailed the girl sent for Hickey. She waited for him in her splendid coach, and the sight of her stunned him. 'But what was all this outside show to the lovely creature within, looking more than mortal. Never did I behold so perfect a beauty.' Sir Joshua Reynolds painted Emily several times, and is said to have declared that he never saw 'so faultless and finely formed a human figure'.

Over the next few months Hickey spent a lot of time with Emily, and he manages to convey the febrile impetuosity of her life as she rushed about wanting to be seen, wanting to be loved, in a narcissistic whirl of pointless activity – she wanted to be what we would now call a celebrity. 'Stepping into the carriage, she almost devoured me with kisses, laughed, cried, and was nearly in hysterics, to the surprise and entertainment of several persons who were passing at the time.' At the theatre: 'Her manner towards me drew the attention of the whole house upon us, which made me entreat her to be less ardent. At my gravity she laughed heartily, adding that she was too happy to be considerate, and could not help betraying her regards to her *bashful swain*.' Thus encouraged, he rushed her off to bed. 'I passed a night that many would have given thousands to do.' But Hickey found that at heart she was empty. 'Although to look upon Emily was to look upon perfection as far as figure and features went, yet my continued intimate acquaintance with her convinced me that she was totally void of feeling, and was indeed as cold as ice.'

Many of Hickey's adventures involved heavy drinking. One night in March 1768 he and a group of what he called wild young men, all 'brimfull of wine', were out on the town. They visited Elizabeth Weatherby's coffee shop, the notorious Ben Jonson's Head in Russell Street off Covent Garden, a haunt of 'rakes, gamesters, swindlers, highwaymen, pickpockets and whores'. Hickey describes Weatherby's as 'an absolute hell upon earth' but it was not the worst

Emily Warren, a beauty groomed for whoredom by the bawd Charlotte Hayes. Reynolds, who painted her several times, was an admirer, but William Hickey, who slept with her, said she was an empty narcissist.

of the brothels and low drinking dens that abounded in the Covent Garden and Drury Lane area.

They rang at the iron-bound door and 'a cut-throat looking rascal' let them in. The scene inside so terrified the young Hickey that he immediately tried to get out again. Men and women were standing on chairs, benches and tables to get a better view of two drunken whores who were fighting on the floor. Their faces were covered in blood, and they had torn each other's clothes off.

In another corner a young man was fighting off three whores and a group of men who were belabouring him with sticks. From time to time he would knock down one of the men or women, but with new men joining in all the time it looked as if he was certain to get a heavy beating until Hickey's friends intervened and after 'a few knock-me-down arguments' restored peace.[1]

William Hickey was born in 1749, the same year as Charles James Fox. It was also the year in which Cleland's bawdy novel *Fanny Hill* was published, and an anonymous pamphlet, *Satan's Harvest Home: or the Present State of Whorecraft, Adultery, Fornication, Pimping, Sodomy etc.* gave a horrifying picture of the lives of wretched street prostitutes:

> What a deplorable Sight it is, to behold Numbers of little Creatures pil'd up in Heaps upon one another, sleeping in the publick Streets, in the most rigorous Seasons, and some of them whose Heads will hardly reach above the Waistband of a Man's Breeches, found to be quick with Child, and become burthensome to the Parish, whose hospitable Bulks [shop stalls] and Dunghills have given them Refuge.

## A wanton little baggage

Such sights were unknown in St Albans Street, Pall Mall, Westminster, where Hickey was born. It was a wealthy and fashionable area which was also the very heart of the elite red-light district, and residents would have been more likely to see successful bawds leading their flocks of well-dressed young whores to take wholesome air in St James's Park on foot or in well-appointed carriages.

William soon had his first experience of 'lovely seducing women'. A pretty young woman named Nanny Harris entered the household as a companion to his mother and to help look after William's younger twin sisters. Nanny, or Nancy, had been strongly recommended by the Duchess of Manchester, who failed to mention that she had discarded the young woman for 'debauching' her own 13-year-old son. Every night Nanny took William into her bed and fondled him: 'nor shall I ever forget my sensations, infant as I was, at awakening one morning and finding myself snugly stowed between her legs, and with one of my hands upon the seat of Love, where no doubt she had placed it, for she was as wanton a little baggage as ever existed.' After a year she was dismissed 'with ignominy', her amours being too numerous and obvious, and took up with a young gentleman of fortune.

William's older brother Henry was mixing with a set of idle and dissipated young men, who lived by gambling, and they invited William to join their frolics. 'Many a bumper of champagne and claret have I drank in the society of this set, at taverns and brothels, accompanied by the most lovely women of the metropolis, and this before I had completed my fourteenth year.' He points out, however, that he never joined in their gambling. 'Would it were in my power to say the same of many other vices, especially those of women and wine; but truth will not admit of it; in those two excesses I have too freely indulged.'

Henry continued to go to the bad until in 1770 he got into a drunken scrape outside Mrs Olivia Harrington's bagnio, the Turk's Head at Charing Cross. The men were 'brimfull' of burgundy, for a change, and a man was killed, run through with a sword. The killer was probably Henry's notorious friend Dick England, but Henry had to go on the run. He went to France and spent three years with a 'respectable Abbé' at Caen. The dead man's widow was bought off, agreeing not to bring any prosecutions, and the friends who had fled abroad returned, including Henry. Hickey's father Joseph, a successful lawyer, bought him a cadetship in the East India Company's army at Madras, but within six months he was dead of a fever. 'Though in the prime of life with respect to years, he was, owing to the excesses already alluded to, very old in constitution, his whole system being so shaken and enervated that he could not stand the sudden and violent change of climate.'

Some months later Hickey wandered through Covent Garden on his way back towards Westminster School, where he was a boarder. Under the Piazza a pretty young girl, not much older than himself, took him by the arm and said: 'You are a fine handsome boy and too young to be walking in such a place as this alone, and I'll take your maidenhead'.

The area around Covent Garden and Drury Lane was infested with street prostitutes, many of whom had their lodgings in nearby courts and alleys, and it was one of these who accosted William. She took him to her apartment in a filthy tenement in a narrow Drury Lane court, and there, in a 'dirty, miserable bed', he enjoyed what he called his first 'exhibition under a roof'– his only previous encounter with a prostitute having been on the grass in St James's Park. 'My companion gave me great credit for my vigour, saying I was a famous little fellow, and should prove an invaluable acquisition to whatever girl was lucky enough to fix me. In this den of wretchedness I passed three truly happy hours.' He offered her half a guinea, a large amount for a street prostitute. She asked him if he had any more, and he at first thought she meant it was not enough. When it became clear that she was reluctant to take his last shilling – she said that if it was all he had she would not take it – he was touched, and became a devoted if infrequent customer. They sometimes met accidentally in the streets, and she always addressed him as 'her dear little maidenhead'.

The delights of female company and what he called 'public places of entertainment' grew on him and made him less inclined than ever to study. His father discovered this by questioning him about the authors he should have been reading. Old Joseph tried persuasion and threats, and when these failed, stopped William's weekly allowance. This didn't work either, and the headmaster of Westminster School asked Joseph to take William away. Accordingly, at the end of 1763 William left the school, 'most deservedly in high disgrace'.

He was sent to another school to prepare for training as a lawyer, but caught smallpox. His good looks, of which he had been only too aware, were lost. He had, he said, become 'quite as plain as my neighbours'. After further sexual adventures his father took him away from the school and apprenticed him to a dissipated attorney. For some months his behaviour was above reproach, impressing among others, he says, the Attorney General, the Solicitor-General, and other prominent lawyers including Lord Thurlow (1731–1806) the abrasive, scheming politician who was later to hold both these posts. But William was stealing large sums from his father's firm to fund his drinking and whoring. He and his raffish friends were customers at three 'notorious bawdy houses' in Bow Street, 'which we took in rotation'. One of these was run by an old Irishwoman named Hamilton, 'with whom I was on remarkable good terms, of which she gave me most convincing proof in many times offering me money, saying "My dear boy, I always have plenty of loose cash about me, and it will do my heart good to furnish your pocket when in want of lining."'

Mrs Hamilton used to contact William when she had 'any particularly smart or handsome new piece'. He says that however low and infamous the brothels were, he sometimes met very beautiful women there. He and his friends would spend three or four hours with the girls, drinking and 'playing all sorts of tricks'. Then they would go off separately with the girl of their choice, either to the girls' lodgings or their own. He still saw Nanny Harris, but preferred 'some fresher and therefore more attractive female'.

That summer of 1767 William and his friends founded a sport club at an inn called the Red House in Battersea Fields, almost opposite Ranelagh. They played field tennis, a game of their own devising, 'which afforded noble exercise'. An added attraction for William was the landlord's pretty daughter Sally. She married shortly after William first met her, but her husband was frequently away, so the affair was untroubled. The group went there two days a week at one in the afternoon, and at two sat down to a substantial 'dinner', which William describes in detail. ' ... capital stewed grigs [small eels], a dish Mrs Burt [Sally's mother] was famous for dressing, a large joint of roast or boiled meat, with proper vegetables and a good-sized pudding or pie; our drink consisted of malt liquors, cider, port wine and punch.'

## Hickey is abominably drunk

That year they held the annual dinner of the club at the Red House in December, and William, who had rowed himself there, got 'abominably drunk'. The others, including Sally, tried to reason with him but he insisted on rowing himself back home. He beached the boat at Millbank and set out to walk home to St Albans Street, Pall Mall. He didn't get far. The paving in the streets around Westminster was being renewed, 'and I in consequence encountered various holes, and various heaps of stone and rubbish, into and over which I tumbled and scrambled'. Just after seven the next morning a party of card-players who had been up all night found him lying in the gutter, 'poor pilgarlic in woeful plight'. They recognised him and took him home.

It must have been a truly heroic bender. When he woke the next day he could not move hand or foot, 'being most miserably bruised, cut and maimed in every part of my body'. He got a fever, and doctors feared he had suffered a serious internal injury. He slowly pulled round, but it was three weeks before he was fit to leave his room.

After this escapade he stayed away from his old haunts for more than two months, and was beginning to believe he could congratulate himself upon 'a complete reformation'. He felt he could join his old chums at Slaughters without falling back into his bad habits, and so one evening in March 1786, he dropped into the club. The wine and punch were flowing, and soon all his good intentions were in shreds. 'I yielded, and drank as deep as the rest.' His friends promised to introduce him to 'two new houses of infinite merit', and they tumbled out into the night, once more 'brimfull' of wine and heading for Weatherby's. What followed was the incident described above.

The night was not yet over. His friends literally dragged him to another low drinking den, Murphy's, run by Mother Jane Murphy just across Little Russell Street from Weatherby's. This low dive was later known as Marjoram's. 'Although there were no actual personal hostilities going on when we entered, the war of words raged to the utmost extent; and such outré phrases never before encountered my ears, though certainly until that night I had considered myself a tolerant proficient in blackguardism.' Murphy's was a place where London's low life went for a drink when Weatherby's closed about three in the morning. Surrounded by thieves and 'the lowest description of prostitute' William and his friends went on drinking until nearly five in the morning.

At about this time he met a fine courtesan named Fanny Hartford, and began an affair. She was kept by a wealthy gentleman, who installed her in a house in Queen Anne Street and also gave her a 'country' place at Hammersmith. He paid for a carriage and a suitable retinue of servants. William observed that many kept women liked to cheat on their lovers, who were usually much older men. She told William that her lover was well known to the Hickey family, but refused to tell him the man's name.

William found out by accident. One night he and Nancy were about to get into bed at the Queen Ann Street house when they heard the maid cry out and a disturbance on the stairs. Nancy's lover had returned unexpectedly and found a door left unlocked by a servant. William jumped into a closet, the man came into the room and William recognised his voice as that of a family friend who was happily married with eight children. He and his wife 'were by the world considered as a rare instance of conjugal felicity in high life. He was then considerably above sixty years old.'

Fanny had the presence of mind to call the maid and tell her to put clean sheets on the bed, meanwhile leading her old lover into the dining room. The servant gathered up William's clothes and took them downstairs to the parlour, where William dressed before slipping into the night. From then on the young couple made sure all the doors were locked and bolted before they began their love-making.

About this time Nanny Harris died, 'a martyr to a life of excess and to venereal taints'. Her death genuinely saddened and shocked William, who reflected on his own dissolute life and the risks he ran by consorting with whores. Although he had the choice of the finest women of the town – he lists Fanny Hartford, Lord Melbourne's mistress Madame La Tour, 'Mrs Sturgess, Miss Larkin etc. etc.', on whom he says he need never have spent a shilling, he often preferred going to a bagnio with 'the most hackneyed and common woman'. He mentions Sally Brent, who wasn't even pretty but nevertheless fascinated William. His description makes her seem almost repulsive: 'much pitted with the smallpox, mercenary in the highest degree, and addicted to drinking'.

About this time his father discovered his embezzlement. Old Joe was distraught, and it took all William's powers of persuasion to make him believe that this time he really would mend his ways. So persuasive was the young man that Joe, who was taking the rest of the family off to Paris, left him in charge of the Twickenham and St Albans Street houses, gave him the use of his horses and the key to the cellar. Joe's fatal generosity extended to giving his son a draft on his bankers', Drummonds, for £75.

Some days later William went to Drummonds and cashed the draft. He was paid in Portuguese 'half Joes', a coin worth 36 pieces, one of several foreign coinages then current in England. He visited Fanny Hartford, who reminded him of his 'sacred' promises to his father and mother, and then set out for a cricket match, in which he was due to play. In the Mall he met two young men to whom he was 'very partial', brothers from the West Indies named Williams, 'according to fame living at a rate greatly beyond their means'. They invited him to a party at the Shakespeare's Head Tavern in Covent Garden. The brothers had little difficulty in persuading him to join them, particularly when they pointed out that two choice whores, Vincent and Newton, would be there. William hoped he would be able to go to the party, stay sober and play cricket. 'Alas! – I never could depend on myself when once embarked in convivial society. The consequences of that, to me fatal, night gave an extraordinary turn to the whole tenor of my future life.'

At the Shakespeare's Head the party consisted, besides young Hickey and the Williams brothers, of a man named Jennings who kept racehorses and lived in 'a most dashing style' but whose source of income was a mystery, a Captain Taylor, who commanded an East Indiaman ship, a banker's son named Lowry, a 'remarkably handsome youth' named Clapereau who was a friend of the Prince of Wales, Misses

Vincent and Newton and two other 'equally jovial damsels'. The party were all what William called 'hard goers', by which he meant they could hold their drink.

## How drunk you was, Sir!

The invitation was a trap. Jennings and the Williams brothers picked his pocket, and he woke in a brothel the next morning.

Eventually a yawning servant appeared, and exclaimed: 'Good God, how drunk and riotous you was, Sir! I never saw anything to equal it.' He told Hickey that he was in the Cross Keys brothel in Little Russell Street, Drury Lane. The Watchmen had taken him there at five o'clock in the morning, after he had been thrown out of Weatherby's. They had to summon reinforcements and at first wanted to hold him in the Covent Garden Watch House until a magistrate was available to hear a charge against him. However, some of the Watch, and a waiter on his way home from Weatherby's, recognised William as a generous man who had given them many a shilling, and so he was taken to the brothel instead.

The Watch had saved William's gold watch, and the servant found seven half-Joes and a letter of credit in his overcoat. 'This was like a reprieve to a man under sentence of death.' William rewarded the servant and the Watch, who were waiting outside, jumped into a hackney coach and, vomiting out of the window the whole journey, made his way home to St Albans Street. There he changed his clothes and drank coffee, then set out for the cricket match at Moulsey, where he was to keep wicket. He rode 12 miles in three quarters of an hour, and arrived as the two teams were about to take the field. In spite of a crushing hangover he kept wicket just well enough to see his team win.

This escapade was the last straw for old Joe. He used his influence with his friends at the East India Company to get his son a job there. Some days later he was formally appointed, and given a cheque for 20 guineas. This was the sum the company gave all young men starting out on their careers, as some of them did not have wealthy relatives to equip them for the voyage. Since he had already been kitted out at his father's expense, William decided to spend the money entertaining some poor whores at the Shakespeare's Head.

He asked Sally Brent if she was acquainted with any. 'Oh, that I am, with many who, I am afraid, fast from not having the means of purchasing food.' She undertook to invite about half a dozen of these wretches to dinner, which she would order.

When William arrived at the Shakespeare's Head at four o'clock the following afternoon he found the room crowded with his friends and with indigent whores, some of whom he knew, including Pris Vincent. William managed to remain tolerably sober, and as the evening wore on he realised that the meal would cost far more than the 20 guineas he had been given by the East India Company. He slipped out of the room to tell Tomkyns that he had not got enough to pay the bill, and was reassured that the men in the party had already taken care of it. William told the others that he would donate his 20 guineas to 'the relief of some unfortunate female', and asked Tomkyns if he knew any such. Tomkyns replied that he had 'that very day' received a letter from Lucy Cooper, who was in the King's Bench prison for debt, 'without a penny in her pocket to purchase food, raiment or coal to warm herself'.

William and his friends, as we have seen, sent her £50.

Hickey duly went to India and returned to England in 1808 a moderately wealthy man. He lived quietly in the country and wrote his memoirs, recalling a way of life the growing middle class already disapproved of strongly.

# The Ruin of the Working Class

On William IV's Coronation Day in 1830 a visitor to Manchester witnessed a public orgy of beer drinking:

> We saw whole pitchers thrown indiscriminately among the crowd — men holding up their hats to receive drink; people quarrelling and fighting for the possession of a jug; the strong taking the liquor from the weak; boys and girls, men and women, in a condition of beastly drunkenness, staggering before the depository of ale, or lying prostrate on the ground ... in every degree of exposure, swearing ... vomiting, but calling for more liquor ... when they could not stand, or even sit, to drink it.

Workers understandably took any opportunity to get drunk. Their hours of toil were long and apart from sex there was almost no other entertainment. Henry Gunning was a tutor in Herefordshire, and remarked the immense quantities of cider drunk by agricultural labourers.

> In years when apples were abundant, the labourers in husbandry were allowed to drink as much cider as they thought proper. It was no unusual thing for a man to put his lips to a wooden bottle containing four quarts, and not remove them until he had emptied it.

I have witnessed this exploit; but I have never ventured to mention a circumstance apparently so incredible, until I read *Marshall's History of Herefordshire*, in which he relates the same facts.

Charles Knight in his *Passage of a Working Life* wrote of the habits of tradesmen early in the 19th century:

Sallying forth to spend their long evenings in their accustomed chairs at the alehouse, which had become their second home. Some had a notion that they secured custom to the shop by a constant round among the numerous hostelries. I knew a most worthy man, occupying a large house which his forefathers had occupied from the time of Queen Anne, who when he gave up the business to his son who, recently married, preferred his own fireside, told the innovator that he would infallibly be ruined if he did not go out to make friends over his evening glass.

Elections were excuses for outbreaks of communal drunkenness. At Horsham, Sussex, in 1844 ...

Every public house and beer-shop in the parish was secured by one side or the other as an electioneering stronghold. At every one of them Pink or Blue flags were flying, the meaning of which could not be misunderstood ... if a voter wanted a drink he could go into any public house and obtain any kind of refreshment without ... being asked for payment ... The labourer whose taste was usually satisfied with small [weak] beer was now in a position to discover and indulge a palate capable of appreciating more aristocratic beverage; and ... no niggardly rule was made as to kind or number of friends a voter might introduce ... it is not too much to say that most of the male population of Horsham were frequently drunk, many were continually drunk and some were continuously drunk for the whole six weeks preceding Election Day.

## Your round
One reason the working classes were more or less addicted to drink was the trades customs which forced workers to buy drinks for their

colleagues. In 1839 John Dunlop, a magistrate, published an exhaustive study of these customs, *The Philosophy of Artificial and Compulsory Drinking Usages in Great Britain and Ireland*. The customs affected many trades. 'A coach builder who ignored hints that "the leather was dry" from the coachman who called to collect a new carriage would soon hear from its new owner that it was badly scratched on arrival' (Longmate, *The Water Drinkers*). Workers were expected to stand drinks for their mates when they had a child. Dunlop reported that in many areas, 'when a wedding takes place in any trade a number of the lower orders surround the house with old pots, kettles, horns etc. and keep up a continual noise until they receive "socket money" or are dispersed by the police'. The 'footing' or money paid to colleagues on admission to a skilled trade ranged from ten shillings in the cotton trade to £7 among calico-printers.

A maid who failed to bring a bottle of whisky for her colleagues when she started a new job was forced out. Her colleagues 'refused to help her in the washing for the family, told unfounded stories to their mistress', and made life so difficult for her that she quit the job after a fortnight. A coal-porter who failed to pay his mates ten shillings drinking money when he first used a cart would find the wheels missing. Printers took revenge by filling with ink the sleeves of apprentices who wouldn't or couldn't pay up. A man might find a pawn-ticket in place of his missing coat, while his mates drank the proceeds. This bullying could be violent – an apprentice shipwright who failed to pay was flogged with a handsaw. A trainee cabinet-maker would be seized from behind, a heavy cloth thrown over him and 'his hands are then tied and he is laid on his face along a bench, his shoes are taken off and he is sharply beat on the soles of his feet with a flat board … he remains after this the object of unrelenting abuse and spite … and is finally sent to Coventry [ostracised]'. Dunlop wondered 'that there are any sober men in the mechanical class at all, when such perpetual drinking domineers over them'.

Things were already changing when Dunlop neared the end of his ten-year investigation. When he began he was sometimes threatened with violence. Later he found a general willingness to talk and to provide information. But, he asked, who could stay unmoved at the still familiar sight of housewives 'on cold wet nights … searching up and down desolate streets for their husbands, sometimes accompanied by several crying, half-sleeping children?' The scene was set for the great Victorian backlash against drinking, the Temperance Movement.

# Victorian Backlash

The Puritan reaction to the loosening of moral stays introduced by the Restoration began in 1698 when William III issued a *Proclamation for Preventing and Punishing Immorality and Profaneness*. He feared 'the open and avowed practice of vice' might 'provoke God to withdraw his mercy and blessings from us, and instead thereof to inflict heavy and severe judgements'. Thousands of secret informers were recruited to spy on their fellow citizens. They were incited to seek out all those who 'impudently dare, in rebellion against the laws of God and man, to swear and curse, to profane the Lord's Day, or be guilty of the loathsome sin of drunkenness …'

In the 19th century successful temperance campaigns in the United States gave a spur to the movement in England. Beginning in the north, where it took root, it gradually spread. It was essentially a working-class movement, strongly supported by nonconformists, particularly the Methodists. There was a strong link to the Liberal Party, whose leader, Lloyd George, was responsible for introducing severe restrictions on drinking hours which outlasted the First World War.

By the time the campaign for reform picked up speed in the 19th century it was up against an immensely powerful brewing industry which was already tightening its grip by means of 'tied houses'. The brewers were taking advantage of calls by justices for improvements in premises before they would grant a licence. Most alehouse keepers could not afford these improvements, and so were driven to borrowing the money from the brewers. In return they had to agree to buy all their drink from the supplier. In some cases the owners sold out to the brewers and stayed on as tenants. Although it was widely agreed that this was against the public interest the brewers were for the moment too powerful to restrain.

Longmate says that by 1816 14,200 alehouses belonged to the brewers, and only 10,800 to the occupiers. There were a further 22,700 which were owned by outsiders. The spread of the tied house was criticised by a House of Commons committee and the Committee on Public Breweries, largely because the publicans were being forced to sell poor beer, but the takeovers continued.

In 1830 Wellington's Tory government decided to amend the licensing laws. There was evidence that the laws were being administered in a capricious way by the justices, who would leave villages without an alehouse because they feared it might become a haunt of poachers, radicals or trade unionists. The Whigs favoured free trade in beer, so backed a measure which would challenge the tied-house system. The brewers were divided, some fearing a decline in the value of tied houses, others seeing new outlets for their products. A few reactionaries warned of the consequences. The measure would 'convert the whole country into a mere grog shop'. The government went ahead, giving everyone who paid a two-guinea excise duty the right to sell beer, without a justices' licence.

The measure came into force on Sunday, 10 October 1830. The immediate result was a Beer Mania. The wit Sydney Smith, formerly a supporter of free trade in ale, wrote: 'The new Beer Bill has begun its operations. Everybody is drunk. Those who are not singing are sprawling. The sovereign people are in a beastly state.'

Queues of people anxious to open two-guinea beer-shops formed outside excise offices. Some of the new beer-shop proprietors were men of bad character who had previously been refused a licence for a public house. In some cases parishes had advanced the two guineas out of poor rates to unemployed labourers. A magistrate complained that some were petty tradesmen 'who would rather get their bread by any other way than hard labour'. Some of the new landlords were thieves who wanted to set up dens for receiving and disposing of stolen goods.

Fifty new beer-shops opened every day in Liverpool, and by the end of the month the city had 800. There were 24,000 beer-shops in England and Wales by the end of 1830: six years later there were 46,000. Even the thinly populated county of Norfolk had 350, while Hanley in Staffordshire, which had 16,000 citizens and already had a good number of public houses, soon had 110 beer-shops. Ingatstone in Essex, which had only 700 inhabitants, got ten. Longmate cites a Lancashire town where six houses in a row of fourteen all sold beer. 'Of fifty houses in an Essex hamlet five were beer shops.'

The brewers sent out salesmen into the remotest areas, where men had never tasted beer, and persuaded householders to open beer-shops in their homes, advancing them the two-guinea excise fee and beer on credit. The butcher, the baker, the candlestick maker, coopers, blacksmiths, carpenters, tailors and grocers set aside rooms to serve beer. In the Commons it was claimed with some justice that the labourer returning home from work 'now has to run the gauntlet through three or four beer-shops, in each of which are fellow labourers carousing, who urge him to stay and drink with them'.

## Palaces of drink

There was the usual moral panic among the middle classes, but the government for the moment refused to rescind the Sale of Beer Act. In June 1831 Lord Althorp said they were not prepared to abandon 'the principle of the measure'. However, the timing of the Act had been unlucky, in that it coincided with a period of serious social unrest. There were riots, with half-starved mobs besieging the homes of the gentry to demand better pay. A wave of rick-burning, cattle maiming and the destruction of machinery led to deaths and official repression which culminated in the trials of the Tolpuddle Martyrs in 1834. The new beer-houses were often the only public rooms in villages, and so the labourers tended to meet there to discuss their grievances. A magistrate complained that the labourers imbibed radical opinions with their beer.

One group which did not suffer were the brewers, despite their earlier fears. The beer-houses gave them a vast new market. And they invented the gin-palace, large and by the standards of beer-shops, splendid emporiums of drink which dazzled and lured the working classes, giving them the illusion of opulence. In 1834 a London grocer described the transformation of 'a low dirty public-house with only one doorway' opposite his house. It became ...

A splendid edifice, the front ornamented with pilasters supporting a handsome cornice and balustrade and the whole elevation remarkably striking and handsome; the doorways were increased ... to three, and each of these eight to ten feet wide ... and the doors and windows glazed with very large single squares of plate glass, and the gas fittings of the most costly description ... when this edifice was completed, notice was given by placards taken round the parish; band of music was stationed in front ... and when the doors were opened the rush was tremendous; it was instantly filled with customers and continued so till midnight.

A campaign against the beer-houses began soon after the passing of the Beer Act. Parliament was told of 'an alarming increase of immorality, pauperism and vice among the lower orders arising from the great number of beer-shops'. Some MPs however supported the shops, particularly those from newly enfranchised industrial towns.

Early in 1833 a Parliamentary Select Committee began an investigation. There were amusing instances of blind prejudice against the pubs, including a former mayor of Arundel who complained that as he returned from shooting he had to get out of his gig three times 'for people coming along, waggoners drunk'. Under questioning he had to admit this happened before there were any beer-houses. A Hampshire clergyman who complained about rural destitution caused by beer drinking had to admit there were no beer-houses in his parish. The most serious complaints were about the unsatisfactory state of many beer-house premises.

The Committee reported in June 1833 and while it acknowledged that 'considerable evils had arisen from the present management and conduct of beer-shops', it merely suggested better premises, that those who ran them should prove their good character and that opening hours should be cut, particularly on Sunday. These and other measures were introduced but the campaign against the beer-houses continued.

# Night and the City

At the beginning of the 19th century the population was practically wallowing in drink. There were estimated to be 50,000 pubs for a population of nine million, as well as innumerable gin parlours. And where there were places to drink there were prostitutes.

Mid-Victorian London teemed with prostitutes. One estimate in the 1830s put the figure at 80,000, many of them children. Bracebridge Hemming, who collaborated with Henry Mayhew on his pioneering *London Labour and the London Poor* (1861–2) gives the same figure for mid-century London. Vice was one of London's biggest industries.

They ranged in price and attractiveness from the sailors' trulls of the Ratcliffe Highway brothels in east London with whom no sober man would risk his health to the demure young beauties in the exclusive nightspots of the West End. The most celebrated of London's disreputable night houses in the 1850s and 1860s was the Café Royal in Princess Street, Leicester Square, known after the woman who ran it as Kate Hamilton's. Only high-class whores were allowed in to mix with the wealthy clientele. Kate had once been a pretty girl with a sweet round face like a Victorian keepsake. In her heydays as a nightclub hostess however she weighed 20 stone 'with a countenance that had weathered countless convivial nights'. D. Shaw, the latter-day Gronow who wrote the lively memoir *London in the Sixties*, describes her as 'shaking with laughter like a giant blancmange' as she sat all night with her favourites drinking champagne. She was now stately rather than beautiful, her bodice always cut low, revealing a formidable expanse of breast, and she herself cut a tremendous figure, ensconced on a platform above the fray, her powerful voice keeping order.

Kate Hamilton's Café Royal in the 1860s. The formidable proprietor is presiding over the revels from a dais in the background. Like the later Café Royal it was a haunt of Bohemians. Only wealthy men and high-class whores were admitted.

High-class night houses such as Kate's made their money by selling food and drink at outrageous prices – champagne and Moselle at twelve shillings a bottle. Only men prepared and able to spend five or six pounds, or even more, were admitted. Mayhew's *London* says that Kate was so selective 'these supper rooms are frequented by a better set of men and women than perhaps any other in London'.

## A police raid

Kate's was approached down a long covered passage, which enabled her servants to keep out unsuitable women and spot police raiding parties. Police regularly raided such nightspots, although Kate's generous bribes probably ensured the incursions were just a formality. *London in the Sixties* describes what happened when a raiding party was spotted: 'An alarm gave immediate notice of the approach of the police. Finding oneself within the "salon" during one of these periodical raids was not without interest. Carpets were turned up in the twinkling of an eye, boards were raised and glasses and bottles – empty or full – were thrust promiscuously in; everyone assumed a sweet and virtuous air and talked in subdued tones, whilst a bevy of police, headed by an inspector, marched solemnly in and having completed the farce, marched solemnly out. What the subsidy attached to this duty, and when and how paid, it is needless to inquire.'[1]

The Portland Rooms, known as Motts, was another luxurious and exclusive nightclub where the most expensive women went to drink and to pick up upper-class customers. Not all were prostitutes, some were actresses, but all hoped to acquire a title by marriage to a lordling or at least to become a courtesan, kept perhaps in a villa in St John's Wood.

Motts was quiet until midnight. Between then and four or five in the morning a dazzling company would assemble from all over London. Gentlemen not wearing evening dress were refused admission. *London in the Sixties* sets the scene: 'Mott's was a unique institution, select it might almost be termed, considering the precautions that were taken regarding admittance. Every man who entered was known by name or sight. A man of good birth or position, no matter how great a roué, was admitted as it were by right, whilst parvenues, however wealthy, were turned away.'

The author sighs for the old days at Motts and particularly for the fragrant young beauties who crowd his memory:

The ladies who frequented Motts, moreover, were not the tawdry make-believes who haunt the modern 'Palaces' but actresses of note, who if not Magdalens [prostitutes] sympathised with them; girls of education and refinement who had succumbed to the blandishments of youthful lordlings, fair women here and there who had not yet developed into peeresses and progenitors of future legislators. Among them were 'Skittles', celebrated for her ponies, and sweet Nelly Fowler, the undisputed Queen of Beauty in those long-ago days. This beautiful girl had a natural perfume so delicate, so universally admitted, that love-sick swains paid large sums for the privilege of having their handkerchiefs placed under the Goddess's pillow, and sweet Nelly pervaded – in spirit if not in the flesh – half the clubs and drawing rooms of England.

Less sentimental than the author of *London in the Sixties* was the Marquess of Hastings, one of the drinking and gambling set who clustered around Edward Prince of Wales, an exuberant habitué of Motts and other nightspots.[2] Ronald Pearsall (*Worm in the Bud*) says that Harry Hastings was a Regency buck 30 years out of his time. He was more than a little eccentric. He once emptied a bag of rats among the dancers at Motts, having first extinguished the gas lighting. This is how *London in the Sixties* depicts the scene: 'To describe what followed is impossible. Two hundred men and women and two hundred sewer rats compressed within the compass of forty feet by thirty, and in a darkness as profound as any that was ever experienced in Egypt.' Despite his pedigree his practical jokes brought frequent warnings from old Freer, the major domo. 'Really, my lord, these practical jokes cannot be permitted.'

Beloved by police and publicans, he occupied a privileged position; nothing vicious characterised his jokes, and he had but one enemy – himself. His advent at a ratting match or a badger drawing was a signal to every loafer that the hour of his thirst was ended, and that henceforth 'the Markis was in the chair'.

His generosity was legendary. 'Six cases of champagne invariably formed the first order' as he treated all and sundry. After breakfasting on mackerel fried in gin, and caviar on toast, he would seek a companion for the day's revels. Here is a specimen of his febrile conversation, as recorded by Pearsall; the Marquess had a hangover at the time.

By Gad, old man, I'm damned glad to see you! To begin with you must dine with me at eight – here. I've asked Prince Hohenlohe and Baron Spaum, and young Beust and Count Adelberg, and if you'll swear on a stack of bibles not to repeat it, I expect two live ambassadors – it's always as well to have a sacred person or two handy in case of a row with the police. First we go to Endell Street – to Faultless's pit. I've got a match for a monkey with Hamilton to beat his champion bird, The Sweep, and after that I've arranged with a detective to take us the rounds in the Ratcliffe Highway. No dressing, old man; the kit you came in is the ticket, and a sovereign or two in silver distributed among your pockets; you're bound to have a fist in every wrinkle of your person – why, if you're dancing with a beauty she'll be going over you all the time. I often used to laugh and shout out, 'Go it, I'm not a bit ticklish!' – still, what the hell does it matter?

*London in the Sixties* describes an expedition Hastings led to the Highway. This notorious stretch of sailors' pubs and brothels was on the riverside east of Wapping. It was dangerous for outsiders, and the police went there only in groups.

> The Ratcliffe Highway, now St George's Street East, alongside the Docks, was a place where crime stalked unmolested, and to thread its deadly length was a foolhardy act which might quail the stoutest heart.
>
> Every square yard was occupied by motley groups. Drunken sailors of every nationality in long sea-boots, and deadly knives at every girdle; drunken women with bloated faces, caressing their unsavoury admirers, and here and there constables in pairs by way of moral effect, but powerless – as they well knew – if outrage and free fights commenced in real earnest. Behind these outworks of lawlessness were dens of infamy beyond the power of description – sing-song caves and dancing booths, wine bars and opium dens, where all day and all night Chinamen might be seen in every degree of insensibility from noxious fumes.

Hastings and his party were accompanied by a detective. He would call out to the drinkers as they entered a pub: 'All right lads, only some gents to stand you a drink'. As they were about to enter the Jolly Sailors in Ship Alley a guard warned them off. 'Keep your money, sergeant. We've got a mangy lot here tonight, they won't cotton to the gents. If they ask one of their women to dance it will be taken as an affront, and if they don't ask them it will be taken as an affront. Leave well alone, say I. Most nights it might do, but not tonight. The drink's got hold of most of them, and there's a lot of scurvy Greeks about who will whip out their knives before you can say what's what.'

Hastings and his party insisted on entering. They found sailors and women dancing feverishly to the playing of a lone fiddler who drank deeply from a mug of gin. 'Here and there couples, apparently too overcome to continue the giddy joys, were propped against the wall gurgling out blasphemy and snatches of ribald songs, whilst in alcoves or leaning over a trestle table were knots of men smoking, cursing, swilling strong drinks and casting wicked eyes at the intruders.'

## What cheer, my hearties?

The visitors are clearly not welcome. One of the sailors wants to know whether they haven't got 'a leg of mutton and currant dumplings at 'ome wi'out coming ere?' Another suggests knifing the intruders. As a group of troublemakers turns on them a giant Scandinavian stops them. 'Bide a while, lads, let's make them show their colours.' He turns to Hastings. 'What cheer, there?' The marquess replies: 'What cheer, my hearties?' and the situation is defused. Soon the two groups are fraternising.

Shaw's portrait of the dangers of drinking in the pubs of Stepney is borne out by other authors. The sailors and their girls are the moral descendants of the gin-crazed poor of more than a hundred years before, still disenfranchised but ready to take some form of direct action.

*London in the Sixties* names a series of public houses around the Ratcliffe Highway which were regarded as too dangerous for outsiders like Hastings' party.

The Jolly Sailors was admittedly the most dangerous of all the dens, even amid such hotbeds of iniquity as the King of Prussia, the Prince Regent, the Old Mahogany Bar, the Old Gun, the Blue Anchor and

Regency bucks slumming in a Ratcliffe Highway grogshop. The scene recalls the Marquess of Hastings visiting such dens with his friends in the sixties.

the Rose and Crown, and had decoys in all directions to lure drunken sailors or foolish sightseers within its fatal portals. Situated at the extremity of Grace's Alley, it led directly into Well Close Square, a cul-de-sac it was easier to enter than to leave.

The reason for this concentration of dangerous pubs in the East End was complicity between magistrates and brewers. Morals campaigners had been trying to clean up the area for years, but they were frustrated by a combination of the brewers and a crooked local government magnate and brothel keeper named Joseph Merceron. The campaigners fought a determined but losing battle to close the worst examples in the Stepney parish of Shadwell. As early as 1819 the First Report from the Committee on the State of the Police of the Metropolis told how the area had become plagued by prostitutes who used 'the superabundance of public houses' in the area. The report stated:

> ... some of them for a long time past have been the constant resort of the most abandoned and profligate women; and being in a situation affording a peculiar convenience for their evil practices, and purposely fitted for their accommodation, they have occasioned the increase of the worst kind of houses of ill-fame, the inhabitants whereof bid defiance to all decency and restraint. The prostitutes and procuresses filled the streets both night and day; and the parishioners have been thereby deprived of their trade; for those public-houses, being situated in the High Street, it was impossible for respectable persons to approach the shops without having their eyes and ears offended by scenes and language the most awful and disgusting ... the parish appeared as if it were doomed to be the receptacle of all the profligates of the neighbourhood.

The exasperated residents complained to the parish trustees and the magistrates. They claimed their servants and sons were constantly exposed to seduction, 'and too often became a prey to the wretched beings with whom they were continually surrounded'. Constables and the Watch were bribed to look the other way. The parish trustees set up their own patrols and found a deplorable state of affairs. Dance-halls attached to the public houses were being used by prostitutes to pick up clients who were taken to nearby brothels, in some cases also owned by the pub landlords.

The trustees applied to the licensing magistrates to have the licences of the pubs suspended. Their petition was accepted with great reluctance, but the licences were suspended pending an appeal by the publicans. The Committee on the State of the Police reveals the network of corruption which the parish trustees were up against: 'The most notorious of these houses was the Duke of York, kept by — Hennekey, but supplied with porter by Messrs Meux and Co. who had lent a large sum of money upon the house, and which was producing an immense return, the draught of beer and spirits being enormous'. In the interval before the hearing Meux and Co. did everything they could to get the petition thrown out. In the forefront of this campaign was Joseph Merceron, himself one of the licensing magistrates. The result, says the report on the police, was that the local publicans, particularly Hennekey of the Duke of York, 'not only continued their indecent practices, but with the greatest impudence ... defied and threatened the parish officers, insulting them in the public streets and daring them to do their worst'.

Despite the powerful advocacy of Merceron and his friends the licences of the three public houses were withdrawn for the coming year. Eventually the brewers produced another publican, apparently a man of good character named Birks, who promised to clean up the place, and he was granted a licence for the King's Arms. 'Within a month the King's Arms was engaged in the lucrative trade of prostitution and liquor on an even bigger scale than the Duke of York, Meux and Co. having paid for extensive alterations to be carried out to the house.'

So the struggle went on. At one time the parish consulted the Attorney-General to see whether they could bring a criminal action against the magistrates. He ruled that there was nothing to suggest that they had acted corruptly, although they might have acted against the public interest. Yet there undoubtedly was corruption in the granting of licences. Merceron, who served a jail sentence for stealing public funds, died in 1861.

Other immoral public houses which drew the attention of morals campaigners were the so-called 'finishes'. These were nightspots which attracted upper-class clients after other hostelries had closed for the night. In 1840 the French socialist and feminist Flora Tristan published *Promenades Dans Londres* in which she described a visit to one:

After the play they move on to the 'finishes'; these are squalid taverns or vast resplendent gin-palaces where people go to spend what remains of the night ...

From the outside these gin-palaces with their carefully fastened shutters seem to be quietly slumbering; but no sooner has the doorkeeper admitted you by the little door reserved for initiates than you are dazzled by the light of a thousand gas lamps. Upstairs there is a spacious salon divided down the middle; in one half there is a row of tables separated one from the other by wooden screens ... In the other half is a dais where the prostitutes parade in all their finery; seeking to arouse the men with their glances and remarks ...

Towards midnight the regular clients begin to arrive; several finishes are frequented by men in high society, and this is where the cream of the aristocracy gather. At first the young noblemen recline on the sofas, smoking and exchanging pleasantries with the women; then, when they have drunk enough for the fumes of champagne and Madeira to go to their heads, the illustrious scions of the English nobility, the very honourable members of Parliament, remove their coats, untie their cravats, take off their waistcoats and braces, and proceed to set up their private boudoir in a public place. Why not make themselves at home, since they are paying out so much money for the right to display their contempt ... The orgy rises to a crescendo; between four and five in the morning it reaches its height.

At this point it takes a good deal of courage to remain in one's seat, a mute spectator of all that takes place. What worthy use these English lords make of their immense fortunes! How fine and generous they are when they have lost the use of their reason and offer fifty, even a hundred guineas to a prostitute if she will lend herself to all the obscenities that drunkenness engenders ...

For in a finish there is no lack of entertainment. One of the favourite sports is to *ply a woman with drink* until she falls dead drunk upon the floor, then to make her swallow a draught compounded of *vinegar, mustard and pepper*; this invariably throws the poor creature into horrible convulsions, and her spasms and contortions provoke the *honourable company* to gales of laughter and infinite amusement. Another diversion much appreciated at these fashionable gatherings is to empty the contents of the nearest glass upon the women as they lie insensible upon the ground. I have seen satin dresses of no recognisable colour, only a confused mass of stains; wine, brandy, beer, tea, coffee, cream etc. ... daubed all over them in a thousand fantastic shapes ... The air is heavy with the noxious odours of food, drink, tobacco, and others more fetid still which seize you by the throat, grip your temples in a vice and make your senses reel: it is indescribably horrible! ... However, this life, which continues relentlessly night after night, is the prostitute's sole hope of a fortune, for she has no hold on the Englishman when he is sober. *The sober Englishman is chaste to the point of prudery.*

It is usually between seven and eight in the morning when people leave the finish. The servants go out to look for cabs, and anyone still on his feet gathers up his clothes and returns home; as for the rest, the pot-boys dress them in the first garments that come to hand and bundle them into a cab and tell the cabman where to deliver them. Often nobody knows their address; then they are deposited in the cellar and left to sleep in the straw. This place is known as the drunkards' hole, and there they stay until they have recovered their wits sufficiently to say where they wish to be taken.

## The flash houses

Flash houses were the low-life equivalent of the finishes. They were squalid lodging houses or brothels, often associated with public houses. Flash houses were central to the criminal enterprise in the 18th and early 19th centuries. Criminals used them to eat and sleep, to plan robberies, to exchange information, to recruit new gang members, to dispose of or acquire stolen goods. Fagin's den in Oliver Twist is typical of such houses.

Most experts agreed that 'flash houses' were responsible for the juvenile crime wave in the first half of the 19th century. Boys drank there with mature thieves and prostitutes and girls of their own age, who were often their mistresses. Henry Grey Bennett, chairman of the 1816 Select Committee on the Police, accused the police of taking bribes for keeping the activities of the flash houses secret from the magistrates, and he named some of the more notorious houses. There was the Black Horse in Tottenham Court Road, frequented by thieves such as Huffey White and Conkey Beau. The landlord, Blackman, 'has been considered a thief for fifteen years ... there is not a regular flash-house in London that is not known to the officers of the police, from the Rose in Rose-street, Long Acre, kept by Kelly, which he kept long with impunity, to the Bear, opposite to Bow-Street office, the infamous character of which is notorious, and which unites the trades of brothel and public-house.' Grey Bennet's efforts at reform were defeated by a combination of police corruption and the vested interests of the brewers.

These lodging-houses abounded all over the country, but were particularly numerous and scandalous in London. In 1851 the Common Lodging House Act was passed in an attempt to control them. Police were given powers to inspect and close them if they failed to reach an elementary standard of decency and cleanliness. Hundreds were closed, and in the remainder put their prices up to meet the costs of the new standards. Some of the poor were thus made homeless because they could not afford to pay.

Unlike the temperance movement, which was largely working class, these attempts to make the poor moral were led by the middle and upper-middle classes. While they went about their work the family at the very top of society was nurturing a dangerous enemy of the new morality.

# Good Night, Sweet Prince

The reaction against Victorian values in aristocratic circles was led by the Queen's son, Albert Edward, Prince of Wales, the last dissolute holder of that title. Victoria's son, known as Bertie, had an almost Georgian appetite for sex and drink. He helped loosen the stays of both the times and his friends' wives. As Anita Leslie wrote in *Edwardians in Love*: 'Albert Edward, Prince of Wales, would personally dictate the code of social behaviour for the next fifty years, and it would be unique in history.'

He was short and fat and ugly, and stank of cigars. But he had the male equivalent of 'It', the secret ingredient identified as sex appeal in the beauties of the time, and besides, he was a prince. It's hard to know how many of the innumerable beautiful women who passed through his bed found him rather than his title alluring. He probably liked sex even more than food and drink, but his weakness for enormous Edwardian meals and cigars eventually broke his health and probably made him impotent.

Edwardian hostesses served guests at their country houses 30-course breakfasts, and apart from snacks, there would be an eight-course lunch, a substantial mid-afternoon meal and a formidable dinner: twelve heavy courses, all accompanied by the appropriate wines, were the norm. If Bertie was not pleasuring his hostess or the wife of a friend in some distant bed he would have a 2am snack of devilled chicken, sandwiches and whisky and soda.

When the women had left the table Bertie and his friends played practical jokes every bit as tasteless as those of his ancestor George IV. The butt was often Christopher Sykes, whose sycophancy deserved a dukedom but who instead bankrupted himself to amuse Bertie.

## Tum-Tum, you're fat

When Sykes got hopelessly drunk at a ball and had to be put to bed, Bertie had a dead seagull put in beside him. The following night he arranged for a dead rabbit to share a bed with Sykes, who was drunk again. When invited to Sykes's country house he would douse his host with his own brandy. His favourite trick was more painful. 'Come here, Christopher, and look at the smoke coming out of my eyes.' However often this trick was played, the obsequious Sykes would obey. He would look into the Prince's eyes and be burned on the hand with the latter's cigar. 'As your Royal Highness pleases' was his servile response to any humiliation, and it became a catch-phrase in Bertie's set. When the cost of entertaining the Prince and his friends proved ruinous and Sykes had to retire into semi-seclusion on his estates at the end of the 1880s, the Prince declared it to be a 'thoroughly bad business'. It was bad form indeed for a friend of his to go bust. Nevertheless he did help Sykes with his more pressing debts.

Perhaps the drink accounted for Bertie's extreme touchiness on these occasions. A friend who referred to his portliness offended him as grievously as Brummell did the Prince Regent when he called him 'your fat friend'. It happened one night at Sandringham, one of the royal residences. Bertie's old friend, Sir Frederick Johnstone, became inebriated and waggish. The Prince said, 'Freddy, Freddy, you're very drunk.' He suggested to Johnstone that he should go to bed. Johnstone pointed to the Prince's mighty belly and said, using a forbidden pet name: 'Tum-Tum, you're very fat.' As Pearsall recounts in *Worm in the Bud*, he was out of the house before breakfast the next morning.

The limits of the Prince's tolerance and sense of humour were demonstrated again during a game of billiards. He played a poor shot, and his opponent joked: 'Pull yourself together, Wales.' The Prince promptly sent for the man's carriage.

Bertie died in 1910 at the age of 69, his lungs weakened by years of heavy cigar smoking. The Queen reluctantly invited his last official mistress, Alice Keppel, to his bedside. Keppel later became a noted

London hostess, as famous for her drinking as her parties. The politician and diarist Chips Channon recalled a dinner party he gave at which Keppel was the 'showpiece'. He wrote in his diary, 'she is so affectionate and *grande dame* that it is a pity that she tipples, and then becomes garrulous and inaccurate in her statements.' Theo Aronson says in *The King in Love* that during the Second World War Keppel was often to be seen 'holding uproarious court to gatherings of equivocal young men in London pubs'.

# The Art of Rebellion

The poet Algernon Charles Swinburne had a shock of flaming red hair, pale green eyes set in a pale face and the physique of a child. He was excitable. Once in the studio of the artist James McNeill Whistler he was reciting a work that had aroused his enthusiasm. As he read he skipped on and off a sofa, 'his little arms and legs jerking like those of a marionette. ... The words went to his head, his excitement grew, his voice rose to a hysterical screech and then suddenly he stiffened, became silent, fell down rigid and unconscious' (Gaunt, *The Aesthetic Adventure*). He was nursed back to health by Whistler's mother, who showed a motherly understanding of this man-child.

Swinburne went to great lengths to outrage Victorian sensibilities. He was addicted to republicanism, drink and flagellation. In 1872, when he was 35, one of his heroes, the Italian patriot Mazzini, died. Swinburne drank alone until it was time to go to a friend's party. It was a crowded literary occasion. He arrived hopelessly drunk and was concealed in the servants' quarters until he sobered up and was sent home. The critic Edmund Gosse bluntly described him as a drunkard. Gosse had watched as a cab drew up at Swinburne's rooms in Cheyne Walk and the critic and aesthete Walter Pater stepped out. Behind him Swinburne fell out of the vehicle on his hands and knees, his top-hat rolling into the gutter. While Pater was taken to the drawing room Swinburne was hurried elsewhere to be sobered up and made presentable.

In those buttoned-up times he was an embarrassment to friends and hosts. He would spout words endlessly, in a loud high-pitched voice, about poetry, republicanism and, as he became more drunk, lesbianism and sodomy, 'variously practised'. His frailty made the performance pathetic, but many were offended.

142

Mrs Hungerford Pollen threatened to banish Swinburne from her house after he drank some sherry and became violent and blasphemous. When she told her husband that Swinburne must never be invited again he replied: 'Oh! my dear, we must never be unkind to him; he is just a child!' Mrs Pollen replied that in that case he was a 'very, very *spoilt* child'. She added that even when sober his idea of rational conversation was 'to dance and skip all over the room, reciting poetry at the top of his voice, and going on and on with it'. She never liked him.

At another house Swinburne disappeared before dinner, and was found in the dining room, having drunk the dessert wine. He was dancing madly round the dining table, watched by the servants.

After the explorer and writer Richard Burton introduced him to brandy he would return at night hopelessly drunk to the Cheyne Walk house he shared with the painter Dante Gabriel Rossetti. One night Rossetti was woken at three in the morning by 'tremendous knocking'. Swinburne was outside, supported in the arms of a policeman and followed by a procession of street urchins. He tried to put him to bed, Swinburne 'screaming and splashing about' until he suddenly subsided. According to Edmund Gosse, if Swinburne saw a bottle within reach while he was dining with friends, he would pounce on it 'like a mongoose on a snake'. The poet would fill a tumbler and drink greedily, 'his lips trembling and his eyelids opening and closing violently'.

Arthur Munby saw him in the drawing room of the Arts Club in Hanover Square, leaping about, blowing kisses and swearing violently. On another occasion there in December 1866 Munby saw him 'obviously drunk ... waving his arms ... talking loud and wild'. He would order a cab and cancel it, and finally staggered down to the toilets. A member came up exclaiming: 'What a sad business! Here is Swinburne come into the club again dead drunk.' Swinburne was lying prostrate downstairs.

## The unbridled Queen

Swinburne was a secret pornographer, something which would have made him a pariah if widely known. Perhaps his finest performance in this genre is *La Soeur de la Reine*, a burlesque drama about Queen Victoria's prostitute sister. The point of the joke is the Queen herself, a woman of rampant and insatiable sexual appetite who preys on the senior servants of state. Lord John Russell and 'Sir Peel' are among her victims.

She was first seduced by Wordsworth, after he gave a highly suggestive reading of his poem *The Excursion*. Meanwhile her twin sister, Kitty, has been plying her trade on the streets. She had been secretly brought up as a prostitute so that there would be no threat to the succession. The Queen's court is peopled by grotesques, including the Duchess of Fuckingstone, Miss Sarah Butterbottom, the Marchioness of Mausprick and Miss Polly Poke.

Swinburne is known to have read portions of *La Soeur* to friends. It is unlikely he read them another of his fantasies about the Queen, quoted in a letter to Dante Gabriel Rossetti in March 1870:

> This is a dildo the Queen used
> Once in a pinch in an office,
> Quite unaware it had *been* used
> First, by a housemaid erratic.
> Soon, though obese and lymphatic,
> Symptoms she felt all that month as it went on
> What sort of parties had used it and spent on.

Swinburne was a sado-masochist. Friends introduced him to a flagellation brothel in St John's Wood, 'presided over by a well educated lady, well versed in the birchen mysteries'. The services were expensive, and Swinburne had money troubles. Other friends, including Rossetti, decided what he needed was a wife. The unlikely woman they chose for him was the famous actress Adah Isaacs Menken. Born in New Orleans, she was slightly older than Swinburne and had been married several times, one of her husbands being the pugilist John Carmel Heenan. Adah's best-known role was in *Mazeppa*, a drama based on Byron's poem. In it she appeared in a skin-coloured costume strapped to the back of a horse, her tights making it appear she was naked.

Adah had written some verses, and when Rossetti suggested she undertake Swinburne's sexual education she was interested. Swinburne was taken to a performance of *Mazeppa* at Astley's in Horseferry Road, and late one night in December 1867 Adah turned up on his doorstep. She said the equivalent of 'I just love your poems and I've come from Paris to love the poet' though in more earthy language. She spent the night at his rooms in Dorset Street, and the experiment continued until January 1868.

Although Swinburne seemed immensely proud of his mistress, it was she who broke it off. She told Rossetti that it was too difficult to get Swinburne 'up to scratch'. His sadistic tendency didn't help. 'I can't make him understand that biting's no use!' Swinburne soon got over his loss. He had found Adah trying at times, especially when she sat on the edge of the bed raising her shapely legs in the air and reading her poems.

Adah took herself off to Paris, where she was photographed sitting on the knee of Dumas the elder. She died there the following year, apparently from drinking too much brandy. Swinburne went back to the two rouged and golden-haired women who performed services for him and other men of similar tendencies in Circus Road, St John's Wood. Eventually he tired, not of the beatings but of the financial demands of the harpies who administered them. 'It was one thing to be beaten like a child, but to be made a fool of over money by such creatures as these was quite intolerable' (Gaunt, *Swinburne*).

Without the distraction of flagellation Swinburne turned again to drink. Burton had introduced him to Charles Duncan Cameron, a diplomat who had suffered greatly on Her Majesty's service. Cameron had been British Consul in Abyssinia, at the Emperor Theodore's court. The emperor believed that the British Foreign Office had insulted him and seized Cameron, holding him in chains. Eventually a British expeditionary force stormed the city and freed Cameron. (Theodore shot himself with a pistol given to him by Queen Victoria.)

## A scandalous noise

Cameron was treated like a hero on his return to London, but his ordeal had driven him to drink. He believed that England would soon be convulsed by armed revolution, which made him a congenial drinking companion for Swinburne. Munby recorded a scandalous visit the pair paid to the Arts Club in June 1869, when Swinburne was 32. They embraced in an indecent way for the entertainment of the members, and made 'a scandalous noise'. The committee called on Swinburne to resign. He did quit just over a year later, after he and Cameron were involved in a famous scandal. They went to the club while a committee meeting was in progress. The cloakroom was full of silk hats. They placed them in two rows on the floor and holding their left ankles in their left hands, destroyed the hats by hopping from one to another.[1]

As often happened, Swinburne could remember nothing of the incident. 'This is the first I have heard of the matter,' he told William Rossetti, who brought news that the club committee wanted him to resign:

I have certainly objurgated more than one waiter, and remember bending double one fork in an energetic mood at dinner ... As to freedom of voice or tone – I am stunned daily by more noise at that place than I ever heard (or, you suggest, made) in my life. If I damaged a valuable article belonging to them, why did they not send in a bill? I have remained in order more frequently to meet a few intimates, who relieve if they cannot redeem the moral squalor of the place.

After a final binge in 1879 Swinburne was rescued by a solicitor friend, Theodore Watts-Dunton, who kept him in semi-seclusion at his home, 2 The Pines, Putney, for the rest of his life. Here he allowed him a bottle of beer at lunch, and tried to shield him from any kind of excitement. He turned away Swinburne's old friends; others were rejected by Swinburne himself. One old drinking crony who turned up on the doorstep of the Pines and addressed Swinburne with the words 'Hullo, Algernon, old buck!' was confronted by the poet, 'speechless with rage, the new-born fire of ascetic disapprobation in his blue eyes'. Swinburne ignored the outstretched hand and slammed the door.

There were rumours that Watts-Dunton was holding him prisoner. Gosse referred to the poet's 'captivity at The Pines', but Swinburne was grateful to his rescuer. Watts-Dunton weaned him off brandy by persuading him port was the real poet's drink – after all, Tennyson drank it. Then he substituted claret for port, on the ground that it was the drink of 'gentlemen'. Eventually he persuaded the poet that one should drink the 'wine of the country', which in England was beer. From then on Swinburne had a glass at the Rose and Crown in the morning, and a bottle of Bass at lunch.

Swinburne was only 42 when he arrived at The Pines, and he lived there for the remaining 30 years of his life. Although he became a reactionary, for a time he retained some of his naughtiness. He planned to write a drama based on a supposed love affair between Queen Victoria and her servant John Brown. They consign the royal children to the Tower so they can indulge in mutual sexual frenzy on the Isle of Wight. However by the Golden Jubilee of 1887 he has become a fan. His poem 'The Jubilee' sheds a benign light on the Queen's record:

> And now that fifty years are flown
> Since in a maiden's hand the sign
> Of empire that no seas confine
> First as a star to seaward shone,
> We see their record shine.

The firebrand who had denounced the execution of Fenians in 1867 turned against Irish nationalism and threatened to throw a Fenian down the stairs. When the Boer War broke out he wrote, 'Strike, England, and strike home'. He was enchanted by babies. Max Beerbohm recalled a visit to The Pines when Swinburne cooed to Watts-Dunton about a baby he had seen in its perambulator during his walk on the heath, 'the most BEAUT-iful babbie ever beheld by mortal eyes'. The poet Robert Graves remembered that when he was a baby the ageing poet 'often used to stop my perambulator when he met it on Nurses' Walk at the edge of Wimbledon Common, and pat me on the head and kiss me: he was an inveterate pram-stopper and patter and kisser'. Swinburne paid this tribute to infant loveliness:

> All the bells of heaven may ring,
> All the birds of heaven may sing,
> All the wells on earth may spring,
> All the winds on earth may bring,
> All sweet sounds together ...

As Gaunt says (*Swinburne*) 'the state to which the disciple of Sade and revolution had been reduced would be hard to parallel in terms of irony, except perhaps in the earlier novels of Evelyn Waugh'.

# La Vie de Bohème

Gradually the heavy after-dinner toping of the Georgian period died out. Some attributed this to the replacement of cigars by cigarettes. The heavy pungent smell of cigars was thought to be offensive to women, so after they had left the table men had an excuse to linger over the port while they smoked. As cigarettes with their lighter aroma became more popular men no longer had this excuse. Besides, women were beginning to smoke cigarettes too.

Men could always escape from the general stuffiness of late Victorian domestic life to their clubs, but even there drinking was more restrained. The pall of Victorian respectability hung over all, and it was beginning to chafe, especially for women. By the end of the 19th century new ideas, feminism, suffragism, modernism and free thought were aching to be born. Some women chose the stern path of politics, some a kind of persuasion by earnest quietism. Some looked to the emerging Bohemia, which welcomed women of a certain kind.

There were enclaves of Bohemianism where artists, journalists and charlatans kept some of the traditions of their forebears alive, foremost among them the Café Royal in Regent Street. Here for about four decades some of the most talented writers and artists of their time mixed with eccentrics, crooks, wits and weirdos. The Café opened in 1865. Its Domino Room, with marble-topped tables, red velvet seats, sawdust-covered floor and mirrored splendour was a Bohemian enclave from the 1890s to the early 1930s. Most of all for the *fin de siècle* decadents. While Oscar Wilde held court, among the listeners were the poet Ernest Dowson, the artist Aubrey Beardsley, the novelist Ronald Firbank and the poet Richard Le Gallienne, sipping absinthe in imitation of Verlaine. Also listening though less patiently might be James McNeill Whistler, George Bernard Shaw, Frank Harris and Augustus John. Whistler was exasperated by Wilde's pronouncements on art. 'What has Oscar in common with Art?' he wrote. 'Except that he dines at our tables and picks from our platters the plums for the pudding he peddles in the provinces. Oscar – the amiable, irresponsible, esurient Oscar – with no more sense of a picture than the fit of a coat, has the courage of the opinions – of others.' Oscar simply smiled.

In November 1883 *Punch* printed a fanciful conversation between the two of them on Art and Life. Wilde sent Whistler a telegram saying: '*Punch* too ridiculous. When you and I are together we never talk about anything but ourselves.' Whistler replied: 'No, no Oscar, you forget. When you and I are together we never talk about anything except me.' Wilde answered: 'It's true Jimmy we were talking about you, but I was thinking of myself!'

Wilde and Whistler were almost founding fathers of London's Bohemia. The younger set of Bohemians was dominated by the extraordinary figure of the artist Augustus John. In his cloak and wide-brimmed hat, this tall, long-striding, red-bearded, gold-earringed, garrulous, hard-drinking, insatiable sexual predator was an archetype of social rebellion. Osbert Sitwell described him as presiding at the Café Royal 'like some kind of Rasputin-Jehovah'. To suburban mothers he was their worst nightmare as he 'pounced' on their starry-eyed art-student daughters. The girls saw it differently: they were more than happy to be initiated by this kind and supportive if alarmingly fiery lover. Early success as an artist had made him relatively prosperous, and many a half-starved young painter or poet was sure of a meal or a drink if John was occupying a table at the Café. Students from the Slade art school would stand in silent homage when he arrived, 'like a pirate king getting onto his quarterdeck'. His drink was hock and seltzer, but he could knock back a whole bottle of brandy or rum seemingly without ill-effects. It was said that he did the drinking while his friends had the headaches.

## Wilde talk

John often sat silent for hours. Until he was imprisoned in Reading jail Oscar Wilde seldom stopped talking. Wilde first visited the Café Royal in the early 1880s. He quickly gained the reputation of being the most captivating talker of his time, although the company frequently included other great talkers and wits such as Whistler and Shaw. Among the brilliant guests at Wilde's table might be Beardsley, Sir Max Beerbohm, Harris, Dowson and the artists Charles Conder and Sir William Rothenstein. Many others would try to get a table nearby to listen to one of his *mots*, which fell thick and fast from those flabby lips.

> More women grow old nowadays through the faithfulness of their admirers than through anything else.
> Meredith is a prose Browning ... so is Browning.
> Bernard Shaw has no enemies but is immensely disliked by his friends.

This is about as close to malice as Wilde ever got. His jabs were usually blunted: 'Do I know George Moore? I know him so well that I have not spoken to him in ten years.' 'The gods bestowed on Max [Beerbohm] the gift of perpetual old age.' Of a butch actress he said , 'Dear ——, she is one of nature's gentlemen.' Some of his aphorisms still work:

> Only shallow people do not judge by appearances.
> Punctuality is the thief of time.
> There are two ways of disliking art. One is to dislike it and the other is to like it rationally.
> Scandal is gossip made tedious by morality.
> Don't tell me you have exhausted life – when a man tells me that, one knows life has exhausted him.

Were they spontaneous? Did he lie awake polishing them? They certainly weren't all original. When Oscar murmured after a Whistler squib that he wished he had said it, the painter replied: 'You will, Oscar, you will.' Occasionally he could be just a little waspish: when an unknown young man greeted him effusively he said: 'I don't know your face, but your manner is familiar.'

Wilde was capable of delivering *mots* at any time of the day or night, but he was at his best after a few drinks. He drank a great deal, but the famed absinthe was mainly for show. His drink was whisky and soda. He was never quite drunk, and seldom completely sober.

Wilde had a fateful lunch at the Café in March 1895, when Frank Harris tried to persuade him to drop his libel action against the Marquess of Queensberry and flee the country. The other guests at the lunch were Bernard Shaw and Lord Alfred Douglas, Wilde's lover and Queensberry's son. Harris, who feared that the tables would be turned on Wilde and he would be jailed, failed to persuade him to flee. Instead Wilde replied: 'I do not think this is friendly of you, Frank.' Wilde went to face his accuser in court, and the sequel is too well-known and painful to repeat.

The consumptive Beardsley, who seemed to have been clinging to life almost all his young life, personified the unreal atmosphere of the decadents' corner in the Domino Room. His emaciated death-mask with its hair plastered down would light up as he talked. Deghy and Waterhouse (*Café Royal*) catch his tone of voice, so reminiscent of early Waugh:

Oh really! How perfectly sweet!
Oh really! How perfectly enchanting!
Oh really! How perfectly filthy!

Another disciple at the table of King Oscar was the poet Edward Dowson, whose slight oeuvre contains a poem that has lasted:

Last night, ah yesternight, betwixt her lips and mine
There fell thy shadow, Cynara! thy breath was shed
Upon my soul between the kisses and the wine;
And I was desolate and sick of an old passion,
Yea, I was desolate and bowed my head:
I have been faithful to thee, Cynara! in my fashion.

All night upon mine heart I felt her warm heart beat,
Night-long within mine arms in love and sleep she lay;
Surely the kisses of her bought red mouth were sweet;
But I was desolate and sick of an old passion,
When I awoke and found the dawn was grey:
I have been faithful to thee, Cynara! in my fashion.

I have forgot much, Cynara! gone with the wind,
Flung roses, roses riotously with the throng,
Dancing, to put thy pale, lost lillies out of mind;
But I was desolate and sick of an old passion,
Yea, all the time, because the dance was long:
I have been faithful to thee, Cynara! in my fashion.

I cried for madder music and stronger wine,
But when the feast is finished and the lamps expire,
Then falls thy shadow, Cynara! the night is thine;
And I am desolate and sick of an old passion,
Yea hungry for the lips of my desire:
I have been faithful to thee, Cynara! in my fashion.

The rhetorical sentimentality of this poem, 'Non sum qualis eram bonae sub regno Cynarae'[1] has always appealed. It also inspired a song by Cole Porter and gave a title to the best-seller *Gone With The Wind*. Dowson was popular among the younger and poorer writers and artists. His great love was a very young waitress in a café in nearby Glasshouse Street. 'She listened to his verses, smiled charmingly, under her mother's eyes, on his two years' courtship, and at the end of two years married the waiter instead …' He wandered the streets and frequented drinking dens and cabmens' shelters ('Dowson found brothels cheaper than hotels'). This alcoholic young poet, gentle and diffident when sober, became loud and foul-mouthed when drunk. 'He fell into furious and unreasoning passions; a vocabulary unknown to him when sober sprang up like a whirlwind; he seemed always about to commit some act of absurd violence' (Julian Symons, preface to Dowson's *Collected Poems*).

He was eventually found dying in the street in 1900, and died at the age of 33, in Catford, a place no poet, however decadent, would choose for his expiring breath. Beardsley had slipped away in 1898, pleading that all his 'obscene drawings' be burned.

Another artist with a fondness for drink who found companionship in the Café Royal was the cartoonist Phil May. He was once discovered in Regent Street so drunk that he could not speak. Instead he made little drawings of his destination for a cabby, who took him there.

## I don't want to die!

The Café Royal did a nice line in doomed youth. One Saturday night in 1925 Ronald Firbank, influential author of ten novels, startled the diners and drinkers by suddenly screaming: 'I don't want to die!' They stared at the tall thin young man and when he screamed the words again offered rough words of comfort. Most of the men in the room were bookmakers celebrating their luck as the flat-racing season drew to a close. One of them offered him a sixpence. Painted women offered to kiss him.

Firbank didn't need money, he had plenty already. What he needed was to be told he didn't have to die, and his doctor had just told him he had not long to live. He died a year later, aged 38.

His rather slight but amusing novels, including *Valmouth* and *Caprice*, influenced Evelyn Waugh. They were written on piles of blue postcards, and this cultivated eccentricity seemed to infect his whole life. He kept a palm-tree in his apartment, and employed a gardener to water it twice a day. Deghy and Waterhouse describe a man tortured by nervous embarrassment. He would watch plays with his knees drawn up around his head, attracting the attention he loathed. With his long thin hands he would slowly tear the programme into tiny pieces, again drawing attention but unable to stop.

Firbank had difficulty in eating, and once at a dinner given in his honour dined on a single pea, perhaps a conscious echo of Beau Brummell, but drank great volumes of champagne. A homosexual, although he made friends he was essentially solitary, and would sit alone in the Café drinking, so highly strung that his hands constantly fluttered to his tie or his hair. Wyndham Lewis described him as 'a talking gazelle afflicted with some nervous disorder'. Those hands were to be a feature of an absurd lawsuit he brought against the author Osbert Sitwell. He accused Sitwell of spreading the rumour that his family's fortune had been made in the manufacture of boot-buttons. Firbank, whose grandfather had been a captain of heavy industry, would recite over and over again to fellow drinkers his planned courtroom *coup de théâtre*: 'Look at my hands, my lord! How could my father have made boot-buttons? Never! He made the most beautiful railways!' Within weeks he was friends with Sitwell again and the lawsuit never reached the High Court.

Firbank had generosity and tact. He would usually insist on paying for drinks. One day he spotted the young artist Gabriel Atkin sitting alone.

He knew Atkin could not afford to stand him drinks, let alone buy him lunch. He walked over to Atkin and asked him to buy him a meal. Atkin said he couldn't, and Firbank gave him a pound note. Saying 'How wonderful to be a guest!' he ordered lunch for the two of them, paid for with the money he had given Atkin.

When Firbank first met the young aristocrat Evan Morgan, who would later admit that they were 'fairly close acquaintances', he whispered in his ear that his name was Rameses. He insisted on taking Morgan to the British Museum to show him his likeness. Morgan, son and heir of Lord Tredegar, said he thought of Firbank 'as one might some rare bird to be cherished for its exquisite exotic qualities, rather than as a human being'.

Because of his shyness Firbank was socially gauche to an extent which was a trial to his friends. Princess Violette Murat invited the artist Nina Hamnett to stay at her converted farmhouse near Versailles. The Princess was a heavy-drinking, opium-smoking lesbian who liked Nina and supported her financially. She asked if she could meet Firbank, who was then living in Versailles. Nina arranged an invitation to Firbank's home, and promised the princess there would be plenty to drink. When they arrived Firbank was speechless with shyness, and worse, he was sober. The best he could manage was to rush to his desk and pick up a stuffed bird of paradise, which he pressed on the astonished princess.

She invited him to lunch the next day, and when he was already impossibly late lunch began without him. He arrived when dessert had been served, did not eat or speak but shoved a copy of his latest book into the princess's hands before rushing out.

### Always my torture!

When the author Aldous Huxley met Firbank for the last time at the Café Royal it was at a wedding breakfast for another man. Huxley sat down opposite Firbank, who gave 'his usual agonised wriggle of embarrassment' and said: 'Aldous – always my *torture!*'

Perhaps the last word on this loveable, exasperating man should be left to Eric Maschwitz, composer of *These Foolish Things*:

He was truly a habitué of that faded, jaded room. Some days he sat from noon to midnight in his accustomed seat ... A thin man with a black felt hat. A narrow man and restless – writhing like a basket of serpents. Clutching at the lapel of his coat, dipping his head like an embarrassed governess. Always paying for drinks … 'My dear, I saw a crossing sweeper in Sloane Street today with the eyes of a startled faun!' … 'My dear, when you talk like that you give me a distinct feeling of plush!' It was he who gave me the life story of the lavatory attendant of the Café, whose children were never told about their father's profession until they were 16 and old enough therefore to know the facts of life. To an undergraduate, hoping to find the Café Royal the embodiment of all that was most fine and free and desperate, Firbank seemed, in his appearance and his talk, to keep alive a little of the spirit of the Nineties.

## Horrible Harris

Shaw said of Frank Harris that he was not first rate, nor second rate, nor tenth rate. 'He is just his horrible unique self.' Harris was also a brilliant journalist, as editor of the *Fortnightly Review*, the *Saturday Review*, *Vanity Fair* and the *Evening News*. He pioneered a provocative and sensationalistic journalism. For the rest we have to rely to a large extent on his autobiography, *My Life and Loves* (1923–7) which was banned for obscenity. He said he was Irish, had run away to New York at the age of 15, been among many other things a bootblack, a cowboy, a bouncer in a gambling saloon, a labourer helping build Brooklyn Bridge. Deghy and Waterhouse say he was variously described by others as 'genius, pornographer, lout, buccaneer, Bohemian, philosopher, Munchausen, Casanova, Rhetor of the Minor Key, buffoon, colour-blind chameleon, Knave of Hearts and – on one occasion – Saint'. He was certainly a liar and a tireless philanderer. He was small, thick-set, swarthy and truculent. He wore what Philippe Jullian calls 'a doubtful diamond' in his tie (Jullian, *Oscar Wilde*).

Harris arrived in London at the age of 26 some time in the early 1880s. Two years later he was editor of the *Evening News*. One story said he got the job by seducing the wife of one of the proprietors. He increased the circulation tenfold. He married a rich widow and used her house in Park Lane to entertain lavishly.

Harris was often insufferable. Sitting in the Café Royal with a distinguished editor and his wife, he became bored with his guest's lengthy dissertation on the Balkans. 'Why bother to trouble with the Balkans when you have so charming a wife?' he roared. 'Is not a woman better worthy of exploring than all the Balkans?' Dining there another night with the Duc de Richelieu after Oscar Wilde had been sent to prison he suddenly roared out in a voice that stopped all other conversation: 'No, I know nothing about the joys of homosexuality. You must speak to my friend Oscar about that.' Then he added as an afterthought: 'And yet, if Shakespeare had asked me, I would have had to submit.' It was this kind of conversation stopper, in a voice that could be heard all over the Café Royal, that caused Oscar Wilde to say: 'Really, Frank, you will never learn how far too far you can go.'

On another occasion he was dining there with Wilde, Sir Max Beerbohm and Aubrey Beardsley. He told at great length a story first told by the author Anatole France. When he finished Beerbohm said: 'What a charming story, Frank. Anatole France would have spoiled that story.' When Harris went on to boast about his social successes Wilde made his famous remark: 'Yes, dear Frank, we believe you – you have dined in every house in London – *once*.'

He was, like several of the inner circle of Café Royalists, a good talker, although he often went on too long. Max Beerbohm said of him: 'He has a marvellous speaking voice, like the organ at Westminster Abbey, and with infallible footwork.'

When the waiters implored him to leave long after closing time he replied: 'Nonsense! It is I, Frank Harris, who am here! You can call them downstairs to telephone, if they like, to the Commissioner of Police at his private address and they will see it is all right. And you can bring us each a large whisky-and-soda when you come back!'

Some young women who wanted to establish their credentials as Bohemians saw losing their virginity as the indispensable first step. Enid Bagnold went through this rite with Frank Harris.

'Sex,' said Frank Harris, 'is the gateway to life.' So I went through the gateway in the upper room of the Café Royal ... As I sat at dinner with Aunt Clara and Uncle Lexy I couldn't believe that my skull wasn't chanting aloud: 'I'm not a virgin! I'm not a virgin!'

Harris's wild drinking and spending might not have overwhelmed his income from journalism, but rash speculations did. They included a luxury hotel at Monte Carlo. After Wilde had been outlawed Lord Alfred Douglas consulted Harris about a legacy of £2000 he had been left. Should he give the money to Wilde? Harris had a better idea. They should invest it in the casino at his hotel. This would bring in £2000 a year for life. Douglas handed over the money and never saw it again.

In 1914 Harris was jailed for contempt of court. He had suggested in the magazine *Modern Society* that Lord Fitzwilliam, one of two co-respondents in a divorce action, was a man of loose morals. He spent a month in prison.

Harris was now poor. Even before his incarceration he had been absent from the Café Royal for some months. He was spotted in the Ritz roaring at a waiter: 'I am Mr Frank Harris, I tell you, the best-known man in London, and I will sign the bill and pay for it when convenient ...' After he left prison he went bankrupt and left for Paris.

## The Great Beast

Perhaps the most exotic of the many weirdos to inhabit the Domino Room was Aleister Crowley, the self-styled Great Beast. He had a following of rich and neurotic women who were interested in his sexual fantasies. He said he planned to produce a monster baby after the ultimate orgasm. Perhaps to this end he sold aphrodisiac pills made from a mixture which included his own semen. He marketed them as the Elixir of Life. He also invented – and drank – a cocktail he called Kubla Khan No 2, containing gin, vermouth and laudanum. Using his specially sharpened teeth he drank blood from Nancy Cunard's neck, giving her blood poisoning.

Crowley, explorer, poet, black magician, organiser of drugs and sex orgies, who liked to be known as 'the wickedest man in Britain', became interested in the occult while an undergraduate at Cambridge. He was expelled from the Order of the Golden Dawn for 'extreme practices' and founded his own order, the Silver Star. When he was accused in print of sacrificing children in the course of his orgiastic rites, he protested mildly that the writer had overlooked the important detail that the children had always to be beautiful and of noble lineage.

He claimed he had a magic cloak which made him invisible. To prove this he would stalk into the Café , a mysterious tall figure in star-spangled conical hat and flowing cloak. 'What could have been more natural than that half-spoken sentences froze on lips, glasses stopped in mid-air and even the waiters stood thunderstruck?' (Deghy and Waterhouse).

Crowley would walk slowly on through the room and out into Glasshouse Street. He would not accept that anyone had been able to see him. 'Why didn't anyone speak to me, then?' he would ask.

He was accused of a wide variety of crimes, from drug-peddling and fraud to high treason and unspeakable cruelty to animals. Newspapers, particularly the *Sunday Express* and *John Bull*, screamed for his prosecution. But he would sit in the Café Royal, surrounded by his lady followers, calmly swilling tumblerfuls of brandy, in the regalia of a Scottish chieftain.

Crowley inherited a fortune, between £30,000 and £40,000, and set himself up with a flat in Chancery Lane intending to prove himself as a poet. The showman and the charlatan proved too strong for the creative urge. He called himself Count Vladimir Svareff, Le Comte de Fenix, Frater Perdurabo, the Earl of Middlesex and Prince Choia Khan. At other times he was Count de Zonaref, Sir Alastor de Kerval or just plain Alastair MacGregor. He assumed the title Laird of Boleskine after buying an estate in Scotland.

Crowley pursued women regardless of age or attractiveness. He founded a cult of Theleme which may have owed something to the Dashwood's Monks of Medmenham – his cult's motto, 'Do What You Will', was more or less the same. It attracted a stream of men and women mostly with the means to pay for his lavish lifestyle. He repaid his hostesses by defecating on their carpets.

He encouraged his disciples to take drugs as part of his rituals. Once they had become addicts their purses and bodies were his. One woman who denied him this, and brought him as near to disaster as he came, was Betty May.

Betty was known as Tiger Woman after a knife fight with a love rival in Paris. Back in London she became an artist's model – at one time she worked for Jacob Epstein – and had many affairs. She was lively: she would take off her skirt and weave it about in front of her as she sang 'The Raggle-Taggle Gypsies'. From time to time she would squat on all fours and lap her drink from a saucer. She recalled nights at the Café Royal before the First World War:

> The lights, the mirrors, the plush red seats, the eccentrically dressed people, the coffee served in glasses, the pale cloudy absinthes – I was ravished by all these and felt as if I had strayed by accident into some miraculous Arabian palace. ...

No duck ever took to water, no man to drink, as I did to the Café Royal. The colour and the glare, the gaeity and the chatter appealed to something fundamental in my nature.

Betty was a friend of another colourful Café Royalist, the promising young artist Nina Hamnett. Nina, an irrepressible character whose life story threaded through the history of London's Bohemia, wrote an autobiography, *Laughing Torso*. In it she mentioned Crowley. She felt so confident that her reference was inoffensive that she wrote to him before publication: 'I have written quite a lot about you, very nice and appreciative. No libel, no rubbish, simply showing up the *sale bourgeois* attitude to all our behaviour.' For the moment they remained friends, Crowley even going to an exhibition of Nina's paintings at Zwemmer's gallery.

In January 1933 Crowley saw a copy of his novel *Moonchild* on sale in a bookshop window in Praed Street with a notice falsely claiming that his first novel, *The Diary of a Drug Fiend*, had been withdrawn 'after an attack in the sensational press'. Crowley sued the bookseller for libel and won £50 damages, the judge ruling that the bookseller wanted the public to believe that *Moonchild* was indecent. Crowley looked about for someone else to sue. He chose Nina Hamnett, and claimed she had libelled him in *Laughing Torso*.

Betty May was a telling witness for the defence in the subsequent trial. She had met Crowley at the Café Royal about 20 years earlier. 'At the time he was exhibiting devil-worship in the Fulham Road, mostly to silly old ladies, at exorbitant admission fees' (Deghy and Waterhouse). War broke out and Crowley went to America. In London Betty May was still one of the stars of the Café Royal. In 1922 she met Raoul Loveday, an Oxford undergraduate. Although she was 12 years older than Raoul he became her third, or perhaps fourth, husband.

Raoul had an unhealthy interest in the occult, and after Crowley returned from America they met. The meeting lasted two days, and when Loveday returned to the flat in Beak Street, where Betty had been waiting, he had been taking drugs. He climbed the drain-pipe to their third-floor apartment. Betty was shocked by his ghostly white face at the window.

Betty had been an addict but had cured herself of drugs, if not of drink, and did all she could to keep Loveday away from Crowley. But eventually he decided to join the Great Beast at his Abbey of Thelema at Cefalu. On their way they met Nina Hamnett in Paris, where she was the companion of artists who included Modigliani. She wrote in *Laughing Torso*:

Betty had married recently her fourth husband, a most brilliant young man named Raoul Loveday, who was only twenty and had got a first in history at Oxford. He was very good-looking, but looked half-dead. She was delighted to meet me and we all sat in the Dome and drank. They were on their way to Cefalu as Crowley had offered him a job as his secretary. He was very much intrigued with Crowley's views on magic. He [Loveday] had been very ill the year before and had had a serious operation. I had heard that the climate at Cefalu was terrible; heat, mosquitoes and very bad food. The magical training I already knew was very arduous. I urged them not to go. I succeeded in keeping them in Paris two days longer than they intended, but they were determined to go and I was powerless to stop them. I told Raoul that if he went he would die, and really felt a horrible feeling of gloom when I said 'Goodbye' to them. After five months I had a postcard from Betty on which was written, 'My husband died last Friday; meet me at the Gare de Lyon.' I could not meet her as I got the postcard a day too late and she went straight through to London. He died of fever. There were no doctors at Cefalu and one had to be got from Palermo, but it was too late when he arrived.

So when Betty gave evidence in the Crowley lawsuit against Hamnett she was hardly neutral. She had found that the Cefalu abbey was in reality a one-storeyed farmhouse, 'built in defiance of modern sanitation and comfort'. Crowley had installed his 'First Concubine' who was also known as 'The Scarlet Woman' and 'The Whore of the Stars'. The Second Concubine, a former governess named Ninette Shumway, was known as Shummy. There were two or three children, who were allowed as much wine and brandy as they liked.

When Betty refused to go along with his mumbo-jumbo Crowley threatened to sacrifice her on the altar. She had seen him sacrifice a cat, and not wanting to suffer the same fate she stayed to support her husband, who had given himself up fully to magical contemplation and drug-taking. There were evening rituals in the temple when Crowley would dance and chant. On Fridays there was the Invocation to Pan. Crowley persuaded a woman to have sex with a goat, then cut its throat because it showed 'an insulting lack of enthusiasm' for the ritual. Loveday was, in a sense, enchanted.

## The man we'd like to hang

Towards the end of 1922, shortly after Crowley had forced him to drink the blood of a slaughtered cat, Loveday fell ill. When it became serious Crowley sent for a doctor. After Loveday died two Oxford undergraduates arrived to investigate the death. They concluded that there was nothing suspicious about it.

On Sunday, 25 February 1923 the *Sunday Express* printed an interview with Betty May about Cefalu. That day there was a copy on every table at the Café Royal. It was the first of a sensational series. *John Bull* called Crowley 'The Man We'd Like to Hang'.

Crowley had been hounded out of Italy, on Mussolini's orders. He sought but was refused a personal interview with the Duce. He went to France where his notoriety got him expelled. He returned to London and the Café Royal. One day he walked in, sat at a table and called for brandy. The diners, who had fallen silent and stared when he came in, slowly began their conversations again.

The Black Magic case was heard in April 1934 and was a sensation. In her amusing and artless memoir *Laughing Torso* Hamnett had written that 'Crowley had a temple in Cefalu in Sicily. He was supposed to practise Black Magic there, and one day a baby was said to have disappeared mysteriously. There was also a goat there. This all pointed to Black Magic, so people said, and the inhabitants of the village were frightened of him.'

Crowley's main objection was to the reference to black magic. His lawyer told the court that he practised only benign white magic. He portrayed his client as a seeker after truth who had taken part in pioneering climbing expeditions to K2 and Kanchenjunga in the Himalayas and had walked across China and the Sahara.

It was easy to make Crowley seem absurd. After three days one of the lawyers invited him to make himself invisible and so prove that he was not an imposter. He declined. The lawyer for Nina's publishers, Constable, read from some of Crowley's privately printed books. Crowley's flippant replies to the lawyer's suggestions that they were obscene didn't help his cause. When the lawyer read verses from *Clouds Without Water* and asked 'Isn't that filth?' Crowley replied: 'You read it as if it were magnificent poetry. I congratulate you.' It was put to him that he had put up with a long campaign of vilification in the Press without taking action. The judge, Mr Justice Swift, asked: 'When you read, "It is hard to say with certainty whether Crowley is a man or beast" did you take any action?'

Crowley replied: 'It was asked of Shelley whether he was a man or someone sent from Hell.' The judge: 'I am not trying Shelley. Did you take any steps to clear your character.' Crowley had to admit that he had not.

Betty May was called. In an attempt to discredit her Crowley produced some letters addressed to 'Bumbletoff'. Betty said it was one of her nicknames, and they were her letters. The judge ruled that Crowley had acquired the letters unlawfully.[2] Shortly afterwards the jury decided they had heard enough and stopped the case. They had listened as the bizarre goings-on at Cefalu were described. A toad had been baptised Jesus, accused of sedition and crucified. Betty May said she watched as Crowley slaughtered a cat, then forced her husband to drink its blood.

The judge summed up:

I have been over forty years engaged in the administration of the law in one capacity or another. I thought I knew of every conceivable form of wickedness. I thought that everything which was vicious or bad had been produced at one time or another before me. I have learnt in this case that we can always learn something more if we live long enough. I have never heard such dreadful and horrible, blasphemous and abominable stuff as that which has been produced by a man who describes himself to you as the greatest living poet.

Crowley lost, of course, and couldn't pay costs. He declared himself bankrupt. Virginia Nicholson (*Among the Bohemians*) says Betty May and Nina Hamnett became household names overnight.

Crowley was by now 59, and showing the effects of years of heroin abuse. The trial had been a major financial setback, but there was no shortage of well-heeled middle-aged women who were anxious to be the next Whore of the Stars. He still made money from 'rejuvenation courses'.

In 1937 Crowley celebrated his sixtieth birthday (he was actually some years older) at the Café Royal. A special guest was a woman of advanced years and interesting financial status who was, he thought, interested in buying a small pot of his Celebrated Magical Sex-Appeal Ointment. Crowley suggested that it was a bargain at £2000.

Crowley, the current Whore of the Stars and the two dozen or so guests met at a nearby tavern for a drink, then went across to the Café Royal. Crowley, a noted connoisseur, had ordered the food and wine with care. Montrachet was followed by Richebourg, then Veuve Cliquot and finally Napoleon brandy. The evening was a success in every detail except the sale of the pot of sex-appeal ointment. The special guest deftly avoided final commitment. The time came to pay the bill, and Crowley had to admit defeat.

The bill was presented to the Whore of the Stars. She wrote a cheque. The head waiter refused it, requesting cash. Finally the *maître d'hôtel* agreed to accept a cheque for the food, but not for the tip. The Whore of the Stars was not carrying any cash. As Crowley looked up and studied the ceiling the Whore made the round of the male guests, whispering in their ears. As unobtrusively as possible they reached for their wallets and handed her notes.

One of the guests, Charles Cammell, saw Crowley and the Whore at the Café Royal some weeks later, 'which proved the solidity of that lady's banking account – and perhaps explained Crowley's attachment'.

The Great Beast's farewell to the Café Royal came soon afterwards. He invited friends to another birthday party, again meticulously planned and prepared, and it was a pleasant evening. Crowley lingered over the brandy, then excused himself and left the room. He went to the cloakroom, got his hat and coat, and left. Shortly afterwards the manager told the guests that their host had left without paying the bill.

## Farewell to the Beast

When Crowley died in 1947 his request to be buried in Westminster Abbey was refused, and he was cremated at Brighton. Even this ceremony was deemed heretical, and the authorities there said they would never again allow such a 'pagan or blasphemous ceremony' (Pentelow and Rowe, *Characters of Fitzrovia*).

Nina Hamnett[3] told some good stories about Crowley in her memoirs which show him as both mystic and lecher:

He always went out at midday to say a prayer to the sun. One day I met him in the Boulevard Montparnasse. Suddenly he stopped in the middle of the street and addressed the sun. I did not know the prayer in question, so respectfully stood behind him until he had finished. In the Quarter was a very celebrated artist's model. She was very beautiful and everyone had enjoyed her favours except Crowley. Someone said to A.C., 'You really must take her out to supper and see what she is really like.'

The next morning everyone was at breakfast in the Dome, and Crowley appeared. They cried, 'Hullo, A.C., what was it like?' and he said rather grimly, 'It was rather like waving a flag in space.'

## Grilled mouse on toast

Betty May and Nina Hamnett became veterans of the hand-to-mouth existence associated with the Bohemian life of occasional carefree enjoyment and long periods of near-starvation. Any sudden arrival of funds meant a party. After they became well-known because of the trial Nina was often in the newspapers. One day a newspaper printed a photograph captioned 'Miss Nina Hamnett, artist and author ... takes a walk in the Park with a gentleman friend'. The woman in the picture was not Nina but Betty May. Nina, who was drinking in the Fitzroy Tavern when the Scottish poet Ruthven Todd showed her the paper, borrowed half a crown for a taxi and drove to Fleet Street, where she accused the newspaper of libel. The paper gave her £25 to forget about it. She rushed back to the Fitzroy Tavern and bought drinks for everybody. When Betty May arrived Nina bought her a double whisky and explained her sudden affluence. Betty dashed off to the newspaper and threatened them with a libel suit for the same reason. Perhaps because of her fearsome reputation as the Tiger Woman of Bohemia she too got £25, which she took back to the Tavern. They drank all evening.

But such windfalls were rare, and didn't last. Betty once cooked grilled mouse on toast, and at times Nina lived on boiled bones and porridge. Even real success could be ephemeral. Nina, who had exhibitions of her work and some good sales, was never able to apply herself for long enough to develop her art, and her talent began to slip away. The pictures became conventional and slipshod.

In her ghosted memoirs, *Tiger Woman,* published in 1929, Betty May said: 'My feeling about my life is in many ways one of great dissatisfaction.' She still had a long life to live – a friend discovered her in a council house in Kent in the 1970s – and from what little is known it had its share of hardships. There seem to have been at least two more marriages but in the end she had only her courage. Perhaps those who burn so bright should burn only briefly.

Nina Hamnett survived the decline of the Café Royal version of Bohemia. She moved on, and is a link to the later Bohemias, Fitzrovia in the Thirties and Forties and the Soho of the Fifties.

The Café Royal remained the centre of London's Bohemia for so long because of the writers and artists who gathered there. Round those great suns gathered a nimbus of lesser talents and pretty girls. The great men died off and the Café changed beyond recognition. The Domino Room was demolished in 1928 and replaced by the smaller Grill Room. Poverty-stricken men and women were no longer allowed to linger most of the day over a cup of coffee. Artists' models could no longer sit at a table and hope some man, known to them or not, would invite them to have a meal. The Grill Room now attracted a set who were more socially successful than Bohemian: J.B. Priestley and Sir Compton Mackenzie, the musicians Harriet Cohen and Sir Arnold Bax, the architect Sir Edwin Lutyens, were leaders in their fields but hardly rebels, at least not any longer. Perhaps the fact that so many had titles tells us something. The Café would never again see a spectacle like Marie Lloyd chasing the head waiter with a pair of hat-pins because she thought she had been charged too much for brandy; a knight striding into the room in a full suit of armour; or Ronald Firbank spreading caviar on his nose instead of his blinis after drinking too much champagne. George Belcher was belaboured with a lobster by a lady friend. A young model ran in, wearing a white overall and screaming: 'I've got leprosy! I've got leprosy!'

# Defending the Realm

Drinkers like Frank Harris and Aleister Crowley did not let tiresome licensing laws restrict their late-night imbibing, but most people had to obey the laws, and they were irksome. In March 1915 Lloyd George had declared: 'We are fighting Germany, Austria and Drink, and as far as I can see, the greatest of these deadly foes is Drink.' He persuaded the King to give up drink, or so he thought, as an example. From then on the King would give his guests a list of soft drinks. Lord Roseberry chose ginger ale and had a severe attack of hiccups. Queen Mary escaped the rigours of this regime by having her jug of fruit cup discreetly laced with champagne, and the King would retire alone to his study once the meal was over 'to attend to a small matter of busines'. 'The matter in question was tacitly assumed to be a small glass of port' (Duke of Windsor, *Family Album*).

The King's gesture had no effect on the habits of the common people, and in June 1915 a Central Control Board was set up to crack down on drinking in areas where it was felt to be impeding the war effort, particularly in munitions manufacture. These measures, introduced under the Defence of the Realm Act, known as Dora, were widely resented, and had far-reaching consequences well into the years of peace. Before the war pubs were open most of the day – in London from five in the morning until half an hour past midnight. Under Dora they didn't open until noon and closed again at half past two until the evening. Customers were forbidden to buy drinks for others. An agricultural worker in East Anglia recalled: 'You couldn't go into a public house, two of you, and say, "Give us two pints of beer and I'll pay for them." That was against the law.' Even more irksome was rationing of alcohol. 'Some of them boys [soldiers home on leave] ... would go into a pub. There was a notice up: Regular Customers

Only, and only one pint! Yes, there were terrible rows down there. Chaps smashed the windows because the landlord wouldn't serve them. ... Before the war some of the pubs would be open all night nearly. Open at six in the morning. I've been down there at 6.30 in the morning and seven or eight of 'em have been drunk as lords. There was more beer spilled on the floor then than is drunk now' (Evans, *The Days That We Have Seen*).

The Dora restrictions on drinking hours continued, with some slight alleviations, after the war. Revellers had to order sandwiches after 11am and in theory could not drink after 12.30pm. To men and women who wanted to forget the privations and horrors of the war years these restrictions were made worse by homilies from physicians and the Church. The young were drinking too much. The *Practitioner* declared that drink robbed them of the 'power of manly self-control'. Cocktail drinking was 'the most reprehensible form of alcoholic abuse'. No wonder men and women went to nightclubs which flouted the laws.

Nightclubs flourished. Some were respectable – 'the Night Light had two princesses and four peers on its committee' (Graves and Hodge, *The Long Weekend*) – while others were squalid.

## Stalking Augustus John

Before the war there was Madame Strindberg's strikingly modernistic subterranean Cave of the Golden Calf in Heddon Street, off Regent Street. Madame Strindberg was the recently widowed wife of the Swedish dramatist August Strindberg. For years she had stalked the artist Augustus John, who dubbed her The Walking Hell-Bitch of the Western World. She faked suicide attempts and hired detectives in her attempts to lure him away from his wife Dorelia. If opening the club was another attempt to win him it failed – he refused to have anything to do with it. In his autobiography *Chiaroscuro* he wrote: 'My attendance was counted upon, but I never entered the place. One look at the seething mob outside its doors, on the opening night, was enough for me. I passed on. Another miscalculation!'

John's conventional, flashy art already belonged to the past, and in snubbing the Cave he was unconsciously turning his back on the future. The club represented the new art: Jacob Epstein and Wyndham Lewis were among those who contributed to the decor, and Eric Gill sculpted an emblematic golden calf. Spencer Gore was in charge of the decorative scheme, and he brought in Charles Ginner.

The performers were not of the same quality. They included Betty May, who danced and sang her theme song 'The Raggle-Taggle Gypsies'. Osbert Sitwell recalled the Cave:

This low-ceilinged night-club, appropriately sunk below the pavement ... and hideously but relevantly frescoed ... appeared in the small hours to be a super-heated Vorticist garden of gesticulating figures, dancing and talking, while the rhythm of the primitive forms of ragtime throbbed through the wide room.

Apart from a gypsy orchestra and the Coppersmiths band playing their 'strident tintinabulation' there were readings of Russians stories 'in a very melodramatic fashion' by Frank Harris, shadow-plays written and performed by Ford Madox Ford, and in November 1913 the Italian Emilio Marinetti recited one of his Futurist broadsides with great élan. Nina Hamnett was an enthusiastic customer. However, although the food and wine were excellent and it was popular the club was not a financial success. Madame Strindberg may have been one of the first proprietors to practise a kind of crude socialism in which the wealthier revellers unwittingly paid the bills of the poorer, but she got heavily into debt, and when the Cave was raided by police for charging non-members for food and drink it never recovered. There was a liquidation sale in 1914. The Hell-Bitch sailed for New York, writing to Augustus John that 'dreams are sweeter than reality. We shall never meet again now ...'

Augustus John himself founded the Crab Tree club in 1914 in Greek Street. His partners included the painter William Orpen and Lord Howard de Walden. The club deliberately avoided the high-style finish of the Cave. John hoped it would be 'amusing and useful at times'. There were tables and chairs and little else. No waiters, and sometimes nobody to take money. Anyone wearing evening dress was fined a shilling, which helped pay for the absinthe and cigarettes. It was not universally popular, and Paul Nash described it as 'A most disgusting place ... only the most pinched harlots attend. A place of utter coarseness and dull unrelieved monotony. John alone, a great pathetic muzzy god, a sort of Silenus – but alas no nymphs, satyrs and leopards to compete the picture.' He was right about the harlots. John said he got crabs at the Crab Tree.

## The Bright Young Things

After the Armistice the rise of the Bright Young Things spurred demand for venues suitable to their need for change and excitement, free of constraint. The wealthy socialite David Tennant opened the Gargoyle Club in Meard Street, Soho, in 1925. It quickly became the place for the fast set and was perhaps the best-known of all Bohemian nightspots. According to Daphne Fielding, it 'transformed conventional people into Bohemians. ... It was easy to imagine David Tennant's first wife, [the actress] Hermione Baddeley, kicking her well-turned legs in a *can-can à la Goulue*, for in its infancy the Gargoyle had a Toulouse-Lautrec atmosphere' (Fielding, *The Duchess of Jermyn Street*). Tennant wanted it to be '"an avant-garde" place open during the day where still-struggling writers, painters, poets and musicians will be offered the best food and wine at prices they can afford. Above all it will be a place without the usual rules, where people can express themselves freely.' The painter Edward Burra did not find it altogether cheap. He called it 'a little bit more expensive than our dear old Maison [Lyons] but still when you are surrounded by lovely Matisses whose price runs into 4 figgers and get a squint of *Vogue* without paying it's not so expensive.' It appealed to a younger generation than the Café Royal set, although the two sometimes mingled. It was also unashamedly upper-crust. One evening two princes, three princesses and the King of Romania were all there. The Prince of Wales, later briefly King Edward VIII, often went. Although evening wear was obligatory and the cutlery was solid silver, Tennant surprisingly asked Augustus John to be president. Even more surprisingly, John agreed. Members came from haut and low Bohemia – the Tennants and Mitfords, Stracheys, Patridges, Bells and Sitwells, Dylan and Caitlin Thomas, Cyril Connolly, and Michael Arlen.

At the Gargoyle you were also likely to meet a set who were more Bright Young Things than Bohemian. Besides the Stracheys and the Mitfords, they included their friend Evelyn Waugh, Brian Howard, Nancy Cunard, and Cecil Beaton. When Waugh was courting the woman who became his first wife, Evelyn Gardner, they would sometimes dine at the Gargoyle. She described how one evening 'an awful old woman in the party insisted on leaning her head on Evelyn's [Waugh's] shoulder and holding his hand. Poor Evelyn simply didn't know what to do about it.'

Other clubs were the Ham Bone, the Harlequin, the Studio, the Bullfrog, the Cave of Harmony and the Nest. The Cave of Harmony was opened in 1924 by the cabaret performer Elsa Lanchester in Gower Street. There was no alcohol but there was music and 'one could foxtrot, enjoy the fruity re-wordings of Victorian love ballads performed by Elsa and the actor Harold Scott, and hobnob with painters and writers until 2am'.

## Queen of the Nightclubs

Mrs Kate Meyrick, an Irishwoman with upper-class links, was described as queen of the nightclubs in Twenties London. She was born in County Clare and was the first woman in Ireland to ride a bicycle. When her doctor husband left her at the end of the First World War with eight children to support, including two sons at Harrow and four daughters at Roedean, she became manager of her first club. Dalton's in Leicester Square was a known pick-up point for prostitutes, and was frequently raided by the police. She moved on and although already in her forties was to open many other clubs.

The celebrity detective Fabian of the Yard described Mrs Meyrick as a neat, stern little woman 'who might easily have run a first-class seminary for well-brought-up young ladies'. She soon found herself among the riff-raff of the underworld. 'An evening-dress constituted no guarantee at all of its wearer's credentials,' she noted. 'A party of apparently quite decent men might easily – only too often did – turn out to be one of the numerous gangs of bullies and racecourse terrorists who held sway.' Mrs Meyrick is referring to the Sabini gang and their rivals, surprisingly large and brutal criminal organisations who terrorised bookmakers into paying protection money at racecourses. In nightclubs they expected free drinks and sometimes staged shoot-outs. One night after a customer in one of her clubs called some of the gangsters 'cads', one of them pulled a gun and shot the place up. When Kate finally refused to serve them one of them knocked her out. The following day another gangster came to apologise. He explained that the man who attacked her was an outsider, and he had been given a beating he would never forget. As the Sabinis were experts in unsubtle violence this was plausible.

Kate found the police far more troublesome than the gangsters. In 1921 she opened the famous 43 club at 43 Gerard Street in Soho. It appealed to a Bohemian mix – Augustus John, Jacob Epstein – and writers, including

Joseph Conrad and J.B. Priestley. The Lancashire millionaire Jimmy White turned up one night with six Daimlers full of showgirls. He spent £400 on a champagne party. The notorious drug dealer 'Brilliant' Chang was a member. Chang's escapades caused a moral panic after the war. Two young women he knew were found dead from cocaine overdoses. Mrs Meyrick claimed she tried to stop him and his gang peddling in her club, but she remained friendly with him. He was later deported.

The 43 was first raided by police in 1923. Mrs Meyrick was fined £300, but allowed to pay in instalments. In 1924 she had her first spell in prison, six months in Holloway, where she was popular with the other women prisoners. There was also much sympathy for her among distinguished clients, who included the Crown Prince of Sweden, Prince Nicholas of Rumania, Talulah Bankhead, Jack Buchanan and Michael Arlen.

Mrs Meyrick ran several clubs at a time, so that if one was raided and closed down the others carried on, even when she was in prison, as she frequently was. In 1925 she opened the Manhattan. Among her customers were the remarkable jockey Gordon Richards, 'Red Hot Mammy' Sophie Tucker, the American singer, and Rudolph Valentino. The American band leader Paul Whiteman played there occasionally. Finally in 1927 she opened her grandest club yet, the Silver Slipper in Regent Street. The dance floor was made of glass, the walls painted with exotic Italian scenes. There were more raids and fines, but while she was away her expensively educated daughters kept the clubs going. A year later she was sucked into the Goddard case. He was a crooked police sergeant who had been taking bribes from club owners. He got away with it, but Mrs Meyrick got 15 months' hard labour. After finishing the sentence she returned to the West End and opened more clubs, but more prison sentences persuaded her to quit. Her health had been broken by prison, and she lost her fortune in the Wall Street Crash. She died a year later and dance bands in the West End fell silent for two minutes as a tribute.

In her memoirs, *Secrets of the 43 Club*, which she wrote in her last months, Meyrick showed the resilience and defiance which won her many friends: 'What does the future hold in store? It may hold disappointment, perhaps. But one thing I know it can never take away from me, and that is the love of Life, *real* Life, brilliant and pulsating.'

Three of her daughters married into the aristocracy by way of the 43 Club: May married Lord Kinnoull, Dorothy Lord de Clifford and Gwendoline the Earl of Craven.

## Rosa's love nest

Another nightclub owner who was hounded by the police was the manager of Chez Victor. In 1929 the *Sunday Express* reported that Victor had moved to Paris to open a new club, and that he had written to Jix, otherwise the ineffable Sir William Joynson-Hicks, Home Secretary, who had deported him, inviting him to drop in at the club when he was in Paris. Jix replied on official notepaper that he would be pleased to. The crackdown on London clubs continued, however, and Lord Byng, the Commissioner of Police, later boasted that London night life was dead.

He was wrong. Clubland changed but survived. Some of the stuffier men's clubs had to change their rules to move with the times. Cocktail bars were introduced in White's and the St James's. Married men were allowed to join the Bachelors' on payment of a small fine, and the Travellers', which originally stipulated that members should have travelled at least a thousand miles in a straight line from London, came to accept many who had never been further than Paris (Graves and Hodge).

There were drinking holes for the well-heeled all over London where the licensing laws did not apply. One was the Cavendish Hotel on the corner of Jermyn and Duke streets. It was run by the remarkable Rosa Lewis, a friend of the Prince of Wales. Lewis is probably best remembered today as the model for Lottie Crump, proprietress of Shepheard's Hotel in Evelyn Waugh's novel *Vile Bodies*. This former skivvy ran the Cavendish from 1902 until after the Second World War, and for much of the time it doubled as a comfortable if eccentric love-nest for members of the aristocracy. There were rumours that Rosa was one of the Prince's many lovers, and that he used the Cavendish for secret trysts, but there is no evidence.

Rosa Lewis was born in Leyton in 1867 and began in domestic service when she was 12. She became a celebrity cook, travelling round great houses and preparing multi-course meals for large numbers of guests at house parties. At different times she cooked for Bertie and the Kaiser. Her services weren't cheap and she became rich.

When she took over the Cavendish there were suggestions that a cabal of aristocrats including Bertie had persuaded her so they would have somewhere to conduct their amours, but although Bertie had a suite there he probably didn't use it much. 'Her rich clients regarded the Cavendish as a naughty nursery where they sowed their spurious wild oats and tippled their champagne, managed all the while by Rosa, their amoral nanny' (Masters, *Rosa Lewis*).

The Cavendish had no bars. Guests would drink in their own rooms, and favoured guests would make their way to Rosa's own parlour where some heavy drinking went on. Those who drank most did not necessarily pay. In her increasingly eccentric way Rosa would charge those she thought best able to pay. Waugh's *Vile Bodies* describes the system.[1]

When Bertie died Rosa, greatly distressed, served champagne and her guests raised their glasses to a portrait of the King. Then she led them down to a special wine cellar where she kept a selection of great vintages reserved for the King's table at country-house parties. There was Veuve Clicquot 1904, Château Pontet-Canet 1895 and Schloss Johannisberg Cabinet 1893, 80-year-old brandies, and vintage ports. Afterwards Rosa locked the door of the cellar and refused to allow it to be opened again during her lifetime, a curious shrine to her beloved Bertie.

## Fitzrovia is born

The Café Royal eventually began to attract too many self-consciously successful artists and writers. The more restless spirits sought a new centre for louche London Bohemia, and one night in 1926 Nina Hamnett and Augustus John, with the critic Tommy Earp, discovered the Fitzroy Tavern. This was a pub on the corner of Windmill Street and Charlotte Street in an area north of Oxford Street which became known as Fitzrovia[2]. The name is generally thought to have been invented by the journalist and politician Tom Driberg, a man as unconventional as the district. Nina had been searching 'for something different', 'a public house with a large saloon bar attached to which was an amiable proprietor' (Hamnett, *Laughing Torso*). The Tavern had sawdust on the floor, First World War posters on the walls, a lively clientele and the perfect proprietors, Pop Kleinfeld and his successor, his son-in-law Charlie Allchild[3]. The Fitzroy was almost too successful as a bolt-hole for artists tired of being gawped at by the slumming middle classes. It was noisy and full of prostitutes and sailors, and when word got out that the Bohemians had moved on there cultural tourists began to appear. The high-society drop-out Nancy Cunard dropped in from time to time. The cabaret singer Elizabeth Welch was taken there by the composers William Walton and Constant Lambert one evening in 1933. 'I was very excited because of course I'd heard so much about it. It was also, I think, my first pub. We used to drop in every so often. Augustus John was always there, I remember – and always singing' (David, *The Fitzrovians*).

Dylan Thomas met Nina Hamnett there and afterwards libelled her in a newspaper. Under the headline 'Genius and Madness Akin in World of Art' he referred to her as 'author of the banned book *Laughing Torso*'. The paper had to apologise.

The Eiffel Tower restaurant in Percy Street was another favourite. It was discovered by Augustus John and Nancy Cunard, and was very expensive. They could afford it, but few of their Bohemian friends could. Never mind, if Augustus turned up he would usually pay. One day he was startled to be charged £43 for lunch for two. The proprietor, Rudolf Stulik, a Viennese, explained: 'Is not for lunch only. Little Welshman with curly hair, he come here. He stay two weeks and eat. He says you pay.' The Welshman was Dylan Thomas.

The Eiffel became a venue for haut Bohemia. Nancy Cunard was so taken with it she wrote:

> I think the Tower shall go up to heaven
> One night in a flame of fire, about eleven.
> I always saw our carnal-spiritual home
> Blazing upon the sky symbolically…
> If ever we go to heaven in a troop
> The Tower must be our ladder,
> Vertically

Nancy was one of a group of upper-class women, some of them fellow students at the Slade, who were prototypes for the Bright Young Things of the Twenties. With the dazzling Lady Diana Manners and Iris Tree she signalled her open rebellion from respectable Society by wearing lavish make-up and exotic clothes. They wore trousers, smoked and drank in public and went about unchaperoned. These were unheard-of liberties at the time. Michael Arlen portrayed Nancy as Virginia in his novel *Piracy*, not only dining alone at the Eiffel Tower in 1916 but walking home alone through the darkened streets of Soho in the early hours:

Swiftly she would penetrate the black solitudes of Soho in wartime: a rich and fragile figure braving all the dangers of the city by night, an almost fearful figure to arise suddenly in the honest man's homeward path: so tall and golden and proud of carriage, so marvellously indifferent to his astonished stare! Sometimes she would have to walk a long way before she could find a taxi – through Soho to Shaftesbury Avenue, and up that to Piccadilly Circus. Sometimes men would murmur in passing, sometimes they would say the coarsest things, and once or twice a man caught at her arm as she swiftly passed him; and Virginia looked at him straightly, for a swift second, as though secretly understanding his desire and mocking it; and then she went on her way as though her way had been uninterrupted … homewards to Belgrave Square.

The three women kept a chaotic studio where they could entertain and be themselves away from their disapproving parents. Nancy was eventually disinherited by her wealthy family – her great grandfather founded the shipping line – because of her affair with the black jazz pianist Henry Crowder. When she heard that Nancy was staying with Crowder at the Eiffel Nancy's mother told Stulik that if he did not throw them out she would see that he 'got the works'. She had been deeply embarrassed when Lady Asquith had asked her over lunch: 'How is Nancy? … what is it now, drink, drugs or niggers?' All three were important in Nancy's life.[4]

Nancy called Stulik 'dear, sophisticated, generous, drunken Rudolf Stulik'. He allowed favoured customers to use his restaurant like a club. They would turn up after closing time and drink into the small hours in flagrant breach of the licensing laws. One night Nina, who was drunk, was persuaded to leave three times by a side door, only to return by the main entrance. Finally a waiter was ordered to take her home.

Stulik would join his guests, sitting at their table and treating them to drinks. But the time would come when he was weary and he would try to get them to go home. The writer and publisher Robert McAlmon wrote:

Every night Rudolf went through his category of invitations, asking us to leave so that he could go to bed. It was, 'Ladies und chentlemen, ve close.' After that he would become fraternal and plead with us as a brother. 'Brudders and sisters, go to ped. I vant to sleep.' He would finally let his head fall on his chest and snooze. After another bottle of champagne had been drunk by the rest of us, Rudolf would wake with a start. 'De sooner you go the bedder I ligk you. Ged oud, blease,' he would declare decisively.

Stulik had a system of charges which soaked the rich and helped the poor, rather in the way of Rosa Lewis at her Cavendish Hotel in Jermyn Street and Madame Strindberg at the Cave. The painter Tristram Hillier described it:

> Stulik maintained a ratio of charges based on what he estimated to be the wealth of his clients. For the fashionable, who liked to gather at night in what they imagined to be a Bohemian atmosphere, his prices were astronomical, but for the likes of myself, once accepted as a friend of the house, there was always a good *plat du jour* of some kind at a modest price, and generally people of interest to talk to or famous ones to watch with respectful awe.

Stulik was too generous. Although from time to time Augustus John bailed him out he gradually sank into bankruptcy. The decline was sad. When the writer John Davenport ordered an omelette he had to give Stulik the money to send out for the eggs. Stulik took to drink, mostly at the Wheatsheaf round the corner and mostly with his dog Chocolate. 'As the evening wore on he and Chocolate became steadily more confused' (Nicholson, *Among the Bohemians*).

The writer Peter Quennell (*The Wanton Chase*) recalled the last days of the Eiffel, with Stulik waiting for customers who never came, pacing back and forth, muttering about debtors and creditors, with his dog slowly pacing back and forth in the opposite direction.

Stulik sold the Eiffel in 1938. Friends contributed to a fund to set him up as proprietor of a small café but he died before it came to anything. Unlike many other proprietors he had successfully ignored the licensing laws, but for Bohemians and drinkers in general they were an important and sad fact of life.

There were clubs to suit every taste. The Gateways Club was a lesbian drinking den made notorious by the film *The Killing of Sister George*, which was partly filmed there in 1968. The club, in Bramerton Street just off the King's Road in Chelsea, was run by Gina Ware and her husband Ted. They married when the beautiful Gina was 31 and Ted 56. Later a trouser-wearing woman known simply as Smithy became part of the Wares' household, and worked as a barmaid in the club. Before the Wares turned the club into a women-only venue it had attracted bookies and tarts, and gangsters such as Jack Spot. *The Killing of Sister George*, which depicted sex between women at a time such things were not mentioned in polite circles, brought the club unwanted publicity. In 1971 it was picketed by members of the Gay Liberation Front, who chanted 'Out of the closets, into the streets'. They objected to the covert lesbianism of which the club was a bastion. Nevertheless the Gateways, which opened in 1944, didn't close until 1985.

## Bottle parties

The private 'bottle party' was invented in the Twenties to beat the police crack-down on late-night drinking. Revellers and those who exploited them discovered that the law could not interfere with private parties. This included the provision of food, drink, music and other entertainment. The organiser pretended to be the 'host', his customers the 'guests'. The liquor had to be ordered in ordinary licensing hours by the 'host'. The first bottle parties were decorous affairs. There were no gatecrashers, as admission was by printed invitation only. The premises were usually luxurious, the waiters polite and the dance-bands first-class. They were all-night affairs, seldom opening before midnight and usually closing about seven in the morning, when early risers on their way to the office would see top-hatted and dinner-jacketed men and women in evening dresses being helped into taxis. Soon, as readers of the early novels of Evelyn Waugh will know, the bottle party became just another clip joint, often in squalid premises with semi-nude cabarets.

The host charged his guests up to 55 shillings for bad champagne and 25 shillings for whisky. Two rashers of bacon and an egg cost five shillings. Gerald Kersh's forgotten but marvellously evocative novel *Night and the City* is a guidebook to running such an enterprise.

Young gents out on the town might resent the outrageous prices but most of the clients could afford them. They were generally what Graves and Hodge call 'businessmen who preferred bank-rolls to cheque books'.

Bookmakers, pools promoters, Soho vice-kings, gangsters, provincial industrialists 'making whoopee away from their families'. They found that the faded beauties who came to sit with them immediately they arrived had to be plied with expensive fake drinks. The girls were under orders to move on to another customer as soon as the first man ran out of money. The vice-kings, who had probably provided the girls, and the gangsters, who probably had a stake in the 'party', were happy to pay.

The old spirit of puritanism hadn't quite died. Sir Herbert Neild complained at a meeting of the Lord's Day Observance Society in 1921: 'We have gone recreation mad.' Temperance societies protested against allowing wireless sets in public houses, lest pubs become even more popular. In Nottingham several publicans were refused licences for the sets. In the capital the Bishop of London said he would rather die on the doorstep of the House of Lords than allow the closing hour in pubs to be extended to 11pm throughout the city. He was not called upon to make the ultimate sacrifice – the Bill was defeated. People were protesting – about jazz, about sex, about fashions, about the young. About drinking. And particularly about the combination of all five.

The Dora regulations, gradually ameliorated, were in effect the last triumph of the temperance movement. One of its greatest achievements was to stigmatise public drunkenness. No longer did women and children wait outside public houses for their husbands and fathers to be thrown out. Consumption of alcohol was cut from 89 million gallons in 1914 to 37 million in 1918 – admittedly war years. Opening hours, 16 or more pre-war, were cut to eight or nine. Deaths from alcoholism fell by five-sixths.

# The Underworld
# Cashes In

The public's response to the petty restrictions of the First World War
was muted. The reaction to the Second World War was more complex
and spirited, largely due to the highly organised London underworld
and the rise of the spiv. The black market, the blackout, bomb-damaged
but well-stocked shops all presented the underworld with a unique
opportunity. A young criminal named Billy Hill, who would later in his
ghosted autobiography style himself Boss of Britain's Underworld, had
the brains and organising ability to exploit it. He and his London gang
acquired an 18th-century manor house in the village of Bovington in
Hertfordshire, which he stocked with the vast quantities of scarce goods
his men stole from warehouses, lorries and railway sidings. He kept a
large stock of those most precious commodities in London's clubland,
genuine gin and whisky.

Our Bovington run-in was packed tight with bent gear, and I now
had a relay of my own cars bringing it up to London as the demand
needed it. All I had to do was take a stroll around the West End and
I was literally besieged by people wanting to buy almost anything
from a pair of nylon stockings to a fresh salmon or a shoulder of
good smoked bacon. There were many times when that barn was
filled chock-a-block with nicked gear – sheets, towels, furniture,
shoes, textiles, rolls of silk, tea, even rare spices, which fetched a

fortune from the Soho Café proprietors who need that sort of thing (Hill, *Boss of Britain's Underworld*).

One of his best lines was whisky. Drink was scarce, particularly spirits. Even scarcer was the genuine article, most clubs selling almost lethal hooch. Hill made another fortune out of whisky.

> Most of the trivial villains were making bombs out of manufacturing their own brands, and sticking the vile rubbish in proprietory brand bottles. I liked to think that if I was crooked, at least I was bent in an honest way. I sold only real whisky. Good stuff at that. I sold each barrel of whisky for £500 a time.

Gradually Hill's gang of robbers supplanted the Whites, the racecourse gangsters and protection racketeers who dominated London crime. It was a happy time in the underworld:

> Money? It was coming to us like pieces of dirty paper. I rarely went out with less than a monkey [£500] or a grand in my pocket. That was spending stuff. Emergency funds in case I got nicked, or in case the bite was put on me [asked for a loan]. That was apart from the remainder of a steady fortune I was piling up … I was making about £300 to £400 a week from all my work … I had my boys working their way finding out where whisky was stored. Then we went in and nicked it by the barrel.

By the end of the war the West End was like the Wild West. Hill said Mayfair and Soho were 'teeming with prosperity. Servicemen of all nations were being demobilised in thousands. … They were loaded with dough. Gratuity money, most of it. They flung it about the West End like ticker tape on Broadway. Afternoon drinking clubs were making fortunes.'

Much of Hill's genuine whisky went to clubs, which were desperate for supplies. There was never enough of the real thing to go round, and it was expensive. During the war the clubs met demand by selling hooch.

In the West End of London bottle parties were still the main way to get an evening's drinking. 'Customers at a Berkeley Square night club or a shabby basement in Soho could drink after hours by signing order forms which were sent to all-night wine retailers. Drink was bought in the customer's name and in theory never belonged to the club' (Graves and Hodges). At the beginning of the war there were between 200 and 300 of these parties every night in the West End. Because their purpose was to fleece their customers, many of whom were now servicemen and women, the authorities took a dim view, but decided there was nothing they could do.

However, police did raid the parties. Usually by the time they arrived drinks had been removed from tables and roulette wheels had vanished. It happened too often to be a coincidence. Sir Philip Game, Commissioner of the Metropolitan Police, asked for an explanation. He was told that Vine Street police station, from which the raiding parties set out, was under surveillance by spies paid by the club proprietors. When a raiding party left the station these spies phoned the clubs. If a club was prosecuted the spies went to court in order to be able to recognise next time the officers who gave evidence. Clearly there was a great deal at stake.

In January 1940 the police set up a new 'bottle party squad'. In May 1940 the owner of the Mother Hubbard Club in Ham Yard was sent to prison for 21 days for serving drinks out of licensing hours. The El Morocco Restaurant Bottle Party in Albemarle Street was raided. Two peers were among the 60 guests whose names were taken. Max Fredericks, organiser of the New Harlem Bottle Party in Old Compton Street, Soho, was fined £150.

In April 1940, with new drinking clubs opening all over the country the authorities finally conceded that people should be allowed to enjoy themselves. The Piccadilly Corner House was given a licence to sell drink until 2am. Other restaurants including the Criterion were later added to the list, and police agreed to draw up a list of approved bottle parties.

## Killer hooch

By January 1942 the problem of the poisonous hooch supplied by Billy Hill's rivals was acute. The Air Ministry warned RAF pilots about what they called the 'hooch racket'. Some of it was so toxic it could cause blindness, madness and death. The threat to RAF personnel was the most obvious and pressing. Within hours of returning from a mission they might be in London, drinking in a nightclub, and due to set out on another mission the next day.

The Home Secretary, Herbert Morrison, had some of the seized hooch analysed. It was found to be more toxic than that sold in America during Prohibition. Much of it was based on industrial alcohol and methylated spirits.

Customs officers uncovered what they termed 'a spider's web' of hooch manufacture and distribution at the Granville Club in Albemarle Street. Using drums of industrial spirit, the six men and two women involved mixed it with boiled water and burnt sugar as colouring. They filled genuine but empty bottles of known brands, paying as much as the equivalent of £5 each for such bottles. Seven gallons of this firewater was sold to unwitting members of the club. Other supplies were sold to bars, bottle parties and nightclubs. The proprietors would be given a bottle of genuine spirits to try, then the rest of their order would be filled by hooch.

As deaths and injuries caused by poisonous alcohol mounted there was widespread public concern. A seaman found in a stupor in a canteen at Waterloo Station dived through a high window to his death in March 1942. He had fought with the canteen manageress and the Navy police after being roused with difficulty. The manageress said there had been several non-fatal incidents, 'and we are attributing them to a kind of doped drink the men get hold of'.

In May 1942 eleven men and three women were killed by hooch in Glasgow. There had been other deaths from hooch in Liverpool, and seven other victims were still being treated in hospital. In another incident in Liverpool two seamen passed out after a single drink. One of them died. Four company directors were paralysed after a small whisky and soda at a London hotel. It took them ten days to recover. This was far more serious than the working classes drinking themselves to death. In the House of Lords, a peer demanded that hooch peddlars should be shot.

When a Canadian airman went berserk in a hotel it took six guards to hold him down. Doctors said he had brain damage and would be a cripple for life. A man who stole methyl alcohol from the oil wharf where he worked added it to his home-made elderberry wine and gave some to two seamen. Both died.

The police had some successes. They traced stills and closed clubs which sold the product. Two men who tried to sell hooch to Forest Hill club were jailed for six months and fined £250 each, the equivalent of £10,000 today. In May 1944 a Dagenham man who was making fake whisky from industrial spirit was ordered to pay £641. He claimed he had nothing to do with the hooch but had 'most idiotically' allowed another man to take over his house and operate the still. 'I have been left to carry the can back,' he said. He was convicted of defrauding the Revenue. It is not known why he was not charged with attempting to poison his victims, which would presumably have carried a much harsher penalty.

As the Metropolitan Police began to have a measure of success against hooch stills in London more and more were established in provincial cities and around military bases. American troops going on leave were given a free bottle of gin or whisky to lessen the temptation to drink bad liquor.

# Modern Times

Bohemias arise like islands in the calm sea of normal social drinking. Some sink and are lost to history, like Atlantis. Others survive and are in time encrusted with accumulations of myth and legend, like coral. By the late Thirties the Café Royal was losing its status as the main attraction for poor rebellious artists. The legends remained but the Bohemians moved on.

For some time the poorest artists had been using pubs. These had been regarded by the often middle-class artists as the domain of the working class, but the Depression changed all that, as Constantine Fitzgibbon points out in his biography of Dylan Thomas. Nina Hamnett discovered the pubs of Fitzrovia, at the time an unfashionable area north of Oxford Street. The editor Tambimuttu warned Julian Maclaren-Ross: 'Only beware of Fitzrovia. It's a dangerous place, you must be careful.'

'Fights with knives?'

'No, a worse danger. You might get Sohoitis you know.'

'No I don't. What is it?'

'If you get Sohoitis,' Tambi said very seriously, 'you will stay there always day and night and get no work done ever. You have been warned.'

J. Meary Tambimuttu, an Indian from Ceylon, was the editor of the magazine *Poetry (London)*. He brought a degree of eccentricity to this task rare even in the world of small and uneconomic literary magazines. Although his publishers Nicholson and Watson provided him with an office, he preferred to ply his craft in pubs. Poems and other manuscripts bulged from his pockets or fell out and were lost. Another editor told how he was summoned to Tambi's flat to read a 'first-rate' new poem by Dylan Thomas. By the time he arrived the manuscript had disappeared. It was eventually found floating in a chamber pot under Tambi's bed (David, *The Fitzrovians*).

Tambi approached Maclaren-Ross, a stranger, one evening in a pub and asked him if he had a book to sell.

'I'm not a bookseller,' I said.
Tambi said: 'No no, I mean a book you have written yourself. I am empowered by my principals to offer a one-hundred pounds advance.'
'Sorry,' I said.
Tambi said: 'One hundred and fifty.'
'Not possible,' I said.
He said: 'Two hundred. That is the top.'
I said: 'We're not in the bazaar.'
Tambi's prehensile pink tongue darted out like a chameleon's from between his purple puckered lips. 'I will have to consult Nick and Wat,' he said, 'before I can go higher.'
When I explained that I was under contract to Cape, he said: 'A pity. My imprint would have added lustre to your work.'

Somehow Tambi persuaded a wide range of noted poets and illustrators to contribute to *Poetry (London)*, which continued to appear occasionally throughout the war. Walter De La Mare, David Gascoyne, George Barker and Kathleen Raine all appeared, and the illustrators included Henry Moore, Mervyn Peake, Graham Sutherland and Ceri Richards.

Maclaren-Ross met a girl named Kitty Banks whom Tambi had once engaged as a secretary. She was just down from Oxford and must have been desperate for a job in publishing. Tambi took her to a bare basement and showed her a pile of rat-gnawed manuscripts in a corner. It was her office and she was now the poetry reader, he told her.

'Poems,' he said. 'Contributions. You know? I have not time to read them. If they're no good perhaps they should be returned. They have been here a long time, the rats have eaten some. We have no typewriter yet but there is ink and paper to write to the authors.'

He then told her he was on his way to lunch with T.S. Eliot and borrowed her last £5. When he returned in a fortnight she was almost hidden from sight behind a pile of stamped envelopes with the manuscripts inside.

> 'But the stamps?' he said. 'Where did you get them? I did not think there were any.'
> 'I bought them.'
> 'Then you still have some money?'
> 'An aunt sent me £3.'
> 'That is good. Give me what remains. I am tonight entertaining Edith Sitwell. You know about Edith Sitwell?' he said, dropping the money in his pocket.
> (Maclaren-Ross, *Memoirs of the Forties*)

When he returned after another fortnight there was a polite note from Kitty saying she had resigned. Rather than starve she had taken a job at the Foreign Office. 'All the same,' she told Maclaren-Ross, 'he's a great editor. No, stop laughing, he is. He has such flair.'

## Pub crawl with Tambi

It was Tambi who introduced Maclaren-Ross to the pubs of Fitzrovia and Soho. Followed by a crowd of his followers, he took him on a pub crawl, first stopping suddenly outside a branch of Martin's Bank. He told Maclaren-Ross he should have an account there, 'near the pubs and you can come quickly down and cash a cheque if you are short or if any of us needs money'. They visited the Black Horse, the Burglar's Rest, the Marquis of Granby, the Wheatsheaf, the Beer House and the Highlander. Maclaren-Ross later woke fully dressed in his lodgings, the room full of smoke from a cigarette which had burned away the corner of a new leather briefcase.

Tambi attracted young poetesses eager to have their work published. They were more often disappointed in this than he was in his hopes of sex with them: 'he was extremely fond of women sexually without caring for them much as a sex.'

Maclaren-Ross remembered a night when Tambi picked up two suburban girls in the Wheatsheaf. They wanted the men to buy them a meal in a distant, newly opened restaurant. As they stumbled through the darkened streets Tambi began to worry that it was near closing time. He turned to the girls.

'Listen, you must tell us please, my friend and I wish to know, do you do it or not?'

'Do it?' they chorused. 'Do what?'

'You know. Sex.'

The girls stated very firmly that they did not 'do it'. 'Then be off' Tambi shouted, and the two men retraced their steps to Soho (*Memoirs of the Forties*).

Years later Tambi tried to talk his way into Michael Walker's aunt's flat in Chelsea. Some relatives had arrived from Ceylon and he hoped to persuade them that it was his flat, and that he was living in style. Michael's aunt politely showed him the door.[1] But if he didn't live in style he had style, of a kind. Michael Bakewell says in *Fitzrovia* that his patrons included several American millionairesses, the Beatles and Mrs Gandhi.

'Only beware of Fitzrovia…' It was too late to warn Nina Hamnett. Drink and a wildly promiscuous lifestyle were coarsening her. She had been the mistress of Roger Fry and the sculptor Henri Gaudier-Brzeska (he made the sculpture of her now in the V and A, 'with me left tit knocked off', the Laughing Torso of her autobiography) and the drinking companion of famous artists in Paris, but by now her own work was conventional. And she devoted less and less time to it. The novelist Anthony Powell, who had a brief affair with her, wrote in his autobiography that her heavy drinking was 'a condition not affecting her gift, but restricting continuous work to a few months at best; human relationships to equally fragmentary associations'. She was particularly fond of sailors and labourers she met at the Fitzroy Tavern. Asked why she liked sailors so much she replied: 'Because they leave in the morning.' She met a young boxer named Vernon Campbell there and went to boxing matches when he was fighting. One night at a party in Augustus John's Chelsea studio she found Campbell sitting on a settee with a young woman named Cowles. In a drunken fury she grabbed Cowles by the hair and dragged her over the back of the settee, leaving her head streaming blood.

## Tours with Nina

Drink was beginning to dominate her life. She was a regular in the pubs of Fitzrovia, going on pub-crawls around the Tavern, the Wheatsheaf, the Marquis of Granby, the Bricklayer's Arms and the Black Horse. As a pioneer Nina was sometimes asked to act as a guide to the pubs of the area, a service she was happy to perform for a few drinks. She recalled two sightseers she was showing round asking her whether there were any 'dope fiends' in the Fitzroy Tavern. When she said there weren't, adding that 'the people in this quarter when they have a few pennies and want to feel excited only drink beer', her companions were disappointed.

In 1936 the public got a fascinating glimpse of Bohemian life when two of the stars of Fitzrovia were involved in a murder case. Sylvia Gough was the daughter of a millionaire. When younger and beautiful she had acted on film and stage, performed in the Ziegfeld Follies in New York and been a model for Augustus John, Sargent and Orpen. Essentially a Twenties figure, by 1936 she had the haunting ghost of beauty, fast fading under assault from drink.

The other woman in the case was Betty May. She was beloved by Douglas Burton, a book reviewer who had met her at the Fitzroy Tavern. Obsessed by what he called her 'pantherine' movements and eyes, he had asked her to marry him. She refused. Sylvia Gough, who was 42, was living with a writer named Douglas Bose, who was half her age. He beat her, and one night when Burton met her at the Fitzroy Bose had given her a black eye. Burton gave her sanctuary at his home for a few days. He took her to a party at a friend's studio, and Bose turned up. Burton sprang at him and killed him with a blow of a sculptor's hammer. He was found guilty but insane, and the judge at his trial called the case 'singularly squalid and unpleasant'. Betty May made some money by selling her version of the events to Fleet Street.

# Sordidness, Boy, That's the Thing

After a while there were too many sightseers at the Fitzroy Tavern and the committed Bohemians moved on to a cluster of pubs just a few hundred yards south, to what the author Anthony Burgess called 'the Maclaren-Ross circuit'. The Wheatsheaf in Rathbone Place became their headquarters for a time. A regular there at opening time was a mysterious woman called Mrs Stewart, an old-age pensioner who had lived in Paris and known Joyce and Hemingway. She would sit by herself sipping a Guinness and doing the crossword. Other pubs on the circuit were the Black Horse in Rathbone Place, the Bricklayer's Arms, also known as the Burglar's Rest after thieves broke in and spent the night drinking there, the Marquis of Granby across the road from the Wheatsheaf, where, according to Maclaren-Ross, 'gigantic Guardsmen went in search of homosexuals to beat up and rob'. Further up Rathbone Street was the Duke of York.

For many of the old Bohemian Fitzrovians the pubs were becoming too well-known and crowded, and Nina Hamnett and her friends were the problem. People were coming from far and wide to see this enclave where the drink was cheap and the drinkers interestingly raffish and amusing. In *Is She a Lady?* her rambling second book of reminiscences, Nina said: 'The neighbourhood of Charlotte and Fitzroy streets was becoming daily more fashionable. The pubs were becoming so full that it was difficult to get a drink at all.'

Some of these visitors were wealthy or upper-class 'tourists' visiting the area as their ancestors (male) had visited the brothels and sailors' pubs of the Ratcliffe Highway. Anthony Powell's wife, Lady Violet, visited a 'raffish-smart, bohemian, mysterious and extremely smoky' jazz club in Soho called the Nest. Powell says that after her second and last visit, Lady Violet objected, 'I had to have my dress cleaned because it smelt so appalling' (Motion, *The Lamberts*).

Julian Maclaren-Ross ran into a mob of what he regarded as these cultural tourists one night in the late Thirties as he searched for a girl called Vicky in the smoky pubs of Rathbone Place:

Through the fog, at its thickest where the Public Bar was partitioned off, I could distinguish, leaning against the glass and wood, a group of young men swathed in scarves and smoking curved pipes, technically known to me as the Slithy Toves. To my dismay I caught sight of Vicky in their midst! A Tove with even more scarves than the rest and wearing a polo sweater to boot swayed in front of her, swearing nineteen to the dozen. She saw me at the same time and waved wildly, calling out: 'Julian! Come and meet Walter.'

I looked round for my drink. It had disappeared ... In a very bad temper I forced my way towards Vicky.

She said: 'Julian, this is Walter. We were up at Cambridge together.'

In an instant I was shaking hands with every Tove in sight. 'You can't all have been at Cambridge,' I said.

'No, I was at Oxford,' a Tove with an orange beard told me. 'I edited a magazine there. Are you an editor?'

'God forbid,' I said.

'Pity, because if you were, I've some poems here I'd like to show you. D'you know Tambi by any chance?'

Maclaren-Ross was a formidable monologist. Dan Davin said in his memoirs *Closing Times*: 'To those who were not prepared to let him have the lion's share of the conversation he seemed a pretentious bore.' Anthony Powell, who depicted him as X. Trapnell in his novel sequence *A Dance to the Music of Time*, said you knew is was time to go when Maclaren-Ross began his impersonation of Sydney Greenstreet. He managed to survive by writing radio thrillers for the BBC. Maclaren-Ross died in 1964, celebrating the arrival of an unexpected cheque for a radio repeat.

## A tripod of drunks

War made the atmosphere in the noisy, smoke-filled pubs of Fitzrovia even more febrile. Writers like Dylan Thomas and Maclaren-Ross got work with the BBC and the Ministry of Information. The usual mix of characters changed. There were more crooks with money – black marketeers, spivs, minor criminals for whom the blackout provided unique opportunities – more prostitutes, deserters, servicemen. Drink and cigarettes would run out but Nina, 'head of Soho's bush telegraph service', usually knew where to find some more (Davies, 'Nina Hamnett, Bohemian'). Among the new faces, apart from Thomas, were several artists – the two Roberts, Colquhoun and MacBryde, John Craxton, Lucian Freud and John Minton. The author and long-time *Listener* arts editor Derwent May described the argumentative but inseparable Roberts, McBryde 'small and dumpy, Colquhoun tall and gaunt. You could hear them shouting to each other, one apparently in Frith Street, the other in Dean Street'.[2]

Ruthven Todd recalled leaving the Highlander pub during an air raid one night in 1942. Coming towards him were three people, drunk and supporting each other, looking like a tripod. 'The legs wobbled and wove and crumpled and it became clear that it was only possible for the three persons to move as a tripod linked by arms over one another's shoulders.' The trio were Nina, Augustus John and Norman Douglas, all 'drunk as sponges'. They were on their way to the Gargoyle club for 'an unneeded drink' (Hooker, *Nina Hamnett*).

Fitzrovia guttered and died in the postwar years. Many old buildings had been destroyed in the Blitz, and higher rents forced the artists and writers out. Even Nina joined the exodus to Soho, although she was still seen from time to time in the Fitzroy.

One of the earliest, and perhaps the best, chronicler of wartime Fitzrovia was Julian Maclaren-Ross. He worked with Dylan Thomas at the BBC, and his *Memoirs of the Forties* has a good deal to say of the poet. They first met in 1943 when Maclaren-Ross started as a scriptwriter at Strand Films. Thomas, then 29, was already there. Maclaren-Ross said

Thomas did not greatly resemble the much-reproduced early photograph known by him as 'the Fucking Cherub'. The poet Louis MacNeice described Thomas as he was at that time in his 'Autumn Sequel' (1954).

> [He] stayed young and gay,
> A bulbous Taliessin, a spruce and small
> Bow-tied Silenus roistering his way
> Through lands of fruit and fable, well aware
> That even Dionysus had his day
> And cannot take it with him. Debonair,
> He leaned against the bar till his cigarette
> Became one stream of ash sustained in air
> Through which he puffed his talk. The nights were wet
> And incomparably alive ...

Although penniless Maclaren-Ross contrived to be something of a dandy. He carried a silver-topped malacca cane, and wore a fur coat and dark glasses. He had recently been invalided out of the army.

After their first working day together they went on a pub-crawl. Maclaren-Ross had already discovered that one of the few places with ample supplies of whisky was the Café Royal, and he drank solidly there at lunchtime. In the evening they worked their way through Soho in search of more Scotch. Dylan was wearing a tight celluloid collar and by the time they reached the Highlander pub, where they found some gin, he was scarlet in the face.

> I suggested he should take the damned thing off.
> 'Why don't you take that bloody jacket off?' Dylan said.
> 'What's wrong with my jacket?'
> 'Fucking dandy. Flourishing that stick. Why don't you try to look more sordid? Sordidness, boy, that's the thing.'
> 'If you'd just come out of the glasshouse [military prison] you wouldn't want to look more sordid.'
> Dylan paused with a double gin suspended. 'The glasshouse?' he said. 'That where you've been? ...'
> Dylan set his gin carefully on the counter, and reaching up wrenched the celluloid collar from its stud. 'Jesus boy,' he said. 'I'm sorry.'

'That's all right. You weren't to know.' ...
He remained abashed for the rest of the evening and later on
somehow I lost him.

The following morning Dylan had a hangover. Maclaren-Ross arrived at
the office as he was trying to dial TIM, the talking clock, to see if it was
opening time. His hands were shaking so much he couldn't dial. When
Mclaren-Ross told him it was only half-past ten he groaned:

'Oh God another hour.' ... His eyes were globular, rimmed with red
right round, nor had he shaved ...
'Was I rude to you last night?'
'No.'
'I bloody was. I was rude to you about your coat. Is the coat all right?
You weren't sick down it or anything?'
'No.'
'What about the stick? Don't say you lost the stick?'
I showed him the stick and he seemed genuinely comforted.
Henceforward he adopted the cane and jacket as though they were
his own especial properties, making sure I didn't leave the cane
behind in pubs and becoming belligerent himself when a chap in one
of them took exception to the jacket.

## Augustus pounces

This shows Dylan Thomas at his endearing best, and the vein of fantasy
that ran through his converesation. Once walking with Rayner
Heppenstall to a pub in Charlotte Street he coughed, spat and examined
the spittle. 'Blood, boy! That's the stuff!' he remarked. He was also very
funny. Heppenstall remembers bar-room recitations of scatological
limericks:

There was an old bugger called God
Who put a young virgin in pod
This amazing behaviour
Produced Christ our saviour
Who died on a cross, poor old sod.

193

Thomas was introduced to his wife Caitlin Macnamara in the Wheatsheaf pub in Fitzrovia by Augustus John, who had seduced her, despite a 35-year difference in their ages. She denied ever loving John and said it was 'a brief dutiful performance for him to keep up his reputation as a Casanova ogre'. But there are reasons to believe that he still 'pounced' on her from time to time. Caitlin added that 'this lofty favour was not reserved for me alone, but one and all of his models, of whatever age and social category, suffered the identical treatment'. She also said he had 'leaped on her, ripped off her clothes and penetrated her like some mindless hairy goat'. John probably felt he still had some right to Caitlin; he once punched Thomas in a drunken row that may have had something to do with her.

In wartime London Thomas's reputation was growing, and not just for his BBC work and his poems. There were many anecdotes about his drinking, his talk, his jokes and fantasies. Some people were enchanted. Elisabeth Lutyens was asked by her husband how she could spend five hours in a pub drinking with Thomas and his cronies. 'But to me it wasn't five hours drinking in a pub, it was five hours of incredibly funny conversation.'

There was a price to pay for being such a generous public entertainer. Dylan Thomas was losing his poetic voice. Never prolific, he was finding it harder to write at all, and would struggle for months over a single poem. His friend John Davenport said: 'When you think of the cloudbursts of laughter, the sheer, roaring gorgeous 17th-century din of laughter that went on whenever he was around, it's difficult to believe that inside was the misery' (Ferris, *Dylan Thomas*). Thomas was suffering. He hated being a mere public entertainer, a role that was to take him over with poetry reading trips to the United States, where he died in 1953. There was an element of showmanship even in that death – he boasted of how much he had drunk in his last binge. He was the prisoner of the image. Once asked why he drank so much he relied: 'Because they expect it of me.'

Some of the anecdotes were about Thomas's carelessness with other people's property, which amounted at times to thieving. It could be as little as a shirt borrowed unasked on a visit, or wholesale plunder. A painter and his wife who lent him their flat early in the war returned to find many things missing, including a fur coat and their silver. One version of the story had them returning and catching Thomas polishing the silver prior to disposing of it. 'How kind, you shouldn't have bothered,' they are said to have remarked. He could do worse: at Caitlin's sister's house he urinated against the living-room wall, and at another of her relatives he defecated on the floor.

In the pubs of Soho and Fitzrovia he was surrounded by a constant gale of laughter. He delivered comic monologues about a funny little man to whom ludicrous things occurred, and whose name happened to be Thomas. The poet John Pudney remembered how Dylan would suggest, 'Let's be dogs.' He would then go down on all fours, biting people. On a visit to Cambridge University where he was to read poems he went into his dog act in an undergraduate's rooms. Professor E.M. Tillyard found the occasion tiresome. 'Luckily there were other people there, for meeting Thomas brought no reward. He was in the feeble, maudlin state of intoxication, and spent his time crawling under the table and round the furniture, making vague noises. He was entirely good-natured, and was kept happy by an occasional stroke of the head or pat on the back.'

## That's the record

The image of Dylan the drinker most people had was of this good-natured, funny boon companion. He changed when drunk. The writer Jack Lindsay saw him like this, when he 'rapidly grew his piggish mask, heavy-lipped and snouted'. Caitlin said on television in 1975 that drink 'ruined him, of course. He'd have been a marvellous old man now if someone had snatched the booze away from him. I don't think he was even all that keen on the booze. It was just the company and the life and the weakness ...' Although towards the end of his life he earned a considerable income he frittered it away. One of the people who kept the Thomases afloat was Margaret Taylor, wife of the historian A.J.P. Taylor. She tried to find him in one of his Fitzrovia pubs, the Stag's Head in New Cavendish Street but he hid behind the bar. 'His hand would sneak round the flap, groping for another pint' (Pentlow and Rowe, *Characters of Fitzrovia*).

Dylan Thomas died in New York in November 1953. He had spent the previous day drinking on and off, but not heavily. At two in the morning he got out of bed saying he must have a drink. After about an hour and a half he returned to his hotel, and told the woman he was sleeping with: 'I've had eighteen straight whiskies. I think that's the record.' He became ill and a doctor gave him a morphine injection. He died later in hospital.

Caitlin lived on until 1994, obsessed for years by her memories of Dylan, her writings about him and her alcoholism. 'Ours was not a love story, it was a drink story,' she observed. They seemed to represent all that was carefree and irresponsible about the Bohemian life. They were penniless, drunk, dirty and dishonest. But Caitlin was also angry. Dylan's womanising and improvidence, and his waste of talent made her bitter. After he died she attempted suicide several times. At last in her sixties she stopped drinking and found a cure in 'swimming, bicycling, horseback riding, badminton, and teaching her son to dance' (Nicholson, *Among the Bohemians*).

By the time the Colony Room, a drinking club in Dean Street run by the extravagantly foul-mouthed but much-loved Muriel Belcher, opened in 1948 the Thomases were seen less often in London. Dylan's only recorded meeting with its best-known habitué, the painter Francis Bacon, was not a success – they both wanted to monopolise the conversation.

Belcher's greetings for favoured members was 'Hello cunty'. Non-members got a brisk 'fuck off'. She referred to men as 'she', 'Clara' or 'Miss'. Hitler was 'Miss Hitler' and when George Bernard Shaw died she said, 'You've got to hand it to her, a clever little woman, that one.'

Many of the younger artists were members. Francis Bacon, whom she called 'daughter', was a favourite. Before he became so wealthy he could have bought the club she gave him free drinks and paid him £10 a week to bring in rich customers. She sensed instinctively that he would be a draw, and she was right. He was popular and sought after, and brought in the kind of people she liked. When he did become rich and famous he was famously generous. He recalled: 'I loved Muriel enormously, and for some reason we both got on very well, and so I went in there a lot. I could drink there for nothing, which was marvellous of course.'

Muriel, the daughter of wealthy Portuguese Jews who ran a theatre in Birmingham, had helped run the Music Box, a wartime club in Leicester Place, before going into business on her own. She particularly liked artists, although she said, 'I don't give a fuck about art'. Lucian Freud, John Craxton, John Minton, Rodrigo Moynihan and the two Roberts (Colquhoun and MacBryde) were among the struggling artists who were more or less regulars. What she most disliked was meanness. When she spotted a reluctant spender she would cry: 'Come on everyone, we'll all have a drink with this vision of loveliness beside me.' Then to the customer: 'Open you bead bag, Lottie.' Few such customers ever came back to face her again.

## A double twice, dear

Nina Hamnett, now a rather pathetic figure, was a regular in another drinking club, the Caves De France, and the French pub as well as the Colony Room. Dan Farson (*The Gilded Gutter Life of Francis Bacon*) remembers her at the Caves, hoisting herself on to a bar stool and gasping, 'Couldn't buy me a drink, could you, love, for old time's sake?' She was trading on a brief affair with Farson's father. She would ask for 'a double whisky, *twice*, dear'. When offers of drinks were not forthcoming she would rattle a tobacco tin for contributions. 'She was a wreck of the woman she had been, once the "proverbial" toast of the Left Bank in Paris, a talented artist herself yet better known as the friend of artists' (Farson).

Although Muriel Belcher liked Nina her habit of urinating where she sat strained relations. At the French pub she peed so often in her favourite seat her ownership of it was never challenged. Hooker (*Nina Hamnett*) says it

Nina Hamnet, exuberant pioneer of the bohemian lifestyle for women. Nina was muse and mistress to great artists. To avoid causing offence she would vomit in her handbag.

was 'not unknown' for her to vomit in her handbag before making her way home. Farson says she tried to keep up appearances, and once on the way from the French pub to the Caves 'was daintily sick into her handbag (which she then clasped shut) in order not to embarrass her companions by doing this in the gutter'.

After a heavy session at the Fitzroy in May 1953 Nina fell and fractured her thigh. The hospital doctor who treated her botched the operation, and when her leg healed it was four inches shorter than the other. She had to use a stick and wear a built-up shoe. She was never free from pain again. When she was at her lowest a radio play by a friend upset her badly. Bob Pocock's *It's Long Past Time*, about Charlotte Street in the Thirties, featured her prominently as Cynthia. Although it was intended as an affectionate portrait Nina felt she had been portrayed as an artistic has-been and figure of fun. A few days later, in December 1956, she fell forty feet from the window of her flat and was impaled on railings below. At an inquest the coroner recorded a verdict of 'accidental death'.

Forty of her friends gathered in the Fitzroy Tavern for a liquid farewell. The following year David Wright's 'Verses at a Bohemian Funeral' was published.

Vanished unwasted hours of being
(Being not doing)
In the religion of alcohol ...

When Henrietta Moraes, later Francis Bacon's model but at the time a cat burglar, was sent to prison for ten days, Muriel Belcher organised a whip-round for her. Henrietta said: '£1000 was waiting for me in the Colony, which was sort of amazing. Muriel was like that, if she liked you.'

Not everyone had such kind memories of her as Moraes. Dan Farson took the author John Braine to the Colony one afternoon and signed him in. Muriel Belcher took one look at Braine and announced in a loud voice, 'She's not a pretty little lady, is she?' Hoping Braine had not noticed this, Farson introduced him to Belcher, saying he was the author of the best-selling novel *Room at the Top*. 'I can see there's plenty of room at *her* top!' Belcher replied.

The other customers laughed. Braine, said Farson, quivered with indignation. 'Madam, I've never been so insulted in my life,' he spluttered.

It was the wrong line to take. 'On your way, Lottie,' she told Braine, opening the door, 'or you'll get a fourpenny one.'

A customer detested by Belcher but beloved by Bacon was the photographer John Deakin. He did fashion and portrait pictures for *Vogue*, producing powerful close-ups which impressed the painter. He was sarcastic and mean. When he stroked a husky dog someone had taken into the Colony Belcher called out: 'Hold onto your sled, gal, or that one will bum a free ride to Alaska!' She eventually barred him for spreading a rumour that she had embezzled money her members contributed to a charity for handicapped children.

Bacon called Deakin a ' very interesting and amusing man' and would accept criticism of his 'doodles' from him that he would not tolerate from anyone else. One night at the Rockingham Club, which was pretentious and full of men Farson described as 'superior shop assistants', Deakin passed out from drink and had to be carried up the stairs. The shop assistants signalled their horror at such behaviour, and Bacon paused on the stairs to shout: 'Even unconscious he's more fun than you lot!'

Deakin was fired from *Vogue* over his drinking. He had been asked to help with the decorations at a party the magazine was giving. Arriving several hours too early he helped himself to drinks, and by the time the distinguished guests arrived he had collapsed and had to be carried out.

## The second-nastiest man

In 1960 Deakin and Farson went on holiday to Tangier with Lady Rose MacLaren – no relative of Julian. Through Rose they were invited to the home of the heiress Barbara Woolworth Hutton, where Deakin made a nuisance of himself.

Hutton, surrounded by fawning admirers, took them on a tour of her palace. 'Do we have to?' asked Deakin, who was looking for a drink. He tagged along, making disparaging remarks about the antique furniture. Hutton abandoned the tour and sat on a throne while her current toyboy lover played the guitar. There was applause, followed by a shout from behind the arras. 'When that second-rate strummer has finished,' Deakin cried, 'I'd like a drink.'

He was sent back to London. At a lunch in Wheeler's Farson, who had stayed on in Tangier for a ball at Hutton's palace, entertained a lunch party at Wheeler's by telling them what Hutton said about Deakin.

'Did Barbara Hutton really dislike me that much?' Deakin asked.

Farson replied: 'She said you were the second-nastiest man she had met in forty years.' Not even the nastiest.

Bacon wanted to paint Henrietta Moraes, but not from life. He told her that when he painted live models people were shocked by the results. Instead he would get Deakin to photograph her, and work from his pictures. Deakin duly took two series of intimate nude photos of her.

One day Henrietta was in a low drinking club in Soho, 'full of sailors'. Deakin was there, furtively showing the sailors pictures. Seizing one of them, she saw it was one of the pictures he had taken of her. He was charging ten shillings each. 'I was really furious at the time. Only ten shillings. How dare he!'

Deakin died in Brighton in 1972. He was recovering from having a lung removed, and went on a giant bender around the Brighton bars and clubs with a friend. When another friend rang him the next day to see how he was he admitted he had drunk too much the night before. When a maid brought him tea a few minutes later he was dead.

Belcher died in 1979. She had been transferred from a private nursing home to the Middlesex Hospital because her obscenities were upsetting staff and patients. Dan Farson gave the address at her memorial service in St Paul's, Covent Garden. He spoke of their 'great good luck in knowing Muriel Belcher, who turned life into a marvellous party'.

# Bohemian Elegy?

Some believed that Bohemia ended with the Second World War. The welfare state, with its safety nets and cradle-to-grave care, took away much of the thrill of the hand-to-mouth existence. When you spent your last penny on a drink in the Thirties, you really didn't know where the next one was coming from. After the war there was the expanding BBC and the Arts Council with the prospect of at least temporary alleviation. Artists and writers put on suits and took jobs in universities and art schools. To remain rebellious and independent tested the Bohemian spirit, but outposts of the old resistance remained, particularly in Soho. There the lazy, the addicted and, in a few cases, the strangely and extravagantly talented held out.

Presiding over the revels was Francis Bacon. He was in a sense the new Augustus John, generous and expansive. He was not, however, heterosexual. He had a talent for friendship but lost friends because of his touchiness. He had courage: when he was 40 he told a group of friends at his favourite restaurant, Wheeler's in Old Compton Street, that a doctor had just told him that his heart was in such a bad state that a single drink could kill him. He then ordered a succession of bottles of champagne. After he had a kidney removed he told the artist Michael Wishart: 'When you've been drunk since the age of fifteen, you're lucky to have even one kidney!' Then he laughed. When he slipped on the stairs of the Colony and knocked his right eye half out he simply pushed it back in and took himself off to a hospital. Although he had a scar he never mentioned the fall.

Farson says his stamina and powers of recovery were remarkable. After a long day's filming for the *South Bank Show* Bacon got its presenter drunk 'possibly for the first time in his life'. The following day

The artist Francis Bacon in expansive mood. His generosity and sense of fun lit up the pubs of Soho in the fifties. Bacon took on Augustus John's mantle of leading Bohemia.

the presenter turned up late at Mario's restaurant and wanting black coffee only to find that Bacon had been there an hour and was already deep into the champagne.

His daily hangovers were a stimulus to work. He would drink and gamble through the night, then begin work at six in the morning in a kind of fever, painting at great speed. Friends wondered at his productivity, which was consistent. Farson says he completed the *Three Studies for a Crucifixion* of 1962 while he was drunk.

When he first turned up at the Colony he never knew where his next drink was coming from. Wealth did not seem to change him. At a time when he could sell all he produced, he would abandon paintings in cupboards as he moved from one address to another – he destroyed or simply abandoned a large part of his production. Sometimes the new tenants sold these discarded pictures. The playwright Frank Norman remembered Bacon spotting in the window of a Bond Street gallery a picture he had left behind in Tangier after a holiday. He asked the price, and when told it was £50,000 wrote out a cheque. He then took the picture outside and stamped it to pieces on the pavement.

Another Colony Room regular was Paul Potts, known as 'the People's Poet'. 'His appearance, increasingly like that of a Soho wino, was tolerated with saintly forbearance by Muriel as he smouldered and stank in a corner, for he rarely washed' (Farson, *Francis Bacon*). Potts resented his lack of success, and one of the people he took this out on was Derwent May, at the time the arts editor of *The Listener*. What riled Potts was May's refusal to commission work from him. One afternoon after menacing May for some time Potts kicked him hard on the ankle, making the editor yelp in pain and fury. He threatened to call the police if Potts did it again, and from then on the poet fulminated in a corner. Farson says Potts remained an outcast until his death in 1990.

Another favourite drinking spot with the Soho crowd was the York Minster in Dean Street, also called the French pub. Bacon first went there in 1949, when Victor Berlemont was the landlord. It was later run by his son Gaston, described by Farson as the doyen of Soho landlords.

## Bacon boos a princess

Bacon could behave outrageously and was no respecter of reputations or status. At a ball given by Lady Rothermere Princess Margaret burst into an exhibitionist frenzy after a surfeit of champagne. She stopped the dance-band and took the microphone from the professional singer. She launched into some Cole Porter songs, to the delight of her ladies-in-waiting. Bacon's friend Lady Caroline Blackwood said he could not stand the caterwauling for long. After a while he began to boo so loudly the sycophantic clapping of the guests was drowned out. Margaret, tiaraed and crinolined, who had begun to wiggle her diminutive figure and her dress with its layers of petticoats reinforced with wooden hoops, faltered in mid-song. She went scarlet and then ashen and was led away by her ladies-in-waiting.

Caroline Blackwood said: 'Among all the guests in Lady Rothermere's ballroom more than a few were secretly suffering from Princess Margaret's singing, but they suffered in silence, gagged by their snobbery. Francis could not be gagged.'

Bacon himself commented: 'Her singing was really too awful. Someone had to stop her.'

Robert Medley remembered a dinner party in the early Fifties at which Bacon met W.H. Auden. 'Francis suddenly turned on Wystan [Auden]: "Never before have I had to submit to such a disgusting display of hypocritical Christian morality!" Declaring that he could no longer sit at the same table with such a monster who considered himself an artist, he leaped to his feet and stormed out of the front door into the street' (quoted Farson). Drink, lots of it, was of course a factor in these outbursts.

Frequently he was outrageous just for the hell of it. Once when the Colony was full of American tourists he asked Jeffrey Bernard which woman he fancied most in the whole world. Bernard called it a 'daft question' but asked Bacon who he most fancied. 'He replied with a languid yet loud tone: "D'yer know, I think I'd really like to be fucked by Colonel Gadaffi." Exit the Americans' (Farson, *Francis Bacon*).

He put up cheerfully with attacks on his art by journalists. In 1985 the Director of the Tate Gallery, Alan Bowness, wrote in the catalogue of an exhibition of Bacon's pictures that he was 'surely the greatest living painter'. This brought a virulent repost in *The Times* by Bernard Levin, then a well-known journalist. Under the headline 'A Genius? I Say Rotten' Levin wrote: 'The puffing and booming of Francis Bacon seems to me one of the silliest aberrations even of our exceptionally silly time.' After his death the journalist Paul Johnson wrote:

He could not draw. His ability to paint was limited and the way he laid the pigments on the canvas was often barbarous. He had no ideas, other than one or two morbid fancies arising from his homosexuality, chaotic way of life, and Irish fear of death. What he did have was a gimmick, something resembling an advertising designer's logo. In his case it was a knack of portraying the human face or body not so much twisted as smeared out of shape. It was enough. Such a logo could easily be dressed up by the scriptwriters of the industry into an 'image of our despairing century'; it fitted their favourite words: 'disquieting', 'disturbing'.

These two journalists were in distinguished company, as Bacon gleefully pointed out. Mrs Thatcher asked the directors of the Tate who was Britain's greatest painter. When they named Bacon she replied: 'Not that dreadful man who paints those horrible pictures!' If he had been there Bacon would have flashed his inimitable smile and called for more champagne, for which he would have insisted on paying. He was a man of more generous spirit than some of his critics.

Bacon died of a heart attack in Madrid in 1992. He had gone there, against the advice of his doctor, to see his new Spanish boyfriend. In old age the passion and vitality that animated his best work had not quite died.

One of those who enjoyed Bacon's largesse was Jeffrey Bernard, the journalist and drinker. Bacon had gone to New York with his boyfriend George Dyer, and they met Bernard, who had no money, as usual. 'I must have been mad, for I was dead broke and it was freezing. Francis bought me an overcoat and every morning I joined him for breakfast at the Algonquin, which consisted of a

Jeffrey Bernard made a living out of being unwell. Drinking at the rate of five double gins in ten minutes helped.

bottle of Dom Pérignon, and every morning he gave me a crisp hundred-dollar bill' (quoted Farson).

This meeting of two of Soho's most significant drinkers is intriguing. They are playing their most important social roles, Bacon as drinker and giver and Bernard as drinker and scrounger. After Bacon died Bernard became Soho's most notorious drunk and made a career of it in more ways than one, writing endless newspaper columns about his progress as an alcoholic. In every other way he was the opposite of Bacon: mean-spirited, pessimistic, constantly complaining. Jonathan Meades described Bernard's Low Life column in the *Spectator*, which made him famous, as 'a suicide note in weekly instalments'.

Bernard first experienced Soho when he was 14. He told Dan Farson: 'Suddenly I was surrounded by pretty girls, booze, nutcases, painters and writers. It was magic, like walking out of Belsen into Disneyland and I've been drunk ever since.'

## Bernard's three loves

His older brother Bruce recalled that Jeffrey used to hang around outside pubs. 'I could get into pubs and he wanted to get into pubs too, but there was no question of the landlord serving him because he was quite small, and looked so young.' Soho, soon to assuage his thirst, also solved his sexual problems. For years he had wanted to ravish his mother, whom he described as a 'very glamorous, very beautiful woman'. He was 'consumed by guilt' over these feelings. When he was 15 he went to Soho every day during the summer holidays, telling his mother he was going to the Science Museum. He met the 18-year-old daughter of a journalist, and she helped him lose his virginity on Hampstead Heath. It was 2 July 1947. Thirty years later he reported in the *Daily Express*: 'Just to make sure I'd lost it I lost it again the following evening.' That same year he also discovered horse racing, the third great love of his life with drink and sex. One of his first jobs was as a dishwasher in Victor Sassie's Budapest restaurant in Dean Street. (This was the forerunner of Sassie's famous Gay Hussar in Greek Street.) Then he discovered the pubs and clubs which were to be the stage on which he acted out the often sordid drama of his life.

Among them was the French pub in Dean Street. Dan Farson remembered the landlord, Gaston Berlemont, for his impeccable manners. Dan was once barred for some forgotten solecism, but never forgot Gaston's grace in expelling him. He murmured, 'One of us will have to go, and it's not going to be me,' showed him out politely and then asked: 'Do me a favour, *monsieur*, and join me tomorrow at opening time for a glass of champagne?'

Berlemont first met Bernard as a very young man. He remembered that even then Bernard became sarcastic and touchy after just a few drinks. By 1961 he was drinking a bottle of Scotch whisky a day and living beyond any means he could earn or scrounge. The American writer Norman Mailer once took him back to his suite at the Ritz, where they drank all night at Mailer's expense. Bernard then persuaded him to pay for his taxi home.

He married five times, and slept with hundreds of women – he once suggested 500, though how he could have remembered is not clear. He sometimes fell asleep while having sex. He could react violently when a partner was unfaithful. When he found out that his second wife, the actress

Jacki Ellis, was having an affair with his friend Barry Bell he confronted them in a restaurant. 'I walked in and he was just putting a fork in his mouth and I walked over and gave his hand a tremendous shove into the roof of his mouth, which made his eyes water' (Lord, *Just The One*).

Many journalists become drunks: Bernard was a drunk who became a journalist. He was introduced to Dennis Hackett, then editor of *Queen*, in 1964, and told him: 'What this magazine needs is a racing column.' Hackett agreed, and at the age of thirty-two Bernard was to embark on a career that lasted until his death and in the end made him famous. He was a born journalist in that he had flair, but because of his drinking and fecklessness he often missed deadlines and so was often sacked.

Bernard had made his first racing bet in 1947, and had since been obsessed by the louche world of jockeys and trainers. He wrote about that world from a new angle, that of the losing punter. His first column for *Queen* began: 'The practice of making excuses for beaten horses is not only the punter's greatest expense, but also allows bookmakers to make off for the Bahamas every winter.' The tone of voice appealed to all the other habitual losers out there. He refined it over the years, but the same wry threnody was the stuff of his Low Life columns in the *Spectator* 20 years later.

In February 1965 Hackett sent Bernard to interview his fellow-Fitzrovian, the racing tipster Prince Monolulu, who was ill in the Middlesex Hospital. Monolulu, who was 82 and well-known for his chant 'I gotta horse', was too weak to help himself to one of the chocolates Bernard took him. Bernard put a chocolate cream in the sick man's mouth, then called a nurse when he began to choke. It was too late – Monolulu choked and died.

Bernard then had a brief stint as a *Daily Mirror* fashion writer. It didn't work out but he met Mike Molloy, who would later be Editor-in-Chief of the Mirror Group. They hit it off at once and became lifelong friends.

His growing reputation as a racing journalist led in October 1970 to a job writing a racing column in the racing paper *The Sporting Life*. Carolyn Cluskey, later the paper's administration manager, says that when he first arrived he seemed impossibly glamorous, trailing clouds of Soho glory. 'We had no panache or style and suddenly here was this vision – he was just beautiful.' When she handed him his racecourse badge which would get him into any racecourse in the country he said: 'I can't believe it. I've always wanted one of these. I've just fulfilled a lifetime's ambition.' Fairly quickly he became unreliable over deadlines. 'There were executive editors who were saying, "there's no room for this rubbish in the paper," and the production editor would be sweating, wondering if the copy was even going to arrive. It couldn't go on.'

But she said, he was great fun. 'He took me to lunch from time to time when I managed to get his expenses paid quickly. He drank so fast we couldn't keep up – five double gins in ten minutes. I don't know who paid, but he still owes me twenty-five quid!' (interview with the author April 2007).

The opportunities to plumb the alcoholic lower depths with his new racing acquaintances were irresistible. He later confessed that the year he worked as a *Sporting Life* columnist was spent 'in a drunken haze'. He was often in trouble. Readers began to write in saying there was too much about drinking and not enough about racing in his column.

## In bed with a jockey

His drinking got worse. He suffered from pancreatitis, a serious and painful condition affected by drink. He was surrounded by heavy drinkers wherever he went, in journalism, in Soho and among the racing crowd, the heaviest drinkers of all. At Ascot he was said by a friend to have vomited at the Queen Mother's feet. In his book *Talking Horses* he told how he woke up one morning to find himself in bed in a Huntingdon hotel with a jockey and a local charwoman. He had no idea how they got there. He was asked by the hotel and a council official never to return to Huntingdon.

He lost the job he loved because of drink. He had been asked to present the *Sporting Life* cup to the leading woman rider of the season at the national point-to-point dinner at a Kensington hotel in October 1971. Nervous about making a speech, he began drinking early and by the time of the prize-giving dinner was paralytic. He fell asleep on a sofa and was carried upstairs and put to bed by waiters. Ossie Fletcher, editor of the *Sporting Life*, sacked him and asked him to return his Press badge. Carolyn Cluskey says: 'He's had verbal warnings and final warnings but this was the last straw. The racing world was much more formal then and he'd really let the side down.'

Bad behaviour was becoming a habit. A friend with whom he got drunk in a pub asked him: 'All right, Jeffrey, I know: you've fucked my wife, haven't you?' 'Yes, and your mother and daughter as well.' He probably would never have been offered his last and best-known job if he had been a nicer man and better behaved. He had been writing a column in the *Spectator* called End Piece. In August 1978 it was reborn as Low Life. It made him even better known, its devastating frankness about drinking, gambling, sex, illness and the utter aimlessness of his life quickly catching on. He said later: 'People like to read about someone who is deeper in the shit than they are.'

For a time he also wrote a fortnightly racing column titled Colonel Mad for *Private Eye*, but once again his feckless disregard for deadlines wore out the patience of the publishers. Richard Ingrams, the editor, said: 'He was just so hopelessly unreliable about delivering copy.' In December 1980 the magazine announced that they were dropping the column. Bernard wrote in his last article: 'A team of psychiatric experts has declared me unfit to continue this column, the strain of having done it for three years having quite unhinged me. I carry though to Banstead Hospital fond memories of the Turf, which are bound to comfort me in my dotage.'

The year 1985 was eventful. He was barred for life from the Coach and Horses by the landlord, Norman Balon, after he squirted soda over a barmaid. He got a writ from Robson Books, who had advanced him £500 for an unwritten book of anecdotes about Lester Piggott. He fell in love with Deirdre Redgrave, ex-wife of the actor Corin Redgrave. He was named the Periodical Publishers' Association Writer of the Year. (He got drunk and lost the £500 cheque they gave him: it was found and returned by a stranger.) Three weeks after he met Deirdre he gave a birthday party for dozens of friends. Jonathan Meades remembered some very distinguished people being very drunk, including the Liberal elder-statesman Jo Grimond. When a friend fell at his feet Bernard kicked him and said: 'I don't want any fucking drunks at this party, cunt!'

He mocked Deirdre's clothes in his Low Life column. 'I was going to lend her to a farmer to frighten the crows,' he wrote. They were interviewed together by the *Sunday Times*. He told the paper: 'She is the most stupid person that I have ever met. She is as daft as a fucking brush but she's got good legs.' She said: 'Come on, Jeffrey, only last weekend you threatened to blow up my block of flats if I left you ... Do you know he suggested someone ought to make a movie of our romance? He said he would be best played by Paul Newman. Personally I think Quentin Crisp would fit the part very well.'

The affair with Deirdre was fizzling out when he wrote what she described as 'a seriously horrible piece' about her in his column. He said: 'thank God it's over with She.' He later told the *Evening Standard* that he had ended it because 'She' hadn't bought him a drink for eight weeks.

From time to time Bernard mentioned in his column that he took illegal racing bets at the Coach and Horses. On a Saturday afternoon the following September he was in the pub taking bets when it was raided by Customs and police. He was arrested by nine policemen and three Customs officers. It turned out that the Customs had been watching him for three months and had placed bets with him on four Saturdays. He was fined £200. Geoffrey Wheatcroft wrote in the *Daily Telegraph*: 'You wonder what assistance the constabulary will need the next time they come to feel the collar of some frail and tipsy scribbler who has forgotten to pay his gas bill. Mounted officers? Sniffer dogs? Police marksmen?'

## Being his own Boswell

Bernard was drinking in the Groucho Club early in 1988 with the writer Keith Waterhouse, who suggested that he would like to write a play based on the Low Life columns. The play, *Jeffrey Bernard is Unwell*, took its title from the line printed in the *Spectator* when he was too drunk or, more frequently now, too ill to write. The play brought him more fame and money than he had known. Most of the money, however, was taken by the Inland Revenue for unpaid taxes. In June 1989 he got a demand for £21,000, with further demands to come. The *Evening Standard* came to the rescue by settling out of court a libel case he brought after they wrote a highly exaggerated account of his drunkenness at the races. £10,000 richer, he said: 'I haven't looked back since then and I haven't been short of funds since then. God bless the *Evening Standard*.' Soon he had even more to thank Keith Waterhouse for. *Jeffrey Bernard is Unwell* opened in September in Brighton. Bernard was played by Peter O'Toole, an old friend. The reviews were dazzling. Bernard became the star of his own life, for once. He and O'Toole faced a mob of Press photographers at a photocall outside the Coach and Horses. There were newspaper and radio interviews. In the *Telegraph Weekend Magazine* Waterhouse reminisced about their drinking days when they were young men about Soho. 'I guess I grew up after a fashion, but Jeff never did. The best and worst thing that happened to him was the gift of his Low Life column in the *Spectator*.

From then on playing truant was more than a vocation, it was a commitment. Being his own Boswell meant that he had to be Jeffrey Bernard all round the clock, seven days a week. No wonder he doesn't look too clever.'

The play opened in London in October at the Apollo Theatre. *Time Out* called it 'a glittering occasion attended by an astonishing assembly of drinkers, hacks and hangers-on, not to mention the usual theatre reviewers wearing ties. Prominent in the audience were Norman Balon, self-styled "rudest landlord in London", and presiding deity of the evening's entertainment, and Jeff himself, who sat smoking and muttering in the stalls.'

Francis Bacon was taken to see the play by Dan Farson. He left after the interval, infuriated at being portrayed as a camp homosexual. The critics were enthusiastic. One or two, however, seized the occasion to make unflattering remarks about Bernard himself, as distinct from the stage character. Michael Coveney in the *Financial Times* wrote: 'The man in question is very probably a shit of the first order.' In the *Spectator* Christopher Edwards mentioned Bernard's 'self-pity and self-censure – the latter being, as Doctor Johnson remarked, an invidious form of self-love'. The *Daily Mail*'s Jack Tinker praised Waterhouse's skill but was scathing about Bernard. 'To be honest I move tables in restaurants in order not to sit next to this self-same Bernard. He cannot be guaranteed to be the amusing creature of his stage legend; and unfortunately I have never seen him behaving as anything other than a sad old drunken bore.' The *Sunday Telegraph* published a bitterly acerbic half-page profile. It said he was 'an absurd amateur' who was just a drunk – 'there is *no* more to him than that'. It spoke of his 'unpleasant temper' and the 'darker side of his personality, offensive to those who can't answer back and ingratiating to those who can'.

Bernard enjoyed being a celebrity almost as much as the relative affluence. Fans penetrated the Coach and Horses in pursuit of him. One woman, who said she had seen the play seven times, repeatedly invited him to tea at Fortnums. He was asked to submit an entry to *Who's Who*. He listed his loves as cricket, racing, cooking and Mozart. Drinking was not mentioned. Perhaps he now recognised it as a compulsion which was not even fun any more. Later, however, when he complied with a similar request from *Debrett's Distinguished People of Today*, he listed 'drinking with friends' as one of his favourite pastimes. In the first list he named only three of his four wives, in the second only one.

Life went on, at least the physically and psychologically tortured version he now endured. In January he was in hospital for five days being treated for malnutrition.

Even the most tolerant of Bernard's friends must have found his treatment of his sister Sonia hard to accept. She had been given ECT for mental illness and had never fully recovered. Between spells in mental institutions she would appear in the French pub from time to time, begging, and Bernard would turn his back on her. Gaston would lead her gently away. When Bernard's biographer Graham Lord tracked her down to a sheltered home Bernard showed no interest. 'There's no one at home,' he said. 'She's mad. I don't see her any more.'

## Bohemian elegy?

Bernard died in September 1997. He had been a long time dying. One leg had been amputated, he had diabetes and his column was filled with references to nurses and 'carers', a word he would have hated. He visited his old watering holes seldom and only when he could find someone to push his wheelchair. The week he died the *Spectator* said: 'Jeffrey Bernard will not be writing this week.'

# The Truth They Talk in Hell

Since the newspapers moved elsewhere, Fleet Street is little more to most people than a bridge between the City and the West End. The stars have gone, both the writers and the proprietors, and with them a way of life that flourished for hundreds of years. Hard-drinking, free-spending, extravagantly non-conformist, the men and latterly women of Fleet Street were a race apart. With a few exceptions they professed to represent the soul of middle-class values for the suburbs and shires, but some lived lives that bordered on, and sometimes tipped over into, depravity. No one who witnessed the rituals of senior *Telegraph* journalists in their element in the Street's King and Keys pub late at night in the old days will ever forget the sight.

The ancient Cheshire Cheese pub at 145 Fleet Street had authentic Bohemian credentials. Goldsmith, Thackeray, Dickens, Wilkie Collins, Beerbohm, Mark Twain, Chesterton and Conan Doyle all solaced their existences there. In his poem 'When I Came Back to Fleet Street' Chesterton caught something of the desperation of the impecunious hack, the inexpressible in pursuit of the ephemeral, clinging to the illusion of gaiety in the bar-room's glow:

I had been long in meadow,
And the trees took hold of me,
And the still towns in the beech-woods,

Where men were meant to be.
But old things held; the laughter,
The long unnatural night,
And all the truth they talk in hell,
and all the lies they write....

The men in debt that drank of old
Still drink in debt today;
Chained to the rich by ruin,
Cheerful in chains, as then
When old unbroken Pickwick walked
Among the broken men.

Fleet Street journalists once maintained a secret Bohemia, separate from yet vitally connected to the other hard-drinking clans of the capital by arteries throbbing with booze and money. When all the major newspapers were located nearby agents loaded with expenses were daily despatched to the furthest ends of bibulous London to bring back news and gossip. From

Drinkers in a 1930s pub. The decor is now cosy rather than grand, the inviting warm glow timeless, the drinking restrained by price and shorter hours.

the bars of the House of Commons, the clubs of St James's, the gambling hells of Mayfair, seedy sex and drinking clubs in Soho, the groaning lunch and dinner tables of the City and all the other places where drink was available at all hours a daily gallimaufry of gossip, rumour and fact was gathered and printed as news.

The borderline between work and drink was blurred. Lunches were long and liquid, and charged to the company. 'Lunch with contacts' was the most bare-faced justification. Lunch supposedly with some named celebrity or magnifico bore the risk that someone else on the paper was also supposedly entertaining him that day. The risk was small, however, as it was accepted all round that expenses were a hidden subsidy. The *Daily Mirror* features-writer who charged for 'Entertaining Mr Sloan' got only a mild ticking-off.

Every few yards in Fleet Street there were pubs which were regarded as the territory of a particular paper or a section of its workers. One at least could be regarded as dangerous for outsiders. In a fetid alley behind the Cheshire Cheese was the odiferous Newspaper Workers' Club, a stronghold of printers. Journalists risked limb if not life in going there. The Stab in the Back a few yards from Fleet Street in Fetter Lane was a *Daily Mirror* reporters' stronghold. One night Hugh Cudlipp, chairman of the mighty Mirror group, was lonely in his eyrie atop the *Mirror* skyscraper. Once a successful tabloid editor, he hankered for the rough camaraderie and convivial atmosphere of the Stab, where he had spent many happy evenings but was now a stranger. At last after long consideration he ventured in unannouned to buy the hacks a drink. Bill Marshall, a volatile features writer who was seldom less than drunk at that time of night, jumped on to Cudlipp's back, shouting, 'He's real, he's warm,' and clung on. For a while Cudlipp tried to pretend that Bill wasn't there, but in the end he had to face the fact that there was a large drunken journalist on his back. He went back to his lonely executive suite and apparently never visited the Stab again.

At another Mirror pub, Barney Finnegan's, a haunt of sub-editors, the venerable foreign correspondent Donald Wise was trying to define what he meant by style. A sub, Ben Noble, fell backwards off his stool with a fearsome crash. 'That's style,' said Wise.

At the nearby Vagabond's Club on a reporter's stag night the chef had a heart attack in the cellar. An ambulance arrived and a nurse rushed in.

The drunken hacks, convinced she was a strippogram, refused to let her in and instead clamoured for her to get her kit off ...

In Manchester, where all the major papers had editorial offices and the London operation was replicated on a smaller scale, the drinking was if anything wilder. Certainly the tales were. Bob Gray, a former *Mirror* night editor, told of a Christmas party at the Mitre Hotel near Manchester Cathedral. It started at lunchtime and by late afternoon the survivors were in a sorry state, 'totally arseholed, falling downstairs ...' Eventually he got a call from the police, who said his staff were making a disturbance outside the Mitre. They were refusing to return to work unless he turned up to lead them back.

Gray told the police to turn their dogs on his staff. 'We have done, Mr Gray. Your staff are on their hands and knees barking at the dogs' (Waterhouse, *The Other Fleet Street*).

New technology and the long and bitter war between newspaper owners and the print unions broke the ancient link between Fleet Street and the industry. In 1986 Rupert Murdoch moved production of his titles, including the *Sun* and the *Sunday Times*, downriver to Wapping, breaking the hold of the unions. Other papers also moved out and the pubs where Dickens and Thackeray, Chesterton and Cudlipp, Waugh and Frayn had drunk welcomed a new kind of client. Those who were left of the men in debt who drank of old in the street's many pubs were scattered to the four corners of London, to Canary Wharf and Victoria and Kensington High Street.

Many retired or were paid off, and were glad to leave a trade where the moronic inferno of technology, of blogs and the like grew ever more intense. They were replaced by earnest young men who stared into their screens, sucked mineral water from plastic bottles and had a lot to learn. One was heard to call out: '*Troilus and Cressida* – one play or two?' The sophisticated metropolitan chatter of the old Cheshire Cheese and El Vino's, likened by one hack to the School of Athens, has been silenced. For a time at least the new young men of the City, with their multi-million bonuses and £17,000 bottles of wine, must take up the burden.

# Appendix 1: Smugglers

Much of the wine and brandy, as well as tea and tobacco and other luxury goods, consumed by the English in the 18th century was smuggled. Large numbers of fairly honest citizens were either smugglers or customers. There were as many as 20,000 smugglers out of a population of about eight million. Sir Robert Walpole, the Prime Minister, used an Admiralty barge to transport his smuggled wine up the Thames. Lady Holdernesse, whose husband was Warden of the Cinque Ports and a former Secretary of State, used Walmer Castle to run a business selling smuggled French lace and furniture. James Woodforde, the Norfolk parson and diarist, wrote on 29 March 1777: 'Andrews the smuggler brought me this night about 11 o'clock a bag of Hyson tea 6 pd weight. He frightened us a little by whistling under the parlour window as we were going to bed. I gave him some Geneva and paid him for the tea ... 3.3.0.' On the Isle of Wight where the writer Elizabeth Sewell was staying with an uncle, smugglers left a keg of brandy at the door. It was their way of thanking him for letting them transport their wares by night through his grounds without interfering. The smugglers were ingenious. Brandy kegs were hidden in lobster pots or transported in packing cases marked 'returned Government stores'.

Smuggling gangs could number as many as 50 men. Some were armed and murderous. The Hawkhurst gang in Kent were notorious for their brutality, daring and the scope of their operations. In 1745 a Parliamentary inquiry heard that the gang could muster 500 men in an hour. From their base at Hawkhurst near Hastings the tentacles of their operations spread over five counties.

The lawlessness of the Hawkhursts led the terrified people of the nearby village of Goudhurst to form a militia. The Hawkhursts, who had already routed the people of Folkestone with a force of 92 men and a pack of savage dogs, reacted to this challenge by marching on Goudhurst. They tortured one of the villagers until he revealed details of their defences. He was sent home with a warning that the smugglers would return on 20 April 1747 to burn the village to the ground, slaughtering every man, woman and child.

When the smugglers attacked they were met by a volley of gunfire from the defenders. Two of them were killed and many wounded. It was a rare reverse. Later that year the Hawkhursts carried out their most audacious exploit. Their ship *The Three Brothers*, with a huge cargo of smuggled tea, had been seized by Customs and impounded at Poole in Dorset. The smugglers' leader, Thomas Kingsmill, rounded up 60 of his gang and they set out on horseback, crossing through Kent, Sussex, Hampshire and finally Dorset. When they arrived they found a Navy ship was moored at the quay with its guns trained on the door of the Customs house. They waited for the tide to ebb. The ship sank below the level of the quay and its guns were useless. Kingsmill and his men broke into the Customs house and retrieved their tea.

On their way home they captured an informer and a Customs man, Daniel Chater and William Galley. The *Gentleman's Magazine* described what happened next:

> They began with poor Galley, cut off his nose and privities, broke every joint of him and after several hours' torture dispatched him. Chater they carried to a dry well, hung him by the middle to a cross beam in it, leaving him to perish with hunger and pain; but when they came, several days after, and heard him groan, they cut the rope, let him drop to the bottom and threw in logs and stones to cover him.

There was widespread revulsion. It took the authorities four years to wipe out the gang, and when Kingsmill and some of his men were tried and condemned at the Old Bailey the court was told that the Poole raid was 'the most unheard-of villainy and impudence ever known'.

In 1775 smugglers forced two witnesses who were to give evidence against one of their gang at Winchester Assizes to turn back to Southampton. There were battles between smugglers and the authorities at Orford and Southwold in Suffolk, and at Cranbourn Chase troops who ambushed 50 smugglers were defeated and disarmed.

The public might express conventional revulsion at the brutality of smugglers, but they regarded heavy Customs duties as unfair and didn't regard smuggling as a serious crime. It was also a fact of nature: as long as there was a great disparity between the cost of luxury goods abroad and in England there would be smugglers. Many Customs officers were corrupt: those in London docks colluded with the gangs who descended nightly to steal cargoes, the capital's most intensively organised crime. In 1825 the entire crew of the revenue cutter *Rose* was dismissed. As Hibbert points out (*The English*) the chief Customs officer at Looe was convicted of collusion, as both his immediate predecessors had been.

Smuggling was eventually reduced to negligible levels by cutting the high Customs tariffs. In our time it has become big business again – smuggling drugs, cigarettes, people, guns.

# Appendix 2: What's Your Poison?

One of the most important aims of alcohol legislation has been to protect the drinker from being poisoned. In the 15th century ale-conners were appointed to check the quality of beer. Brewers were required to hoist a sign whenever they were brewing so the inspectors could test it.

In the 19th century there were fears that the brewers were doping beer and spirits with drugs to make them more addictive. In 1824 a drinker complained:

> It has seldom been my fortune, in a great number of years, to taste unadulterated purchased ale ... At present the chief articles of adulteration which my well-practised palate can discover are seeds, sugar and salt ... cocculus indicus (Indian berry), a most intoxicating and deleterious drug, the flavour of which I well know, was formerly much in use.

Adulteration of beer and other drinks with poisonous preservatives was common in the 18th and 19th centuries. Sulphuric acid and oil of turpentine were mixed with gin, and various toxic substances were added to beer. In 1820 the leading analytical chemist Frederick Accum revealed the extent to which beer was being adulterated with poisons. His *Treatise on Adulteration of Food and Culinary Poisons* named a range of illegal substances used, including poisonous *Cocculus indicus*, capsicum, 'mixed drugs' and many others. Between 1813 and 1819 there were nearly a hundred convictions of brewers, publicans and 'brewers' druggists' for defrauding the Revenue. The effect on public health does not seem to have immediately concerned the authorities. Of the great brewers only Thomas Meux was successfully prosecuted – for using salts of tartar to give a frothy head to his porter. Most of the adulteration was being carried out by small brewers.

Legislation followed, if rather tardily: the Adulteration of Foods Act 1860 and the Adulteration of Food, Drink and Drugs Act 1872. Campaigns for purer beer followed, and in 1900 the fears of the reformers were justified. A mysterious disease broke out among heavy drinkers in Manchester and the Midlands. By the end of the year 3000 people had died. A firm making brewing sugar had been adding arsenic. Legislation was introduced to limit the amount of arsenic allowed.

# Brief Lives

**Francis Bacon** (1909–92) Irish artist, homosexual and Bohemian. Regarded by many as the most important British painter of the postwar period, Bacon was at the centre of a hard-drinking set which met in the pubs and clubs of Soho. He was generous with money and drink.

**Muriel Belcher** (1908–78) Landlady of the Colony Room Club in Dean Street, Soho. A foul-mouthed lesbian who addressed her customers by women's names. She called Francis Bacon, one of her favourites, 'daughter' as a term of affection. He called her 'ma'am'. Most kinds of misbehaviour were tolerated at the Colony, though Brendan Behan and Dylan Thomas were barred for trying to vomit on the carpet. When Elizabeth Smart wrote Belcher's obituary she described the Colony's members as 'painters, writers, tinkers, tailors, editors, art editors, cartoonists, singers, African chiefs, burglars, strippers, composers, dress-designers, lords, landowners, barrow-boys, advertising people and unclassifiable people'.

**James Boswell** (1740–95) Diarist and biographer of Samuel Johnson. He met Johnson in London in 1763, and was soon on intimate terms. He had many mistresses, many affairs and many doses of clap, and his journals are frank. He was an unsuccessful lawyer and a heavy drinker. He wrote a good deal, but the *Life* of his friend, a conscious work of art, is his masterpiece.

**George Gordon Byron** (1788–1824) Dissipated poet, the type of the doomed romantic hero. His drinking companions included Sheridan and Thomas Moore, who wrote his biography.

**Charles II** (1630–85) King of England from 1660. The eldest son of the executed Charles I, he returned from exile in 1660 and proved an astute ruler, steering a way past Protestant and Catholic extremists. He had many mistresses, and although there were no legitimate children his illegitimate offspring were plentiful. Easily bored, he surrounded himself with perhaps the most dissolute and talented followers of any English court.

**Samuel Taylor Coleridge** (1772–1834) Poet, critic and drug addict. With Wordsworth he wrote *Lyrical Ballads* (1798). His poetic gift ebbed in a tide of drink, laudanum and talk – he was one of the great talkers, if not conversationists.

**Theresa Cornelys** (1723–79) Former mistress of Casanova who ran a highly successful place of entertainment in Soho Square. She had great flair and her masquerades, balls and recitals attracted the *ton*. In his memoirs William Hickey writes of her 'truly magnificent suite of apartments ... So much did it take that the first people of the kingdom attended it as did also the whole beauty of the metropolis, from the Duchess of Devonshire down to the little milliner's apprentice from Cranbourn Alley'. Cornelys was a poor businesswoman and went broke.

**William Crockford** (1775–1844) Founder in 1827 of the famous gambling club in St James's. He had been a fishmonger, and opened the sumptuous club after winning £100,000 in a 24-hour gambling session against a group of dandies. His club made him £1,200,000 in a few years.

**Aleister Crowley** (1875–1947) Satanist and poet who liked to be known as 'the wickedest man alive'. He founded a cult with a centre in Sicily where Betty May's husband Raoul Loveday died. Crowley brought a sensational libel lawsuit against Nina Hamnett and lost. He spent much time and other people's money in the Café Royal.

**Nancy Cunard** (1896–1965) Heiress, a leader of the rebellion by wealthy young women in the Twenties which marked the end of Victorian hypocrisy. With Augustus John she made the Eiffel Tower restaurant an alternative to the Café Royal. She championed racial equality and was disinherited by her family because of her long affair with a coloured man.

**Sir Francis Dashwood** (1708–81) Chancellor of the Exchequer and founder of the Hell-Fire Club at Medmenham. The obscene cavortings of his Knights of St Francis have stoked the fantasies of authors and filmmakers. He was a serious politician and a generous friend.

**Henry Fielding** (1707–54) English playwright, novelist and magistrate. His plays and satires against the Walpole government prompted the introduction of the Theatrical Licensing Act of 1737 which ended his career as a playwright. He wrote a series of novels, including *Tom Jones*, and as a magistrate helped his brother Sir John set up the Bow Street runners, the first modern police force.

**Ronald Firbank** (1886–1926) Influential novelist and regular at the Café Royal, where he drank prodigious quantities of champagne. Homosexual and lonely, crippled by shyness, he was a generous friend. His novels influenced Evelyn Waugh.

**George IV** (1762–1830) Spendthrift King who ran up huge debts and became a drunken drug addict. He was a treacherous friend and a faithless lover. His contributions to the arts were a strange palace at Brighton, Regent's Park, vast sums spent on buildings some of which he pulled down, and a great many clothes, shoes, uniforms and snuff boxes.

**Nina Hamnett** (1890–1956) Talented artist who became a familiar figure in the pubs of Fitzrovia and Soho. An exuberant pioneer of the Bohemian lifestyle for women, she was promiscuous and eventually alcoholic. She fell to her death from a window at her flat.

**Frank Harris** (1856–1931) Irish writer and combative and successful newspaper editor. Harris claimed that he had been a cowboy, a bootblack and a bouncer in a gambling saloon. He was certainly a liar and a philanderer. He and Oscar Wilde passed long evenings in convivial conversation at the Café Royal – they were not competitors either sexually or as writers.

**Charlotte Hayes** (c.1725–1812) The most successful brothel-keeper of the 18th century. She married an Irish con-man, Dennis O'Kelly, who later owned the wonder-horse Eclipse, which never lost a race. She had brothels in King's Place, a narrow alley near Pall Mall in which all the houses were high-class bordellos. The Prince of Wales was among her customers. Her greatest triumph was the staging of a 'Cyprian Fête' at which gentlemen 'of the highest breeding' first watched athletic young men copulating with 'virgins' as young 'as twelve' and then joined in themselves.

**William Hickey** (1749–1830) Memoirist who left a lively picture of the demi-monde and gave his name to the gossip column in the *Daily Express*. He drew a lively picture of the racy side of London during the reign of George III, when vice was probably more self-confident and flagrant than ever before or since.

**Billy Hill** (1911–84) London gangster who supplied black market liquor to clubland during the Second World War. Hill, who called himself Boss of Britain's Underworld, achieved a temporary dominance of the West End which no later gangster could match, including his successors, the Kray brothers.

**William Hogarth** (1697–1764) English painter and engraver, born in Smithfield. His moral narrative series including *A Rake's Progress* and *Marriage à la mode* were popular and influential. He drew attention to the problems of drink in *Gin Lane* and its counterpart, *Beer Street*.

**Theodore Hook** (1788–1841) Novelist, playwright, civil servant and convict, regarded as the 'wittiest man in England'. He could draw and sing well, and he was perhaps the worst practical joker in history. Coleridge said of his talk that he 'never before conceived such amazing readiness of mind, and resources of genius to be poured out on the mere subject and impulse of the moment'.

**Augustus John** (1878–1961) Artist and arch Bohemian. Leader of the Café Royalists. Generous friend and patron, father of innumerable bastards, alcoholic who continued painting with varying success into old age. He introduced Dylan Thomas to the woman who became his wife, Caitlin Macnamara.

**Charles Lamb** (1775–1834) Essayist, letter writer and talker of genius. Lamb devoted himself to looking after his sister after she stabbed their mother to death in a fit of mania. She was released into his care and he renounced marriage. His friends included most of the progressive writers of his time, particularly Coleridge, and on convivial evenings he was often the leader of the revels.

**Julian Maclaren-Ross** (1912–64) Writer whose *Memoirs of the Forties* enhanced the reputation of Fitzrovia as a wartime enclave of hard-drinking Bohemianism. He worked at the BBC with Dylan Thomas and at night pub-crawled with him, winning a reputation as a garrulous, hard-drinking dandy.

**Caitlin Macnamara** (1913–94) Wife of Dylan Thomas. They were introduced by Augustus John, who had seduced her. Their life together was tempestuous, marked by wilful poverty and mutual alcoholism. She wrote about the marriage in *Leftover Life to Kill* and *Double Drink Story*.

**Betty May** (1901–70s?) A prototype for the liberated woman. May was born in London's East End, modelled for the sculptor Jacob Epstein, became a cocaine addict and a star of the Café Royal set. Her husband died after drinking cat's blood at Aleister Crowley's Satanist cult centre.

**Samuel Pepys** (1633–1703) English diarist. He rose rapidly in the naval service through the patronage of the Earl of Sandwich. He became secretary to the Admiralty in 1672 but was removed from office and imprisoned for alleged complicity in the Popish Plot (1679). Five years later he was reappointed, and in the same year became president of the Royal Society. The highlights of the diary are the Great Plague (1665), the Great Fire (1666) and the Dutch fleet breaching the defences on the Thames (1665–7). He was frank about his weakness for drink and women.

**William Pitt** (1759–1806) Highly successful statesman, Britain's youngest Prime Minister at the age of 24. He saw the country through the early years of the wars against Napoleon and achieved considerable reforms, but failed to emancipate the Catholics. His private life was lonely and he drank heavily, once being sick behind the Speaker's chair.

**Richard Porson** (1759–1808) Classical scholar of uncertain temper. Porson was precocious, and educated by benefactors at Eton and Cambridge. He contributed hugely to Greek scholarship, and to the history of the great age of drinking by his tireless witty talk and enormous and undiscriminating capacity for drink. He was said to threaten to settle arguments with a poker.

**Richard Savage** (1697–1743) Poet and friend of Samuel Johnson. He claimed to be the illegitimate son of noble parents, a lifelong obsession reflected in his bitter poem *The Bastard*. He killed a gentleman in a tavern brawl, narrowly escaped the gallows and lived a disorderly life. *The Wanderer* (1729) is regarded as his major work.

**James Meary Tambimuttu** (1915–83) Eccentric poetry magazine editor and Fitzrovian. He would turn up in pubs with his pockets bulging with manuscripts. Those that didn't fall out and get lost he kept in a chamber pot under his bed. Nevertheless he attracted some of the best-known poets of the war years, including Louis MacNeice, Stephen Spender, David Gascoyne, Gavin Ewart and Harold Pinter to his magazine, *Poetry (London)*. T.S. Eliot was said to be an admirer, by Tambi himself, of course.

**Dylan Thomas** (1914–53) Hard-drinking poet and Fitzrovian. He worked at the BBC during the war, and married Caitlin Macnamara, who had been seduced by Augustus John. He died after a heavy drinking session in America.

**Edward 'Ned' Ward** (1667–1731) Innkeeper and writer, born in Oxfordshire. Best known for the *London Spy*, published in monthly parts from 1698, an invaluable guide to the city's low life. He was sentenced to the pillory for attacking the Whigs in *Hudibras Redivivus* (1705). Wrote coarse satirical and humorous verse.

**Evelyn Waugh** (1903–66) Writer whose early novels chronicle the rise and fall of the Bright Young Things. His letters and diaries record his hard drinking. He was briefly an art student, then a schoolmaster and finally the most acclaimed novelist of his generation.

**Oscar Wilde** (1854–1900) Playwright, novelist and wit, imprisoned for homosexuality. A regular at the Café Royal, where he was the centre of a circle of wits and artists, his sexual ambiguity was tolerated as long as it did not cause scandal.

**John Wilkes** (1727–97) Politician, journalist and rake. His private life was scandalous – he was a prominent member of Sir Francis Dashwood's Hell-Fire Club and took part in the orgies at Medmenham Abbey. As a politician he helped secure the right of the Press to report Parliamentary debates, and deserved the epitaph which he wrote for himself: 'A friend to liberty'.

**John Wilmot, Earl of Rochester** (1647–80) Poet, courtier and rake. His good looks and lively wit made him a favourite at the Restoration court of Charles II. In 1667 he married Elizabeth Malet, a wealthy heiress. He wrote satires against the King and fine lyric poems, but also poetry as obscene as anything serious in the language. See his 'Sodom'.

# Notes

### Last Orders, Please!

1. Ale was made from fermented malt, water and spices. It did not keep well, and so good alehouses made fresh brews every few days. Beer, which cost about the same, was made from fermented malt, water and hops, had a better, stronger flavour, was clearer and kept better. It gradually supplanted ale for city drinkers, ale becoming more of a rural drink. Spirits were drunk, particularly brandy, or *aqua vitae*. There were many mixtures, including Pepys's improbable half pint of Rhenish wine mixed with beer. Others were braggett, fermented ale and honey with spices; caudle, warm wine or ale with eggs, bread, sugar and spices; buttered beer, hot beer with eggs, butter and spices; hippocras, hot wine sweetened with spices; and syllabub, ale, sack or cider with milk or cream, and often bread. Possetts were similar.

2. The distinction between alehouses and taverns was sometimes blurred. In theory alehouses sold only ale, beer, cider and rough spirits. Taverns sold only wine. Inns sold a wide range of drinks and also had decent food and accommodation. They were the precursors of hotels.

### The Gin Mania

1. Oliver Goldsmith saw alehouses as pernicious. He wrote in *The Bee* (1759): 'Alehouses are even an occasion of debauchery and excess, and either in a religious or political light it would be our highest interest to have the greatest part of them suppressed. They should be put under laws of not continuing open beyond a certain hour, and harbouring only proper persons. These rules, it may be said, will diminish the necessary taxes; but this is false reasoning, since what was consumed in debauchery abroad

would, if such a regulation took place, be more justly and perhaps more equitably for the workman's family be spent at home: and this, cheaper to them and without loss of time. On the other hand our alehouses, being ever open, interrupt business.'

## Vice and Drink

1. Elizabeth Chudleigh, Duchess of Kingston (1720–88) beauty tried in the Great Hall of Westminster for bigamy. She was notorious when a maid of honour to the Princess of Wales for appearing in public in a costume so scanty she was practically naked. Mrs Elizabeth Montague wrote: 'Miss Chudleigh's undress was remarkable ... the maids of honour were so offended they were lost for words'. She continued this exhibitionism even after she joined the aristocracy. In 1774 she married the noted philanderer Lieutenant Augustus Hervey RN. They kept the marriage secret because otherwise she would have lost her position in the royal household and her salary of £400 a year. Hervey sailed away to other adventures and in 1769 she married the elderly Duke of Kingston, having persuaded herself that the ceremony she had gone through with Hervey was 'such a scrambling shabby business and so much incomplete' that it was not a real wedding. When the duke died she inherited a fortune. One of the duke's sons challenged the will and the marriage, and she was found guilty. During the trial she abused the peers for their insolence. The Attorney General tried to have her burned in the hand but strings were pulled and she avoided this punishment. She was ordered not to leave the kingdom but went to Russia, where she became a friend of Catherine the Great. She died in Paris in 1788.

2. When the hopelessly extravagant Mrs Cornelys went bust the great cabinet-maker was among her creditors.

## The Hell-Fire Clubs

1. In November 1763 Wilkes was accused of libelling Archbishop Wharton in notes to the *Essay on Woman*. This was a parody of Pope's *Essay on Man*. Pope's work begins:

Awake, my St John! leave all meaner things
To Low ambition, and the pride of kings.
Let us (since life can little more supply

Than just to look about us and to die)
Expatiate free o'er all this scene of Man;
A mighty maze! but not without a plan.

The Wilkes/Potter parody, dedicated to Fanny Murray, begins:

Awake, my Fanny, leave all meaner things,
This morning shall prove what rapture swiving [copulation] brings.
Let us (since life can little more supply
Than just a few good fucks, and then we die)
Expatiate free o'er that lov'd scene of Man;
A mighty maze! for mighty pricks to scan.

Wilkes was attacked in the House of Lords by Sandwich, his fellow carouser at Medmenham. In fact Sandwich was deeper into the Medmenham orgies – he was a member while Wilkes was probably never more than an involved spectator. And they were on opposite sides politically, Wilkes having tormented the administration in his paper, the *North Briton*.

Sandwich read from the *Essay* with obvious relish. The comic irony of the situation, of Sandwich, one of the most depraved men of the age, expressing shock at Wilkes's puerile pastiche, was not lost on the Lords. Dashwood reportedly remarked in a stage whisper that it was the first time he had heard Satan preaching against sin. Wilkes fled to Paris.

## High Stakes
1. Fox is said to have won £10,000 by betting that he had not shat in his breeches. The footnote to a poem called *The Gamblers* explains:

The adventure is recorded of Mr Charles Fox, by which it is said he recovered ten thousand pounds – a sum he had lost the same night at the Hazard table. Charles [Fox] suddenly retires from the company, and bribing a vile Livery [servant] for the decent purposes of fouling his breeches, returns in full perfume to the Knights of the Black Table. Reynard [Fox] as might be expected, is immediately accused … Charles denies it with a laugh and turns it off by saying, 'Foxes, you know, are sometimes apt to smell.' The Knights positively charge him with having befouled himself. Charles affects to be angry, demurs and hesitates a bet ... they take him up, with different bets, to the amount of the sum he had just lost ... Charles rings for [the servant] of whom he enquires, 'John, who —— in my breeches?' 'I did, your honour' (Baker, *George IV, A Life in Caricature*). He was luckier in that sense than other Regency rakes and gamblers, including Beau Brummell, Scrope Davies and 'Golden Ball' Hughes, who fled to the Continent to escape their creditors.

The allure of drink and sex in a low grog shop around 1816. The poor drank to forget, as ever. The figure of death hovers over the proceedings.

## The Prince of Whales

1. Fanny was the sister of the notorious kiss-and-tell courtesan and blackmailer Harriette Wilson, who reported in her unblushing memoirs how she slept with the Duke of Wellington among many others.
2. Cruikshank was a noted drunk until he signed the pledge shortly after publishing *The Bottle* in 1847. He told a temperance meeting: 'My mother first lifted the poisoned chalice to my lips.' (His aged mother was startled when she heard about this and remonstrated with him angrily.) He said he had grown up in times when 'no man was considered a gentleman unless he made his companions drunk'. There are many anecdotes of his tipsy adventures, 'riding home in Dickens's carriage on his head, or

grabbing armfuls of tablecloths and antimacassars for a costume performance of "Lord Bateman"' (Wynn-Jones, *George Cruikshank*). He was arrested from time to time in the early hours 'having been found in the street in an insensible condition', and his publisher David Bogue would be roused from his bed to bail him out. A friend recorded a drunken frolic in 1846, which seems to have been typical of his behaviour. Cruikshank, who was 54 at the time, dropped in after dinner: 'The guests departed, leaving the hilarious George with two others to finish the evening; and when the trio had got into the street, they found the old difficulty in restraining Cruikshank's boisterous spirits. After trying in vain for something more than an hour to lead him home, they left him – climbing up a lamppost!'

He eventually gave up political satire for the more lucrative career of book illustrator – his image of Fagin in his death cell in Dickens's *Oliver Twist* is unforgettable – and with him the art died for generations, to be revived in our own time.

3. After George died the pension was continued by William IV, but it was supposed his niece Victoria would cancel it when she came to the throne. However, she asked whether it was true that Lade was old and broke, and on being told that he was 78, penniless and alone – Lettie having died in 1825 – she ordered that the pension be paid until his death. He died a year later.

4. The Prince demanded that the authorities prosecute over this 'most infamous and shocking libellous production that ever disgraced the pen of man' but failed to get them to act.

5. Perdita Robinson.

6. Hastings was eventually cleared, although the great fortune he had brought back from India had gone to pay for his defence. The East India Company gave him a generous pension to keep him comfortably in old age. Seventeen years later he met Sheridan at Brighton, where both were visiting the Prince of Wales. The Irishman assured Hastings that he felt no personal animosity, 'that any part he had ever taken against him was purely political, and that no one had a greater respect for him than himself, etc.' (Creevey). Hastings replied that 'it would be a great consolation to him in his declining years if Mr Sheridan would make that sentiment more public.'

## Six-Bottle Men

1. Exactly what amounts to heavy drinking is of course subjective. The Roman poet Martial (c.40–c.104) blamed the five bottles of wine he had drunk beforehand for his inviting someone he disliked to dinner. Roman wine is said to have been about half as strong again as the wine we drink now (Tannahill, *Sex in History*), so he had more than seven bottles *before* dinner.

2. John Gibson Lockhart (1794–1854), Scottish biographer, novelist and merciless and sarcastic critic. His masterpiece is the seven-volume biography of Sir Walter Scott, whose daughter he married. He was editor of the *Quarterly Review* for 28 years.

3. Her protector Sir Orlando Bridgeman left her an annuity on condition she mended her ways. She couldn't. The *Meretriciad* makes the point in its stumbling metres:

> When Bridgeman made his last dear will and groan,
> A good annuity was then thy own.
> With this proviso – that you'd rake no more
> Nor play the vagrant mercenary whore.
> Alas! thy many actions since have shown
> Thou could'st not quit the bottle and the town;
> Oft has the Muse beheld thy tottering feet,
> And prayed that instant for the widest street.

One evening two Jews were murdered in the Cider Cellars, and the *Meretriciad* raises the squalid event to epic status – 'a greater ruin Derry's never saw'. Lucy was involved in some way, and the poem suggests she was a troublemaker:

> At other times more riotous than lewd,
> Then nought but swords, blood, tears and oaths ensued,
> So dire a conflict surely ne'er was known,
> A worse sedition Helen had not sown.

Lucy was held overnight in the Bridewell prison. She was soon back in business, and the local taverns again rang with her drunken laughter. 'The Shakespeare Head, the Rose and Bedford Arms / Each Alike profit from my Cooper's charms.' Soon she was imprisoned for debt. In 1776 William Hickey and some friends had a whip-round for her. 'Tomkyns [a tavern keeper] had that day received a letter from Lucy Cooper, who had long been a prisoner for debt in the King's Bench [prison] stating that she was almost naked and starving, without a penny in her pocket to purchase food, raiment or coal to warm herself.' The friends raised £50, and 'this seasonable aid had probably saved the life of a deserving woman who, in her prosperity, had done a thousand generous actions'. After her release she opened a brothel but it failed, and in 1772 she died in poverty, 'without friends or money and now destitute of beauty and past the time when youth supplied the place of charm'.

## Hickey Among the Ladies

1. That this whole episode is based on a misunderstanding makes it none the less terrifying. On a later visit to the brothel William was amazed to recognise one of the drunken termagents who had fought on the floor when he was last there. She was sober, charming, her name was Burgess, she sang 'admirable' songs and explained the 'horrid broil' which William had seen. She and her opponent were utterly drunk, having consumed 'an unusual quantity' of spirits, and quarrelled. The other fight was not what it seemed: '[It] arose from the man (who was a notorious woman's bully [pimp]), having basely robbed the two who attacked him; that the rest concerned were the friends of one party or the other, and acted accordingly.'

## Night and the City

1. Kate's was one of a chain of night houses and brothels run by a Jewish syndicate headed by David Belasco, according to Henry Mayhew, the pioneering social observer. This is one of the few glimpses we get of the shadowy figures behind the chains of Victorian brothels. Belasco went bankrupt, and was later reported to be working as a waiter.

2. Three of those companions had been the Prince's contemporaries at Oxford and were later part of his drinking and gambling set. Hastings, the fourth and last Marquess of Hastings, has been compared to the Earl of Rochester. Sir Frederick Johnstone was a gambler and ladies' man. Henry Chaplin was a vastly wealthy magnate. They were just the kind of idle pleasure-seeking young men whom the Queen despised.

3. Hastings and Henry Chaplin both fell for the Lady Florence Paget, daughter of the Marquess of Anglesey. She accepted Henry's proposal and the wedding was set for the end of summer 1864 at St George's, Hanover Square. Had it taken place it would have been the society wedding of the year. But just a fortnight before the wedding Florence went shopping in Marshall and Snelgrove's in Oxford Street. She went in by a side entrance and shortly afterwards emerged from the front entrance with Harry Hastings, and married him that same day at St George's. (Three years later Hastings ruined himself by betting against Chaplin's colt Hermit in the Derby. He died, broken and bankrupt, at the age of 26.)

Society was shocked. The Queen was outraged. She had reason to remember an earlier scandal involving the Hastings family, although the fault was all on her side. Lady Flora Hastings had been lady-in-waiting to Victoria's mother, the Duchess of Kent. Because of some obscure domestic infighting the Queen had come to dislike her. At Christmas 1838 Lady Flora, who was 27, felt unwell and consulted the Queen's physician Sir James Clark. He noticed that Lady Flora's figure looked unusually full for an unmarried woman, and speculated unwisely to one of the Queen's ladies that she might be pregnant. The Queen got to hear of this and wrote in her journal: 'We have no doubt that she is – to use the plain words – with child.' The Queen insisted on Lady Flora being medically examined. Two doctors testified that she was not pregnant. News of the affair got out and there was a public scandal. Flora's brother Lord Hasting's wrote to the *Morning Post* to clear her name. Four months later Lady Flora died and the cause of the swelling was revealed: she had incurable liver disease.

Perhaps it would be too much to expect public remorse from a sovereign. The Queen certainly remembered that she had lost face because of the Hastings family, and now told her son that she was disgusted that he was mixing with such people.

## The Art of Rebellion

1. There are other versions of this story. In one Swinburne, drunk, is unable to find his own hat and tries all the others, flinging them to the floor when they don't fit. At last in a frenzy he destroys them.

## La Vie de Bohème

1. His other well-known poem, little longer than its title, 'Vitae summa brevis spem nos vetat incohare longam', could be a requiem for the *fin de siècle*:

> They are not long, the weeping and the laughter,
> Love and desire and hate:
> I think they have no portion in us after
> We pass the gate.
> They are not long, the days of wine and roses:
> Out of a misty dream
> Our path emerges for a while, then closes
> Within a dream.

2. A year later Crowley went on trial at the Old Bailey accused of being in possession of the letters knowing them to have been stolen. He was fined £50.

3. She also told an amusing tale about the address where she first had sex. 'I read frequently the poems of Paul Verlaine and ... Arthur Rimbaud. One day I ... discovered to my amusement that the rooms where I had left my virginity behind were those Verlaine and Rimbaud had stayed in ... One day I said to Walter Sickert, 'Do you think they will put up a blue plaque on the house for me or will they put up one for Verlaine and Rimbaud?' and Walter said, 'My dear, they will put up one on the front for you and one on the back for them.'

## Defending the Realm

1. Rosa, who never lost her Cockney vulgarity, was furious with Waugh after the book was published, and barred him from the hotel with the words: 'Take your arse out of my chair.' In his biography of Waugh Christopher Sykes says Rosa used to screech in rage: 'There are two bastards I'm not going to have in this house. One is that rotten little Donegall and the other is that little swine Evelyn Waugh.' Donegall was a gossip columnist.

2. The area can be defined as bordered by the Euston Road in the north and Oxford Street in the south, with Tottenham Court Road and Portland Place as its eastern and western boundaries.

3. In 1955 Allchild was prosecuted for running 'a disorderly house', in effect a brothel. The police claimed that they had found between 50 and 80 prostitutes and homosexuals there. People 'paraded themselves unashamedly' with 'rouged' cheeks. A police constable told the court that a prostitute asked him 'are you looking for a naughty girl or a naughty boy?' Allchild was convicted but cleared on appeal.

4. Lady Cunard, originally Maud but later the more colourful Emerald, was a celebrated hostess. She devoted herself to an affair with the conductor Sir Thomas Beecham. When Nancy returned from being educated abroad in time to come out as a debutante in 1914 she found her mother's attention was elsewhere. She told Lady Diana Cooper: 'My mother's having an affair with Sir Thomas Beecham, I can do as I like.' Detectives were hired and Sir Thomas wrote to Nancy about her behaviour. This gave her an added incentive to misbehave. She wrote an open letter to her mother, Black Man and White Ladyship:

> With you it is the other trouble – class.
> Negroes, besides being black (that is from jet to as white as yourself but not so pink) have not yet 'penetrated into London Society's consciousness'. You exclaim: they are not 'received!' (You would be surprised to know just how much they are 'received'.)

## Modern Times
1. Conversation with the author May 2007.
2. Conversation with the author, Feb 2007.

# Bibliography

Accum, Frederick, *Treatise on Adulteration of Food and Culinary Poisons*, 1820

Acton, Harold, *More Memories of an Aesthete*, Methuen, 1970

Alcock, Thomas, *The Famous Pathologist or the Noble Mountebank*, Nottingham University 1961

Anon, *Satan's Harvest Home: or the Present State of Whorecraft, Adultery, Fornication, Pimping, Sodomy etc.*, 1749

Anon, *Life, Adventures, Amours and Intrigues of ... Jemmy Twitcher*, 1770

Archenholz, Baron J.W. von, *A Picture of England*, 1789

Aronson, Theo, *The King in Love*, Corgi, 1989

Ashe, Geoffrey, *Do What You Will*, W.H. Allen, 1974

Ashley, Maurice, *Charles II: Man and Statesman*, 1971

Baker, Kenneth, *George IV, A Life in Caricature*, Thames & Hudson, 2005

Bakewell, Michael, *Fitzrovia: London's Bohemia*, National Portrait Gallery Publications, 1999

Beer, E.S. de, *The Diary of John Evelyn*, 6 vols, 1955

Berendt, Stephen C., *Royal Mourning and Regency Culture*, Macmillan, 1997

Bernard, Jeffery, *Talking Horses*, Fourth Estate, 1987

Blunden, Margaret, *The Countess of Warwick*, Cassell, 1967

Blyth, Henry, *Old Q, The Rake of Piccadilly*, Weidenfeld & Nicolson, 1967

   *The High Tide of Pleasure*, Weidenfeld & Nicolson, 1970

Boulton, W.B., *The Amusements of Old London*, 1901

Brown, Maria, *Memoirs of the Life of the Duke of Queensberry*

Burford, E.J., *Royal St James*, Robert Hale, 1988

*Wits, Wenchers and Wantons*, Robert Hale, 1986

Burnet, Gilbert, *History of my Own Time*, 1724–34

    *Some Passages in the Life and Death of John Earl of Rochester: Written by his Own Direction on his Deathbed*,1680

Carswell, John, *The Old Cause*, Cresset Press, 1954

Chancellor, E. Beresford, *The Lives of the Rakes*, 6 vols, Philip Allen, 1925

Chapman, Hester W., *Great Villiers*, Secker and Warburg, 1949

Chesterton, G.K. 'When I Cam Back to Fleet Street', Burnes & Oates, 1915

Clarendon, Edward Hythe, First Earl of, *The History of the Rebellion and Civil Wars in England*, Folio Society, 1967

Clark, Peter, *The English Alehouse: A Social History, 1200–1830*, 1983

Cleland, John, *Fanny Hill*, 1749

Cole, Edward, *History of the English Stage*

Creevey, Thomas, *Creevey Papers*, 1903

Curzon, Lady, *Lady Curzon's India: Letters of a Vicereine*, Weidenfeld & Nicolson, *1974*

Dangerfield, George, *The Strange Death of Liberal England*, 1966

David, Hugh, *The Fitzrovians*, Michael Joseph, 1988

Davin, Dan, *Closing Times*, 1975

Davis, I.M., *The Harlot and the Statesman*, Kensal Press, 1986

Davis, Norman, *Paston Papers and Letters of the Fifteenth Century*, 1971

Davies, Rhys, 'Nina Hamnett, Bohemian', *Wales Magazine*, 1959

Deghy, Guy and Waterhouse, Keith, *Café Royal*, Hutchinson 1955

Dickens, Charles, *Sketches by Boz, Illustrative of Every-Day Life and Every-Day People*, 1836–7

Dunlop, John, *The Philosophy of Artificial and Compulsory Drinking Usages in Great Britain and Ireland*, 1839

Evans, G.E., *The Days That We Have Seen*

Farington, Joseph, *The Farington Diary*, edited James Grieg, 8 vols, Hutchinson 1922–28

Farson, Daniel, *The Gilded Gutter Life of Francis Bacon*, Century, 1993

Ferris, Paul, *Dylan Thomas*, Hodder & Stoughton, 1977

Fielding, Daphne, *The Duchess of Jermyn Street*, Eyre & Spottiswoode, 1964

Fielding, Henry, *An Inquiry in the Causes of the late Increase of Robbers etc.*, 1751

Fosbroke, Rev T.D., *British Monachism*, 1817

Fraser, Antonia, *King Charles II*, 1979
  *The Weaker Vessel*, Mandarin, 1993

French, R.V., *Nineteen Centuries of Drink in England*, Longmans Green, 1884

Fuller, Ronald, *Hell-Fire Francis*, Chatto & Windus, 1939

Gaunt, William, *The Aesthetic Adventure*, Jonathan Cape, 1975

Goldsmith, Oliver, *The Bee*, 1759

Goldsworthy, Cephas, *The Satyr, An Account of the Life and Work, Death and Salvation of John Wilmot, Second Earl of Rochester*, Weidenfeld & Nicolson, 2001

Graves, Robert and Hodge, Alan, *The Long Weekend*, Norton 1994

Greene, Graham, *Lord Rochester's Monkey*, Bodley Head 1974

Gronow, Reese Howell, *The Reminiscences and Recollections of Captain Gronow*, 1892

Hamilton, Anthony, *Memoirs of the Comte de Gramont*, Folio Society, 1965

Hamilton, Elizabeth, *The Illustrious Lady*, Hamish Hamilton, 1980

Hamnett, Nina, *Laughing Torso*, Constable, 1932
  *Is She a Lady?* Alan Wingate, 1955

Hanger, George, *The Life, Adventures and Opinions of Col. George Hanger, written by Himself*, 1801

Harris, Frank, *My Life and Loves*, 1923–7

Harrison, William, *Description of England*, 1577

Hawkins, Sir John, *Life of Samuel Johnson*, 1787

Hearne, Thomas, *Remarks and Collections*, 1885–9

Henriques, Fernando, *Prostitution and Society*, 3 vols, MacGibbon and Kee, 1962–8

Hibbert, Christopher, *The Roots of Evil*,
  *George IV, Prince of Wales*, Longman 1972
  *Edward VII: A Portrait*, Allen Lane, 1976
  *The English, A Social History 1066–1945*, Grafton Books, 1987

Hickey, William, *Memoirs*, Hurst and Blackett, 1948

Hill, Billy, *Boss of Britain's Underworld*, Naldrett Press, 1955

Hill, C.P., *Who's Who in Stuart Britain*, Shepheard-Walwyn, 1988

Hooker, Denise, *Nina Hamnett – Queen of Bohemia*, Constable, 1986

Huish, Robert, *Memoirs of George the Fourth*, 2 vols, 1831

James, Robert Rhodes (ed.), *Chips, The Diaries of Sir Henry Channon*,

Weidenfeld & Nicolson, 1967

Jerdan, William, *Autobiography*, 1852–3

John, Augustus. *Chiaroscuro*, Jonathan Cape, 1952

Johnson, James William, *A Profane Wit, The Life of John Wilmot, Earl of Rochester*, University of Rochester Press, 2004

Jullian, Philippe, *Oscar Wilde*, Constable, 1969

Keppel, Sonia, *Edwardian Daughter*, Hamish Hamilton, 1958

Knight, Charles, *Passage of a Working Life*

Langtry, Lillie, *The Days I Knew*, Hutchinson, 1925

Lees-Milne, James, *The Enigmatic Edwardian*, Sidgwick & Jackson, 1986

Leslie, Anita, *Edwardians in Love*, Hutchinson, 1972

Linnane, Fergus, *Encyclopedia of London Vice and Crime*, Suttons, 2004
*London the Wicked City*, Robson Books, 2003

Longmate, Norman, *The Water Drinkers*, Hamish Hamilton, 1968

Lord, Graham, *Just The One*, Penguin, 1992

Macky, John, *Memoirs of the Secret Service*, 1733

Maclaren-Ross, Julian, *Memoirs of the Forties*, Alan Ross, 1965

Magnus, Philip, *King Edward VII*, John Murray, 1964

Malcolm, J.P., *Anecdotes of the Manners and Customs of London During the 18th Century*, 1810

Marsh, Charles, *The Clubs of London*

Martelli, George, *Jemmy Twitcher*, Jonathan Cape, 1962

Masters, Anthony, *Rosa Lewis, An Exceptional Edwardian*, Weidenfeld & Nicolson, 1977

Masters, Brian, *The Mistresses of Charles II*, 1979

Matthews, R., *Prostitution in London: An Audit*, Middlesex University Press, 1997

May, Betty, *Tiger Woman*, Duckworth, 1929

Mayhew, Henry, *London Labour and the London Poor*, 1861–2

McCormick, Donald, *The Hell-Fire Club, The Story of the Amorous Knights of Wycombe*, Jarrolds, 1958

Melville, Lewis, *The Beaux of the Regency*, Hutchinson, 1908

Middlemas, Keith, *Edward VII*, 1975

Moreton, Maria, *Memoirs of the Life of the Duke of Queensberry*

Morris, Corbyn

Motion, Andrew, *The Lamberts*, Chatto & Windus, 1986

Murray, Venetia, *High Society in the Regency Period*, Penguin, 1999

Nicholson, Virginia, *Among the Bohemians*, Viking, 2002

Nouse, Timothy, *Campania Felix*, 1706

O'Toole, Fintan, *A Traitor's Kiss, The Life of Richard Brinsley Sheridan*, Granta, 1997

Parissien, Steven, *George IV, The Grand Entertainment*, John Murray, 2001

Peakman, Julie, *Lascivious Bodies*, Atlantic Books, 2004

Pearsall, Ronald, *Worm in the Bud*, Pimlico, 1993

Pentelow, Mike, and Rowe, Marsha, *Characters of Fitzrovia*, Pimlico, 2002

Philipps, Guy (ed.), *Bad Behaviour*, Elm Tree Books, 1988

Picard, Lisa, *Dr Johnson's London*, Weidenfeld and Nicholson, 2000

*Piers Ploughman*, modernised by H.W. Wells, 1935

Porter, Roy and Hall, Leslie, *The Facts of Life*, Yale University Press 1995

Powell, Anthony, *A Dance to the Music of Time*, 12 vols, 1951–75

Priestley, J.B., *The Prince of Pleasure*, Heinemann, 1969

Pryme, George, *Autobiographic Recollections*, 1870

Quennell, Peter, *The Wanton Chase*, Collins, 1980

Richardson, *Recollections of the Last Half-Century*

Rodger, N.A.M., *The Insatiable Earl*, HarperCollins, 1992

Samuelson, J, *The History of Drink*, 1878

Saussure, Cesar de, *A Foreign View of England in the Reigns of George I and George II*, trans. 1902

Shaw, D., *London in the Sixties*, 1908

Sitwell, Edith, *English Eccentrics*, The Folio Society, 1994

Smollett, Tobias, *The Life and Adventures of Sir Launcelot Greaves*, 1760

Stubbes, Philip, *The Anatomie of Abuses*, 1583

Swift, Jonathan, *Journals to Stella*, 1710–13

Symons, A.J.A., *English Wits*, Hutchinson, 1940

Tannahill, Reay, *Sex in History*, BCA, 1980

Thackeray, W.M., *The Four Georges*, 1879

Thomas, Peter D.G., *John Wilkes, A Friend to Liberty*, Clarendon Press, 1996

Thompson, Commodore Edward, *Meretriciad*, c.1760

Timbs, John, *Club Life of London*, 2 vols, 1866

Trevelyan, George Otto, *Early History of Charles James Fox*

Tristan, Flora, *Promenades Dans Londres*, 1840

Turner, Thomas, *The Diary of Thomas Turner, 1754–1765*

Uglow, Jenny, *Hogarth, a Life and a World*, Faber & Faber, 1997

Walpole, Horace, *Memoirs of the Reign of George III*, Yale University Press, 2000

*The Last Journals of Horace Walpole During the Reign of George III*, 2 vols, 1910

Ward, Ned, *The History of The London Clubs*, 1709
  *The London Spy*, 1698–1709; Folio Society edition, 1955

Warwick, Frances, Countess of, *Life's Ebb and Flow*, Hutchinson, 1929
  *Afterthoughts*, Cassell, 1931

Waterhouse, Robert, *The Other Fleet Street*, First Edition Limited, 2004

Waugh, Evelyn, *Vile Bodies*, Chapman and Hall, 1930

Wells, Henry W., 'The Construction of Piers Plowman', *PMLA*, vol. 44, no. 1, March 1929

Wilson, Harriette, *Memoirs*, Folio Society, 1964

Wraxall, Sir Nathaniel, *Historical Memoirs of my own Time*, 1772–1784
  *Posthumous Memoirs*, 1884

Wright, David, 'Verses at a Bohemian Funeral', in *New Poems*, a PEN anthology, Michael Joseph, 1957

Wynn-Jones, Michael, *George Cruikshank, His Life and London*, Macmillan, 1978

Young, Thomas, *England's Bane or the Description of Drunkenness*, 1617

# Index